GLADYS COOPER

GLADYS COOPER

a biography

by

Sheridan
Morley

HEINEMANN : LONDON

417, 595 | 920 Coo

William Heinemann Ltd
15 Queen Street, Mayfair, London W1X 8BE

LONDON MELBOURNE TORONTO
JOHANNESBURG AUCKLAND

First published 1979

© Sheridan Morley 1979

434 47896 2

Set, printed and bound in Great Britain by
Cox & Wyman Ltd,
London, Fakenham and Reading

for Joan:
her daughter, my mother

also by Sheridan Morley

A TALENT TO AMUSE (*the biography of Noël Coward*)
REVIEW COPIES: *London Theatre in the Seventies*
OSCAR WILDE
MARLENE DIETRICH
SYBIL THORNDIKE: *A Life in the Theatre*

Contents

Grateful acknowledgement is made to the following for their copyright material:

VICTOR GOLLANCZ LTD
  Excerpt from *Round the Next Corner* by Denys Blakelock

CURTIS BROWN LTD & DOUBLEDAY & CO INC
  Excerpt from *Gerald* by Daphne du Maurier

WEIDENFELD (PUBLISHERS) LTD
  Excerpt from *The Rise and Fall of the Matinee Idol* edited by Anthony Curtis
  Excerpts from *Beaton's My Fair Lady* and *The Parting Years* by Cecil Beaton
  Excerpts from *Indirect Journey* by Harold Hobson

JONATHAN CAPE LTD & ALFRED A. KNOPF INC
  Excerpt from *The Life of Noël Coward* by Cole Lesley

GEORGE G. HARRAP & CO, LTD
  Drawing from *Caught in the Act* by Newman

WHITE LION PUBLISHERS
  Excerpt from *Ivor Novello* by Peter Noble

MACDONALD & JANE'S LTD
  Excerpt from *Buck's Book* by Herbert Buckmaster

TOM HUSTLER
  Photographs by Dorothy Wilding

HUTCHINSON PUBLISHING GROUP LTD
  Excerpts from *Gladys Cooper*, an autobiography

The majority of the photographs which appear in this biography are from the author's private collection. Certain of the photographs used as illustrations are of unknown provenance and are believed not to be the subject of claimed copyright. If copyright is claimed in any of them the publishers will be pleased to correspond with the claimant and to make any arrangements which may prove to be appropriate.

Illustrations

GLADYS COOPER'S FAMILY TREE

JOHN FREAME
Quaker

ROBERT BARCLAY = KATHERINE GORDON
Quaker Apologist (of Gordonstoun)

Robert Barclay (1672–1747)

Robert Barclay
II of Urie (1672–1747)

Robert Barclay
III of Urie (1699–1760)

Robert Barclay, M.P.
IV of Urie (1731–99)

Lucy Barclay
1st wife

Lucy Barclay
mar. 1777
Quaker

David Barclay (1682–1769)
Banker

Mary Freame
mar. Thomas Plumstead

Priscilla Freame
Quaker

Priscilla Plumstead
mar. James Farmer, Birmingham

Catherine Barclay
mar. Daniel Bell, *Merchant*

Samuel Galton
F.R.S. (1753–1832)
Banker

Samuel T. Galton
(1783–1844)
mar. aunt of
Charles Darwin

John H. Galton
(1794–1862)
D.L., Worcester
mar. Isabella Strutt

Sir Douglas Galton,
F.R.S.
(1822–99)

Sir Francis Galton,
F.R.S.
(1822–1911)
Founders of the science of Eugenics

Priscilla Bell
Writer (1751–1832)
mar. Edward Wakefield

Catherine Bell
mar. John Gurney
of Earlsham

(1) Mrs. Eliz. Fry
Prison Reformer
(2) Hannah Bell
(Lady Buxton)

Hence
Noel and Roden
Buxton
Writers

Edward Wakefield
(1774–1854)
Farmer; Writer

Edward Gibbon
Wakefield
Colonial Publicist
(1796–1862)
mar. (1) Emma Pattle

Mary Farmer (1748–1828)
mar. Charles Lloyd (1748–1828)
Banker; Translator

Charles Lloyd
(1775–1839)
Poet
Friend of Lamb

Priscilla
Lloyd
mar. 1804

: Rev. Christopher
Wordsworth
(1774–1846)
Master of Trinity

John Wordsworth
(1741–83)
Attorney

William Wordsworth
(1774–1850)
Poet Laureate
Brother of Dorothy

John
(1805–39)
Don

Charles
(1806–92)
Bishop

Christopher
(1808–85)
Bishop

Isabella
Lloyd
Poet

= Henry Russell
Composer
(1812–1900)

–. Russell

Henry Russell
Musician

= Lady Patricia Blackwood
dau. of 2nd Lord Dufferin

Miariam Russell
mar. Frederick
Manasseh Brandon

Annie Brandon
mar. Herbert
Edward Lemon

Muriel Lemon
mar. Frank Nevill Wyatt

Sir Landon
Ronald
Musician

Doris
Cooper
Actress

Grace
Cooper

William Clark Russell
Novelist (1844–1911)

Fanny Russell
1st wife

(1) =

Charles Frederick Cooper
Journalist
(1848–1939)

(2) =

Mabel Barnett
2nd wife, dau. of
Capt. Barnett

Sir Herbert Russell,
K.B.E.
Journalist

Henry St. John Cooper
Novelist
(1870–1926)

Herbert
Buckmaster
("Bucks Club")

(1)

(2) =

Nellie Taylor
Actress
(1894–1932)

Gladys
Cooper
Actress
mar.
3 times

=

Sir Neville
Pearson
Publisher

(1) =

Viva Birkett
Actress (d. 1934)

Philip Merivale
Actor (d. 1946)

(3) =

James MacBrien

(2)

Rupert Young

John Buckmaster
Actor

Joan Buckmaster
m. Robert Morley
actor

Sally (Pearson) Cooper
Actress
mar. Robert Hardy
Actor

Jack Merivale
Actor
m. Jan Sterling
Actress

Rosamund Merivale
Actress

Caroline

Jane

John Buckmaster
Actor

Annabel
mar. Charles Little

Wilton

Sheridan
mar. Margaret Gudejko

Hugo

Alexis

Juliet

Emma

Justine

Acknowledgements

This is my fourth biography and it has taken me something like seven years to complete, partly because I have paused along the way for other projects, such as making a living, and mainly because the material here has taken me that long to collect from around the world. Gladys was not a lady who believed in the past, and she therefore kept very little of it with her: letters, press cuttings, programmes, photographs and playscripts have usually turned up not among her own papers (which were almost exclusively concerned with the adoption of ducks and the transport of large amounts of furniture to and from California at regular intervals) but among those of her relatives and friends and fellow-players, most of whom have been kind enough to supply not only these but also their own recollections of her in public and in private across three-quarters of a century.

My thanks are due first and most of all to her immediate family: to my mother (her elder daughter Joan) who saved all her letters, to her younger daughter Sally, to her two sons-in-law, Robert Morley and Robert Hardy, and to her sister Doris who has invaluable memories of their shared childhood in the 1890s.

My thanks are then due to my own family, Margaret and Hugo and Alexis and Juliet, who put up with me and at least one room entirely filled with Cooper memorabilia while the book was being written, and to Alan Coren the editor of *Punch* who gave me the time off to get the final typescript into shape. It was another professional colleague, John Knight (a producer in what's now the Sound Archive Production Unit at the BBC), who made possible the first and most important half-dozen of the many interviews I was to do at home and abroad about Gladys, those that were   xiii for a radio obituary we recorded soon after her death in 1971.

What follows is an alphabetical list of those people who have also helped me along the way: most by giving me long reminiscent interviews, some by writing to me with accounts of Gladys at different moments in a long and eventful life. One or two of her contemporaries and near-contemporaries who were among the most helpful to me, in that their memories went back the farthest, have not alas lived to see here the result of their kindness; but to all the following I am most grateful:

Adrianne Allen	Harold Hobson
Frith Banbury	Gavin Lambert
Cecil Beaton	Cole Lesley
Dirk Bogarde	Micheál MacLiammóir
Noël Coward	Jack Merivale
George Cukor	Cathleen Nesbitt
Nan Culver	Beverley Nichols
Roland Culver	David Niven
Zena Dare	Laurence Olivier
Michael Denison	Paul Scofield
Angela du Maurier	Sebastian Shaw
Daphne du Maurier	Marti Stevens
Hugo Dyson	Sewell Stokes
Edith Evans	Sybil Thorndike
Peter Graves	Una Venning
Dulcie Gray	Arnold Weissberger
John Gielgud	Derek Williams
Edward Halliday	Alan Lambert Woods
Rex Harrison	Norman Wright
Richard Haydn	Rosamund (Merivale) Young
Wendy Hiller	Rupert Young

In further research, I am especially grateful for the help given to me by Jennifer Aylmer and the staff of the Enthoven Collection at the Victoria and Albert Museum, the staff of the British Film Institute Library, the theatre department of the University of Southern California, the Lincoln Centre Library for the Performing Arts and our own library at *Punch*. I am also, as always, deeply grateful to Raymond Mander and Joe Mitchenson for textual and illustrative help.

A list of source books will be found in the bibliography, but

my thanks are also due to the owners and editors of the following newspapers and magazines, some of which are now defunct, for quotations both direct and indirect: *American Register, Daily Express, Daily Mail, Daily Telegraph, Evening News, Evening Standard, Glasgow Citizen, Good Housekeeping, Illustrated London News, London Mail, Morning Post, News Chronicle, New Statesman, New York Times, The Observer, Play Pictorial, Plays & Players, Saturday Review, The Sketch, Spectator, The Sphere, Sporting and Dramatic, The Stage, Sunday Express, Sunday Pictorial, Sunday Times, The Tatler, Theatre World, The Times, Variety.*

Last, but by no means least, my thanks to Charles Pick at Heinemann in London and to Beverly-Jane Loo at McGraw Hill in New York, the former for his infinite patience and the latter for her boundless enthusiasm.

'She had all the charm of an electric carving knife.'

Dirk Bogarde

'She was one of the great hurdlers of the twentieth-century British theatre.'

Laurence Olivier

'She used to say it was ridiculous of me to expect her to have learnt my words by the first rehearsal, but it wasn't the first rehearsal I worried about. It was the first night.'

Noël Coward

'She has made naturalism into a form of dramatic art.'

James Agate

'Acting was something she did for a living, not something she had ever really thought about.'

David Niven

'She was one of the four best actresses I have ever seen.'

Harold Hobson

'She gardened the way that other people play Hamlet.'

Robert Morley

'She was a darling girl.'

Sybil Thorndike

Preface

It wasn't until a year or two before her death at eighty-two in the autumn of 1971 that I began to realize how very little I really knew about my grandmother Gladys. I knew of course that she was an actress who'd started out as a Gaiety Girl and ended up as a Dame of the British Empire; I knew that she had been one of the very first pin-ups of World War I, and I'd met Chelsea Pensioners in their eighties who'd carried her picture on a post-card through the trenches. I knew that a whole window of Selfridge's had once been occupied by posters of her advertising her own patent beauty cream, and that she'd only narrowly missed being the first woman to loop the loop.

More seriously, I knew that she'd gone on from the Gaiety to become one of this country's very few actress-managers running her own company at the Playhouse Theatre under Hungerford railway bridge by the Thames. 'What did you do about the noise of the trains overhead?' Dirk Bogarde once asked her: 'Trains, dear?' she replied, 'We had them stopped on matinee days, naturally.' There, between 1927 and 1933, she premiered the best of the Somerset Maugham plays: already she'd worked with Hawtrey and Hicks and Gerald du Maurier and Ivor Novello, and later she was to work with Laurence Olivier and John Gielgud and Noël Coward.

In 1939, with thirty-five years in the English theatre already behind her, she went to Hollywood with Hitchcock to make *Rebecca* and turned a three-week contract into a stay of nearly thirty years during which she was three times nominated for an Oscar. That, in essence, was her professional life: in private I knew she'd married three times, had three children of whom the eldest is my mother, and that of all her husbands the only one with whom she was entirely happy died less than a decade after their marriage.

But most of that can be found in the reference books and in any case none of it finally explains anything at all about who she really was, or where she came from, or what she thought she was doing with her life. She herself, as I discovered when I started tentatively to work on this book a year or so before she died, had remarkably little interest in looking back. Like the Go-Between she believed that the past was a foreign country where things were done differently, but unlike him she saw no virtue or point in trying to gain a re-entry visa. Gladys never understood about nostalgia, any more than she ever understood about fear or exhaustion or illness or old age, and she was not one to believe in the existence of something she couldn't understand.

Olivier once said that she was one of the great hurdlers, striding over all the epochs and fashions of the British and American theatre in her lifetime; and it was Robert, my father, who first pointed out that Gladys chose her films and plays and television shows the way most of us choose our aeroplanes – because they happened to be going where she wanted to go. On more than one occasion a plane would have been the more reliable vehicle, but Gladys cared about her failures only fractionally less than she cared about her successes.

Not that she was an especially modest or unselfish lady: like Sybil Thorndike and Edith Evans and the other grand Dames of that extraordinarily resilient and long-lived 1880s generation, Gladys had a very secure idea of her own position in the world and brooked little interference from those who wished to invade or shift that position. Yet the theatre (and the cinema and television, which she regarded simply as its subsidiary if often more convenient manifestations) was not for her, as for some of the other Dames, a temple of the arts or a religious calling. It was work. Enjoyable sometimes, infuriating and occasionally heartbreaking at others, acting was to Gladys nothing more nor less than what she did for a living.

Never very poor, and for that matter never very rich either, Gladys had certain periods in her life when she enjoyed the comparative financial security of an earning husband or an MGM contract: but into her eighties she was still providing for a sister deaf from birth and a son whose working life had been prematurely halted by mental illness. Gladys neither expected nor gave pity for any of this, and though she would occasionally accept advice and other forms of help from her two actor sons-in-law, Robert Morley and Robert Hardy, her life and her responsibilities were always very much her own affair.

Her daughters, Joan and Sally, were frequently roped in to help sort out the innumerable pets, houses, cars and relatives which Gladys had a habit of gathering around her on one side of the Atlantic and then temporarily abandoning while she crossed over to sort out the other lot on the other side. Through three marriages, a theatre company and countless individual shows and films (a career chart will be found in the appendix) Gladys collected around her what seemed like half California and most of the Thames Valley, but in her expectations of family help she made the limits very clear indeed: what she wanted was efficient secretarial and managerial assistance, not a takeover of her life by anyone else.

Independence was at the very heart of her: only once in her life, I believe, did she meet somebody into whose hands she was willing to put herself to some extent, and that man was her third and last husband Philip Merivale. Along the way she met many others – husbands, lovers, children, grandchildren, co-stars, fellow players and quite often comparative strangers – to whom she would unstintingly give parts of herself. Merivale got more than most.

In the manner of many born of her late-Victorian generation Gladys kept herself to herself; she did not ever delve too deeply into her innermost self, nor did she expect others to try and discover whatever lay at the heart of her existence. Psychiatry and self-analysis were, to her generation, both new-fangled and unnecessary.

She viewed the coming of the gossip column and the television interview with a certain amount of alarm, not because she had anything much to hide but because instinctively she felt that self-exposure was bad form. Form she understood, and good manners too, in an immensely Royal way: it wasn't so much that she was never rude or late or careless, all three of which she was occasionally capable of being, but that she knew what to do and say afterwards.

But before we get too deeply into Gladys's life and the mem-   xix

ories of those with whom she shared it, I had better declare the
interests and qualifications which are bound to colour and
condition what follows. The eldest of Gladys's five grandchildren, I was born in December 1941 thirteen days before her
fifty-third birthday: she had been Mrs Philip Merivale for four
years and the two of them were living in California where they
had bought a prospective homestead for the seven children they
had acquired in previous marriages and their prospective grandchildren, though sadly it never became quite that: by the time
most of us got there after the war, Philip was already dead.

The first time Gladys and I met was in 1945 when Metro sent
her to London to do a film. I was already nearly four and, never
a small child at the best of times, was I think even then too old
and too chubby to qualify as the sort of grandchild she liked best
and later luckily got in abundance. Her love for babies and the
very small was legendary and indeed almost eery: she lived just
long enough to know Hugo, my son, and my elder daughter
Alexis, who was eighteen months when Gladys died, and looking
at them playing together by the river one afternoon in the last
summer of Gladys's life, with nothing but eighty years separating
them, I realized that they knew something the rest of us in
between them did not. Certainly Gladys was not the kind of
domesticated, cuddly great-grandmother this picture of domestic
bliss might otherwise convey: she had no great love for children
at their messiest or most inconvenient, but when they were at
their absolute best then so in a curious way was she.

Despite that, I never found it very easy to think of her as my
own grandmother, certainly not the kind of grandmother who
might one day need trays of tea and biscuits taken up to bed.
If there were ever any trays to be carried around her house, it
was Gladys who invariably carried them.

My sister Annabel, five years younger, was I think closer to
Gladys as a grandchild (the two of them used to feed stale bread
to the ducks in Henley until Annabel took to lunching off the
bread herself) and certainly Emma and Justine, the two daughters of Sally's marriage to Robert Hardy, shared with their
grandmother Gladys a unique and unquenchable alliance made
up of old Victorian nursery songs, a great deal of mutual love and
respect, and a kind of energetic enthusiasm which seemed to be
the exclusive property of Gladys and the very young.

xx   I can claim no such alliance, though in some ways I am not sorry: this book would not I think be possible had Gladys and I ever been very close. As it was, we met again in 1948 when she came (briefly) back to London in an indifferent early Ustinov play called *The Indifferent Shepherd*, and then again in the following year when our whole family went to live with her in California for a summer on our way from New York to Australia whither my father, Robert Morley, was bound in his play *Edward My Son*. By that time Gladys was several years into her MGM contract and playing the housekeeper (a regular role) in *The Secret Garden* for them: every morning she would set off early to work while the rest of us, or I at any rate, would slouch around her pool sampling the newly discovered delights of bananas and all-day swimming. Once I remember her taking me to downtown Los Angeles to purchase a tortoise, yet one more beloved animal to add to the menagerie of dogs and cats and geese she was then running in her house and garden, and on another occasion I remember her and her old friend the actor Roland Culver patiently if unsuccessfully trying to discover whether I had any aptitude for golf. Gladys was then already over sixty and had been a widow for two years, but I remember no signs of age or grief: she seemed, then as almost always, immensely busy, immensely cheerful and still immensely unknown to me.

Then we were off to Australia and for the next ten years, after our return to England, my memories of Gladys are a blur of increasingly frequent home visits, huge weekend tea parties at Barn Elms, her house on the regatta stretch of the Thames at Henley, and a gradual awareness as I lumbered through my teens that I was still a good long way off being the dynamic, svelte, attractive grandson she'd have liked. Luckily her grand-daughters came a good deal closer to the mark, and Gladys was never less than marvellous to me: indeed the combination of her innate good manners and my innate insensitivity meant that several more years had elapsed and I was already well into my twenties before I realized that our relationship left something to be desired.

Then, as I began to get myself faintly established as a writer and television interviewer in England, we seemed to draw a little closer; though here again we were doomed, this time by my increasing fascination with the theatrical past and her increasing determination to look nowhere but ahead. Getting On was Gladys's philosophy: I don't think it always mattered to her which precise destination she was getting on towards, as long as there was discernible forward movement of some kind. Like Noël Coward and Somerset Maugham, both of whom wrote plays for her, she was a compulsive traveller – but unlike them she saw little point in discussing where she had been. What Gladys always wanted to talk about was where she was going next.

Despite that, I did manage to persuade her in the last few months of her life that we should do a book to update the two already published: her own (ghost-written) autobiography which dates from 1931, and my godfather Sewell Stokes's 1953 biography *Without Veils*. Gladys was still not keen: up to the very end she retained a touching if sometimes irritable astonishment that people would or could wish to save her old postcards, collect her autograph or remember performances that she herself had long since entirely forgotten. She agreed, however, that she might quite like to do, with me, a book about some of the people she had met and liked in her life, and from there we finally began to approach the idea of a full-scale biography.

Even then she was not, however, easy to pin down: until the last few weeks of her life she was playing on tour in a revival of *The Chalk Garden*, and although her mind remained as active as ever (one of her last letters, written a week before her death to *Time* magazine to complain about a cover story they had done on the new permissive theatre, ended '*HAIR* is a four-letter word') her health was increasingly shaky and she did not at the last have the strength or I think the will for long retrospective interviews.

Nevertheless we managed to tape quite a few, and in the years that have elapsed since her death I have added to them the recollections of around a hundred friends and relatives and colleagues on both sides of the Atlantic. What follows is, I hope, a book she'd have liked to read: more probably however it would have gone somewhere about halfway down the pile of unread biographies on her bedside table, underneath the dog-leads and the photographs of the younger grandchildren and the note about gravel for the drive and the other note about food for the ducks on the winter towpath below her window.

Gladys took the view that her life was for her to lead and others to follow as they pleased, and it was a belief which carried her undaunted and undefeated through to the very end. Perhaps now we'd better go back to the very beginning.

1
Gaiety Girl

chapter one

1888–1895

SHE was born Gladys Constance Cooper in Lewisham on December 18th, 1888: I don't think she ever much cared for the Constance (the name turns up on her birth certificate but almost nowhere else) and the Gladys didn't subsequently please her all that much either, even though it was a rather more fashionable and elegant appellation then than now. G was how she signed herself towards the end of her life, and G is still how most of us think of her to this day.

Her father was Charles Frederick Cooper, the journalist and founding editor of *The Epicure*, a pioneering food and drink magazine, and her mother was his second wife, Mabel Barnett, the daughter of a Captain in the Scots Greys. The Cooper family tree, not a document in which G ever took much interest (some months after her death I eventually located it buried deep in a mouldering cardboard box beneath a large number of documents relating to the adoption of ducks and the purchase of land in Jamaica, subjects infinitely closer to her eccentric heart) shows some impressive if rambling connections: whoever compiled it has managed to trace lines back to William Wordsworth and to Elizabeth Fry the prison reformer, to say nothing of Samuel T. Galton who married an aunt of Charles Darwin, and Galton's son Sir Francis who co-founded the science of eugenics.   **3**

Sadly for that science itself, it is hard to see any direct influences on Gladys going further back than her father, whose work as a journalist took him frequently into London's theatres. Indeed at the time of her birth, Charles Cooper was freelancing as a drama critic, and it was Mabel Barnett's firm belief that their first child would actually be born in a theatre while Cooper was reviewing a first night – a happening which was actually avoided by rather less than twelve hours.

Cooper's first wife, Fanny (a distant member of the Bertrand Russell family), had already borne him two other daughters and two sons, one of whom, Henry St John Cooper, was to become a prolific hack writer of 'clean, healthy love stories' which he churned out at an alarmingly rapid rate – on one occasion, required to provide a story of thirty-two thousand words for a Christmas annual which was already going to press, he completed the task in barely twelve hours, though this was more one suspects a tribute to his stamina than to his prose style.

Of Charles Cooper's second family, Gladys was the eldest child: following the collapse of his first marriage (to which he never referred again except on his deathbed, when he acknowledged that Fanny had been 'difficult') he had found in Mabel Barnett a wife who was to stay with him until the very end of his life, at which time, though now well into his nineties and totally blind, he was still at work on books and magazine journalism. Mabel was by all accounts a mild and sensible and eminently dependable lady who'd originally been employed as a companion for his mother, and the virtues of thrift and economy had been instilled in her by the memory of her own father who had gambled his way through several fortunes during her childhood while her mother drove around Europe in a catastrophically expensive procession of horse-drawn carriages.

Soon after G's birth, and before the arrival of her two younger sisters, the Coopers left Lewisham for a house in Chiswick Mall where in the early 1890s it was still possible to gather mushrooms for breakfast from the fields lying open behind the buildings. Though not at the head of his profession, Cooper was a respected and widely well-connected journalist only briefly tarnished by the scandal of a divorce: the immense respectability of his second wife (had not Mabel's great-grandfather saved the life of the Duke of Kent, later to father Queen Victoria, during the mutiny in Gibraltar in 1801?) was of no little help to him, and

4

Gladys at three (unfinished oil on wood panel by M. H. Carlisle)

apart from his daily work on *The Epicure*, he had been able to carve out a good career for himself freelancing in other publications as an early expert on what was then known as 'pure' and would now be known as health food.

There was much talk, that autumn of 1888, about 'the refuse of society': the Whitechapel murders of Jack the Ripper were causing widespread fear, though in more cheerful vein 1888 was also the year of the first-ever beauty contest, the year they invented the Kodak camera, and the year Dunlop patented the pneumatic tyre. It was a year of birth G shared with Irving Berlin, Maurice Chevalier, T. S. Eliot and Lawrence of Arabia.

The year of G's birth was also the year the British avenged General Gordon's death at Khartoum, the year of the 'Parnellite' murders in Kerry, and the year which celebrated Queen Victoria's half-century on the throne. On the morning of December 18th itself *The Times* was reporting an attack by Lord Randolph Churchill on Kitchener's policies in the Sudan, a decision to install full electric lighting in the House of Commons (even if it should do 'immeasurable damage to the woodwork') and the failure of the paper's African correspondent to locate Mr Stanley who was

5

then proving as elusive as Dr Livingstone himself. It further reported that the Sunday opening of pubs was 'under earnest consideration' and that a number of letters had been received questioning the Prince of Wales's right to pre-empt other travellers' previously booked berths on the Orient Express for his own personal use.

The arts page reported the opening of the Lyric Theatre in Shaftesbury Avenue on the previous night, and the fact that Mr Irving would be joined by Miss Ellen Terry for the December production of *Macbeth* at the Lyceum. In the classified columns a cook was wanted for £48 per year and a housemaid for £18.

Of early life in Lewisham, or indeed Fulham where the family went next, G seems to have had no recollections at all, but Chiswick Mall she remembered very clearly indeed: her sisters Doris and Grace were born at two-yearly intervals after her, and the three of them shared a large nursery overlooking that stretch of the Thames on which the annual Oxford and Cambridge Boat Race is rowed. Doris was the middle sister, halfway from Gladys to Grace who was the one born stone deaf: all three were to survive into their eighties and both Doris and Grace are indeed alive and well at the time of this 1978 writing. Doris it was who recalled their family life along Chiswick Mall:

> There never seemed to be a lot of money but somehow we weren't very poor either: we weren't aware of needing or wanting for very much and the family could still afford to keep a living-in maid. My parents were a very devoted couple, she much younger than him, indeed only a year or two older than his eldest daughter by his first marriage. I often wondered if my mother broke up that first marriage of father's, but I never found out and certainly I wasn't encouraged to ask.
>
> I think father's first wife was much more ambitious, too ambitious for him, perhaps; my mother was much more inclined to follow in his footsteps and look up to him. She was very artistic and they used to have 'at homes' and go to all the social events. She was a Burne-Jones sort of lady, very sensitive, and father adored her.
>
> We lived on his journalism and the books, because there was no inherited family money of any kind: he had a stepmother who lived in Richmond and wore lace caps but that was all we ever really knew of his family, and all the children

6

of his first marriage were virtually grown up by the time we came along.

A French governess came to look after us for a while, but she was hideous and wore glasses and was a total wash-out: Gladys and I taught her English and she taught us nothing at all. Then we went to Chiswick Convent which was lovely, not Gracie of course who had to go to a special deaf school, but Gladys and I used to go there and when the river was very high we had to climb over all the neighbours' garden walls to get home from school because the towpath was flooded.

G never lost her love for rivers in general and the Thames in particular, on the banks of which she spent the first and last decades of her life. River racing was, too, a constant factor: towards the end, when she lived on the regatta stretch at Henley, the BBC took to televising the finals from a camera position almost exactly opposite her house. By this time a fair number of the children and step-children and grandchildren and great-grandchildren were living around her in the Thames Valley and television sets in various houses would be tuned to the racing: then we'd phone G, tell her to go and stand on the towpath outside her gate and wave as the boats passed, and we'd have yet again the pleasure of seeing her on television.

But in those early years along Chiswick Mall they had to find other diversions: grapes grew in the garden and the early photographs show a cheerful, chubby-cheeked Gladys growing into an elegant little girl dressed in Kate Greenaway clothes, topped on at least one occasion by a straw hat designed to look alarmingly like a halo. She was, recalls Doris, a happy if somewhat bossy little girl:

> We weren't very alike in either looks or character, though in old age we grew more alike and now that she's dead people look at me and think they're seeing a ghost. She was fairer than me in skin and complexion, a pink-and-white child, very ambitious and determined, and inclined to rule her sisters with a rod of iron. Mother encouraged her, liked the idea of her being rather 'special', and worked off all her own inhibitions by pushing Gladys forward so that people were forever being encouraged to admire and photograph her: not that they ever needed much encouragement.

7

With her sister Doris, at the start of a long photographic career

G herself always took the view that neither she nor Doris were especially 'nice' children; both were tomboys with a passion for sliding down the stairway railings at a local station, thereby putting the fear of God into an aged porter, and then came the arrival of their youngest sister:

'One day,' remembered Gladys, 'while Doris and I were being wheeled home in the two-seater mailcart in which we were given our daily outings, one of our half-sisters met us and said "Would you like to have a new sister?". "No, we wouldn't" I replied firmly, speaking for both of us. "Well you've got one anyway," she said, whereupon Doris and I set up a howling that lasted until we were hurried indoors – and for some time afterwards. Thus did we welcome Grace to the family circle.'

A theatrical child then, even if in those days the idea of a daughter on the stage was not one to be entertained even by so stagestruck a father as hers. Mr Cooper had indeed once written a play based on one of his own books, *The Ring of Gyges*: the ring was however supposed to make its wearer invisible, a problem of stage management Mr Cooper could never satisfactorily solve, and the play thus lay unperformed in his desk while he channelled his enthusiasm for the footlights into a deep though entirely respectable passion for the actress Mary Anderson. Never for a moment did he think Gladys would become an actress, nor did he approve of well-brought-up young ladies going into a profession still considered fairly despicable.

Mrs Cooper was however less hostile to the idea, and by the time Gladys was twelve she was regularly acting in school plays organized by the convent to raise money for local charities: the Chiswick paper reported in 1900 that 'Miss Gladys Cooper by her beauty and talent won all honours in her clever performance as the Prince of Something-or-other'. By then G was also regularly in demand as a photographic model, a career which was to haunt her and occasionally thwart her other ambitions for many years to come.

It all started when, at the age of six, G's mother took her to be photographed at the Downeys' studio in Ebury Street: old and young Mr Downey were among the most fashionable court and society portrait photographers of the period, and their study of Gladys shows her sitting on a high throne-like chair clutching what appears, mysteriously enough, to be a croquet ball. Flowers are strewn at her feet, and she has that clenched-lip look

9

which denoted either extreme concentration or extreme boredom: the light is beamed on to her face as through a cathedral
window and Queen Alexandra, attending a later sitting at the
same studio, asked for a print of the picture showing 'the little
girl with the beautiful hair'.

Visits to Downeys', as often as not accompanied by Doris and
sometimes Gracie too, became a regular feature of G's childhood
and for a while she appeared to be the most photographed little
girl in London. Then still in its infancy (G had after all been born
in the same year as the Kodak), photography was nevertheless
already being taken very seriously indeed by its first few practi-
tioners, and a sitting would be a half-day affair treated as
reverently as a portrait session for an artist. The techniques
required by the sitter (immense patience, an ability to take
direction and a talent for looking good) were not so far removed
from those required by any actress in rehearsal or performance,
and it was indeed at Downey's studios that G met her first real
actress, Marie Studholme.

One of the great beauties of the age, and a considerable
musical-comedy star of the early 1900s, Marie Studholme had no
children of her own and took an immediate professional and
private liking to Gladys. Professionally, she would have G standing near (but not too near) her in glossy postcard pictures, little
suspecting that one day Gladys was herself to flood the postcard
market. Privately, she would invite G and Doris to stay at
Thames Cottage, her (again riverside) house at Datchet. From
there, on July 4th, 1895 when she was just six and a half, G had
written home:

> Dear Mother: I have got a new doll and a new pram. I have
> been on the river in Miss Studholme's boat. My doll has a lot
> of new dresses. I am going to the theatre on Saturday morning
> with Miss Studholme. I have a pretty new hat which Miss
> Studholme made for me. I am enjoying myself very much.
> Love to all from your loving daughter Gladys.

Another guest at Datchet that summer was the impresario
George Edwardes who eleven years later was to give G her start
at the Gaiety: at this time however there was no real thought of
the theatre except as an exciting place to visit. In the summer
of 1895 Miss Studholme invited G and her mother to a matinee of

10

Edwardes's *An Artist's Model* in which she was then starring at Daly's, and when at the end of the performance the star bowed to her audience G stood up in the stalls and waved back, assuming it to have been a personal greeting. She then went backstage and Hayden Coffin put her on his shoulders and took her off to Miss Studholme's dressing-room for tea. It was a sort of beginning.

With her first admirer, Marie Studholme, photographed at Downey's in 1894

chapter two

1896-1907

T HE matinee visits to Daly's increased, though G was always to insist they were not formative: 'I liked going to see Marie Studholme' she told her first biographer Sewell Stokes, 'but the fact that she was an actress didn't mean very much to me. I'd have liked going to see her if she'd been in a shop or an office or a factory.'

All the same, hers was in some senses by now a theatrical childhood: her face was becoming faintly familiar via the Downey postcards, familiar enough indeed for the celebrated artist Holman Hunt to ask for G and Doris to pose for a religious painting in which, obscurely, he had them both wearing red fisherman's caps.

Yet it wasn't until the summer of 1905, coming up to her seventeenth birthday, that Gladys went into the theatre professionally—albeit accidentally. Her earlier teens had been spent comparatively quietly at home, which she liked, and at school, which she didn't:

> I was born and brought up in the days when girls were not caught young and directed towards earning their own living. I lived quite happily at home, spending a lot of time on the river, for the first fifteen years of my life, giving no particular thought as to what was to become of me. That was the way

then, in families where no urgent necessity for the girls to go out and work existed. Certainly I had no real idea of going on the stage.

G did however have a schoolfriend called Mary Henessey, and Miss Henessey's determination it was to go on the stage: she had discovered, furthermore, that the Vaudeville Theatre in the Strand was holding 'voice trials' which it was possible to enter if you sent off a postcard to the stage door. She persuaded Gladys also to send in a card: Mrs Cooper approved wholeheartedly, and even gave G sixpence to buy a songsheet to practise on. When Mr Cooper heard of the plan he was however markedly less enthusiastic. 'You're mad,' he told Gladys, 'so's your mother. I wash my hands of the whole affair.'

Surrounded by a houseful of fairly domineering daughters, Mr Cooper was to spend increasing amounts of his time washing his hands of their affairs. Came the fateful day, G arrived at the stage door of the Vaudeville only to find that her friend had baulked at the last moment and there was no Mary Henessey.

Unafraid (the word which should appear on her memorial), Gladys went in alone, got past the stage-doorkeeper and sang a number which was Phyllis Dare's current hit from *The Catch of the Season* by Seymour Hicks, then playing at the Vaudeville itself:

My sublime ignorance of the ordeal into which I had plunged myself [remembered G some years later] and the fact that I didn't at that time in the least care whether I got on the stage or not, left me perfectly calm. They let me go on for a bit, then they said 'Well now, take this scene away and learn it' so I did, though I still wasn't taking any of this very seriously. I'd never been to drama school, remember, because I don't think my parents could have afforded it even if father had been more enthusiastic, and it all seemed a bit of a joke.

Anyway I went back and read them the scene, and after that they asked me what stage experience I'd had: quite brazenly I began to lie, and say that I'd been in this play and and that play and they said all right I could take over from Phyllis Dare who was due to leave the cast for a little while.

One full rehearsal was however enough to reveal G's total lack   13

of any stage experience, and the idea of her replacing Miss Dare
(who was in fact two years younger than G) was rapidly abandoned. She was however instead offered the job of principal
understudy:

> I suppose I should have been grateful for the chance to
> understudy a leading role in the West End, having done
> nothing at all in the theatre, but I wasn't: I was horrified.
> Understudy? Me understudy? I was appalled. 'No thank you'
> I said and was graciously sweeping out of the stage door
> again when the chorus master, who must have seen something
> in me he liked, rushed after mother and told us that another
> Seymour Hicks show, *Bluebell in Fairyland*, was casting for a
> tour at the Denton Agency down the road; so I went along
> to those auditions instead and got a job.

The money was three pounds a week, the part was the title
role itself, and the tour opened at Colchester on Gladys's seventeenth birthday, December 18th, 1905. The critic of the *Essex
Telegraph* was enthusiastic ('the company was carefully chosen
. . . Miss Gladys Cooper, a talented actress with a beautiful voice,
was an adorable Bluebell') and Mrs Cooper delighted that she at
last had a daughter on the stage. Mr Cooper was still less sold on
the idea, but resigned to being outvoted and outnumbered in a
family of which he was the only male member. To be a theatre
critic and to adore actresses like Mary Anderson was one thing –
to wake up and find an actress over the breakfast table each morning was something altogether else, and G's father took a good
many more years to acclimatize himself to the reality of her
career.

From Colchester on to Oxford, where *The Times* critic praised
her beauty first and her acting second, an arrangement of priorities
which was to be followed relentlessly in every review G got until
the beginning of World War II.

Then Brighton, where it was reported that 'the local press is
unanimous in declaring the young lady to possess a charming
face and figure, considerable grace of movement and great
histrionic ability'; G was thus now to be considered a professional
actress, a sudden change of status which was grasped more rapidly by Doris than Mr Cooper:

*Her first performance: Bluebell in Fairyland, Theatre Royal,
Colchester, December 1905*

Father never had us taught properly, so if you weren't going to marry or go on the stage straight from school there was really nothing else for a girl to do at that time. But our mother had it put in Gladys's first contract (for *Bluebell*) that her sister had to go on tour too, because she thought it would be nice for us to be together. I had no real ambition to go on the stage at all, but there I was, forced to be a mushroom or something in that ghastly little play. I wasn't really there as a chaperone, just for companionship, and I only had one line in the play which most nights I used to forget.

We had a Miss Lake who travelled around with us to keep an eye on where we were living and see that we ate properly and didn't get into any trouble: in those days, you know, children like Gertrude Lawrence and Noël Coward were constantly travelling around the country in shows long before they reached their teens. Nowadays of course they make you stay in school longer, but I was jolly glad to escape because I hated school anyway and so did Gladys.

But she began to get rather good parts, whereas I was always in the crowd scenes. She was a show-off child but very good, and totally without nerves of any kind. A very attractive, pretty child and always ambitious: cheek was what she had, sheer cheek, but it worked very well. She had, even at the first, an immensely determined character, no nonsense, would never tolerate fools gladly, nor illness nor inefficiency, even in those days. We were a rather intolerant family. I don't think her character ever really changed much: very efficient, always did everything for herself because she could never bear to wait for the rest of us to catch up, nor did she really trust us to get anything quite right. She was frightfully bossy and expected immense obedience from those around her – curiously enough, she usually got it too.

The Christmas after *Bluebell*, Gladys got a job in pantomime at Edinburgh where she was visited in her dressing-room after one matinee by J. A. Malone, the assistant to George Edwardes, who wondered if she'd like a job in the chorus at the Gaiety, then London's leading musical comedy theatre. Failing to realize the importance of the man or the theatre, G dismissed Malone somewhat abruptly: what annoyed her most, later on, was not the error of judgement but that when she finally did get to the

Gaiety it was via a theatrical agent to whom she had to give
ten per cent of a still small salary – money she could have kept
had she taken the job direct from Mr Malone.

In the meantime however she found a job for the summer of
1906 at the Vaudeville in *The Belle of Mayfair* starring Edna May.
G's contract specified three pounds a week.

The Belle of Mayfair (score by Leslie Stuart, he who wrote
Lily of Laguna, Soldiers of the Queen and half a hundred other hits
of the period) was the big musical success of 1906 and marked
G's West End debut, though she herself didn't much care for it:

> For one thing I was put to dress with show girls who were
> much older than I was, and I felt thoroughly out of it with
> them. For another, I could not get my two pig-tails to remain
> coiled up – the hairpins always fell out just as I was going on
> the stage or just as I got on it – and I found that I did not
> know how to make up properly. Previously, as a child actress,
> I had been helped to make up, but here I was supposed to
> know how to do it myself. I remember plastering my face
> with layer after layer of grease paint and so making myself
> the laughing-stock of the dressing room. I was constantly in
> tears while I was in *The Belle of Mayfair*, and began to feel
> that I wanted to have no more to do with the stage.

Then, early in 1907, she auditioned successfully for the George
Edwardes company at the Gaiety, though still without tremendous enthusiasm:

> I felt that I was never going to set the town on fire as a singer
> or a dancer, and I was already beginning to make up my mind
> that if I did stick to the stage I wanted to become a dramatic
> actress. I could see myself much more in, say, Mrs Patrick
> Campbell parts than as a second Gertie Millar or Edna May.
> I began arguing with George Edwardes even before I agreed
> to go under his famous management: he offered me a three
> years contract at £3, £4, and then £5 a week. I said that I did
> not want to bind myself to him for three years.

But sign she did, and admitted many years later that though
the shows themselves did not constitute her favourite kind of
theatre the Edwardes training was invaluable. This, after all, was   17

GAIETY THEATRE

MANAGING DIRECTOR: Mr. GEORGE EDWARDES.

TO-NIGHT AT 8 (Doors open 7.40), A New Musical Play entitled

The Girls of Gottenberg.

Written by GEORGE GROSSMITH, Jun.
Music by IVAN CARYLL and LIONEL MONCKTON.
Lyrics by ADRIAN ROSS and BASIL HOOD.

Otto ... (Prince of Saxe-Hildesheim) Mr. GEORGE GROSSMITH, Jun.
Albrecht (Capt. of Dragoons) Mr. W. LOUIS BRADFIELD
Brittbott! (Sergeant of Hussars) Mr. ROBERT NAINBY
General The Margrave of Saxe-Nierstein Mr. F. J. BLACKMAN
Colonel Finkhausen { Officers Mr. A. J. EVELYN
Fritz { of the Mr. T. C. MAXWELL
Hermann { Blue Mr. J. REDMOND
Franz { Hussars Mr. SOMERS BELLAMY
Karl Mr. GEORGE GRUNDY
Burgomaster ... ... Mr. GEORGE MILLER
Kannenbier (An Innkeeper) Mr. ARTHUR HATHERTON
Adolf (Town Clerk) ... Mr. CHARLES BROWN
Policeman ... ... Mr. ROBERT BURNS
Waiters Messrs. GRANDE & HILL
Corporal Riethen { Blue { Mr. J. R. SINCLAIR
Private Schmidt { Hussars { Mr. H. RAYMOND
AND
Max Moddelkopf ... ... Mr. EDMUND PAYNE

Elsa ... (The General's Daughter) Miss DOLLY CASTLES
Clementine (The Burgomaster's Daughter) Miss VIOLET HALLS
Lucille ... (Maid to Elsa) ... Miss OLIVE MAY
Kathie ... ... Miss TOPSY SINDEN
Hilda ... ... Miss KITTY LINDLEY
Gretchen ... Miss FLORENCE TOMES
Minna (Captain of College) Miss JEAN AYLWIN
Freda (Head of the Alemannia Corps) Miss CRISSIE BELL
Anna (Head of the Pomerania Corps)
Eva (Head of the Saxonia Corps) Miss MAY CHARTERIS
Lina (Head of the Borussia Corps) Miss GLADYS COOPER
Katrina (The only Girl in Rottenberg) Miss JULIA JAMES
Barbara Briefmark (The Postmaster's Daughter) Miss KITTY HANSON
Betti Berncastler (The Doctor's Daughter) Miss ENID LEONHARDT
Miss GLADYS DESMOND
AND
Mitzi (The Innkeeper's Daughter) Miss GERTIE MILLAR

ACT I. Scene 1 ... ... The Barracks, Rottenberg (Alfred Terraine).
Scene 2 ... ... The Market Place, Gottenberg (Joseph and Phil Harker).
ACT II. Scene ... The Gardens of "The Red Hen," across the River, near Gottenberg. (Joseph and Phil Harker)

Orchestra under the Direction of Mr. IVAN CARYLL.

Costumes designed by Mr. PERCY ANDERSON.

Dances arranged by Mr. FRED FARREN.

One of the Gaiety Girls, and starting to climb up the cast list (1907)

a time before the advent of many drama schools and before the creation of subsidized companies where an actress could pick up a training for her profession as she went along. With Edwardes, known as the Guv'nor, said Gladys:

> We were taught elocution, fencing, singing, dancing, stage movement, everything and all for free. In addition to that we worked every night on stage either in the chorus or playing small parts and understudying the leads. It was a musical repertory company in a way, and looking back on it of course I realise how lucky I was to get in. I could never quite forget, though, that it wasn't really my kind of theatre.

Programmes of this period for the Edwardes musicals at the Gaiety and his other theatre, Daly's, indicate that G was in *The Girls of Gottenberg* (1907), *Havana* (1908), *Our Miss Gibbs* and *The Dollar Princess* (1909) and vintage *Play Pictorial* photographs show her slow but sure progression from a chorus group in *Gottenberg* to 'Miss Sadie von Tromp' in *The Dollar Princess*. For a girl still approaching her twenty-first birthday, and temperamentally more suited to light comedy or even high drama than all-singing all-dancing extravaganzas (a fact which did not prevent her singing and dancing in a Walt Disney musical as late as 1967) G's period as a Gaiety Girl must be considered a fair success. 417. 595 / 920 Coo

Though she was forever in dispute with Edwardes about money and the kind of work he was assigning her, she liked the security of being a Gaiety Girl, constantly chaperoned and employed and trained for the profession to which she now knew beyond all doubt she wished to belong . . . albeit eventually in a different division.

Gladys was not however the kind of Gaiety Girl taken to Romano's by wealthy young men about town who would then drink champagne from her slippers, surely one of the nastiest social habits of the time: those were the 'show girls' employed by Edwardes specifically to attract the carriage trade. Gladys belonged at this time to the chorus, an altogether different group whose members were rather more carefully chaperoned and strictly forbidden even to talk to the show girls, let alone their patrons, in or out of the stage door.

Gertie Millar and George Grossmith were the stars of *The Girls*　　19

of Gottenberg and Gladys was one of the 'six bright young things' who drifted in and out of the action. Not much liking her allocated costume, during a break in rehearsals Gladys went out and bought a more stunningly fashionable creation which she then unwisely wore at the next runthrough. 'If that girl is going to appear in that frock,' said Miss Millar, 'I'm not going to appear at all,' and Gladys was ordered to return to her original costume. 'I suppose it was rather small-minded of me,' said Miss Millar when challenged by Gladys during the years of their later friendship, 'but I'd never had such tough competition at the Gaiety before: even then you seemed to have life by the throat.'

Play Pictorial thought *The Girls of Gottenberg* was 'the most emphatic success that Mr George Edwardes has ever had at the Gaiety' and the show had another admirer, too.

He was a twenty-six-year-old Boer War veteran called Herbert Buckmaster.

chapter three

1907-1908

BORN in November 1881, seven years before Gladys, Herbert John Buckmaster was the youngest son of a Ramsgate clergyman: his family connections, he once noted proudly, included two first cousins who were to become respectively 'the finest polo player in all England' (Walter Buckmaster) and the Cambridge professor of mathematics, Alfred North Whitehead. Buck, as he was always to be known, inclined more towards the sporting than the academic life, and after captaining his preparatory school at cricket, football and hockey in the mid-1890s he went on to Sherbourne and then found himself as one of the Public Schools Volunteers being reviewed by Queen Victoria in Windsor Great Park during the Diamond Jubilee celebrations of 1897: 'drawn up two deep,' he wrote later, 'the 3,769 boys extended three-quarters of a mile from a point opposite Shaw Lane deer pen to Queen Anne's Mead. The flower of English youth! I wonder how many of us, reviewed that day, perished in the Boer War and the Great War?'

Buck fought in and survived both: against the fervent wishes of his father, who wanted him to go up to Cambridge ('personally' said Buck, 'I have always thought that a Varsity career is a ridiculous waste of time except where a literary career is contemplated') he sailed at eighteen for Cape Town and the Boers, intending to enlist there in the Colonial Corps which was 'by far the best', as a schoolfriend had told him, 'if you want to see real fighting'.

Arriving in Cape Town after seventeen days at sea, Buck had managed to get himself enlisted in the Imperial Light Horse, known locally and somewhat disrespectfully as 'vanishing targets at five bob a day'. But Buck was deeply impressed by their courage and the friendship that he found and cherished among soldiers was one that he managed to preserve until the end of his days, largely by creating and running a London club many of whose founder members had been with him in a variety of trenches.

By early in the January of 1901 Buck had been at war with the Boers for nearly six months: his diary for the period is as crisp and unemotional as he always was:

January 6th: Slack morning, off at 3pm and rode to Riet-fontein. Good supper of steak and bacon; lucky to be able to commandeer things as rations are scarce. On half rations for some days. There was a rather melancholy sale by auction of the kit belonging to those killed yesterday. Bag of coffee stolen from me while I was asleep.

January 7th: Off early. Camped on veldt near where we did on 3rd. Had wash in river and washed clothes. Have only two handkerchiefs. Clean rifle with one. Corporal Scott goes to hospital with fever.

January 18th: Went off early. Captured two Boers. Looted houses. Got ripe peaches, potatoes which I dug myself, sack of onions, a three-legged pot and two frying pans.

January 19th: Went off on patrol. Our horses shied and I saw a snake about 12 feet long. Very cold night.

January 20th: Slack day. Had a bathe. On wood fatigue.

January 21st: Dad writes he has sent £25 to Standard Bank, Cape Town as a Christmas present. Boers captured a patrol of 7th Hussars.

January 23rd: The squadron go out and bring in forage. I wash clothes and myself. We hear Queen Victoria is dead. Very sad. Would have liked the Old Lady to live to see this wretched affair brought to an end.

But before it was eventually brought to an end, Buck had suc-
cumbed to a combination of malaria and jaundice and been sent

reluctantly back to England: there, after a briefly unsuccessful career as a farmer, he'd settled in London and was eking out a living as a full-time backer of horses, a choice of job which more or less put an end to whatever friendship still existed between himself and his family.

Buck had four good years with the horses, but then found himself with £355 owing to Ladbrokes, his bookmakers, and no clear way of paying the debt. Fortunately a friend and fellow man-about-town was Arthur Bendir, Ladbrokes' managing director, who agreed to take Buck on to the staff and let him pay off the debt as a bookmaker himself. The poacher had now turned gamekeeper, and it was at about this point in his life that my grandfather first met his future wife Gladys Cooper:

> In May 1907 I was having tea at the Carlton Hotel with a friend and she said 'Here is that pretty girl there is so much talk about'. I looked up and saw Gladys Cooper for the first time. Dressed in a dark green plaid coat and skirt, she was with two men, obviously young subalterns. She was then about eighteen, but even in the fashionable crowd who used to take tea in those days at the Carlton, it was obvious that she was not in the least self-conscious but perfectly self-possessed . . . a few days after I was lunching at Romano's with some men and, the place being packed as it always was in Luigi's day, I accidentally bumped against the back of a lady's chair at the next table. I apologised to her, and then saw it was Julia James who was in the *Girls of Gottenberg* with Gladys Cooper. She was with friends of mine who introduced me and I sat down with them for a few moments. A few days after, I wrote and asked Julia James if she would bring Gladys Cooper to lunch the following Saturday at Oddenino's Restaurant before their matinee: and that was when I actually first met Gladys Cooper. The lunch was a great success, and we arranged to take the girls on the river at Maidenhead the following day.

The Girls of Gottenberg ran on at the Gaiety through to the end of 1907 by which time Buck had become a regular escort, allowed to wait for her at the stage door once it became clear to the Edwardes management that this was no casual flirtation. Throughout 1908 they were an inseparable couple, despite the   23 fact that Buck once slammed a door accidentally in G's face, thereby fracturing her nose and accounting in his view for the remarkable beauty for which she was later to be praised. 'Before the accident,' he once wrote, 'she had no bridge to her nose at all: after it she had a lovely nose. I told her she ought to be very grateful to me as it improved her looks no end.'

While Buck continued to work for Ladbrokes, Gladys divided her time between the Gaiety and the studios of Messrs Foulsham and Banfield, postcard manufacturers, who had engaged her on an exclusive contract to sit for them once a month.

> I had almost a monopoly there for a while. Mine was a new face, and they'd put me into ordinary profile shots as well as special series – I once did a whole series of cards as Juliet though I'd never actually played the part. In the end it became a handicap, being better known on postcards than on the stage, but at this time it was all very helpful and I was certainly in no position to turn down regular work.

The lyricist Herbert Farjeon and his young brother were among many postcard collectors of the period:

> We were unanimous about Gladys Cooper. She, even more than Phyllis Dare, topped the lot. She did not need to smile, maintaining a certain but by no means forbidding dignity. And the whole nation endorsed our verdict. Other nations apparently saw the point too. Even when I went to Italy, one of the first things that met my gaze in Sienna was a photograph of Gladys Cooper framed in silver.

G's postcards, and there were more than four hundred of her in different costumes and poses published between 1905 and 1920, add up to an intriguing collection. Many of them are stamped on the back 'This is a Real Photograph of a British Beauty' in case there might otherwise have been some doubt: they show her in all shapes and sizes, wearing a variety of clothes and hats ranging from the alluring to the hideous, and managing in some curious way to change her personality almost entirely from shot to shot. In some, she appears immensely tall, angular and haughty; in others, hugely chubby and jolly, as if about to play a seaside landlady. Hair up or down, hats on or off, clearly the cards were intended for many different purposes: birthday messages of

24

Over four hundred picture postcards of Gladys were published
between 1905 and 1920

WE TWO.

unique banality were often printed across the bottom ('Though Life may be a tangle, May all your Birthdays ring, With bells that never jangle, But only sweet songs sing') and many also bore her flamboyantly legible signature across the lower right-hand corner. Others are totally unidentified, either because the publishers thought her already well enough known, or because her name was at that stage in her career by no means as important as her face.

Another card, also intended for a birthday, has two pink roses and G mysteriously clad in golfing kit complete with putter: on a third she's dressed like Tallulah Bankhead and perched on a cocktail cabinet, while in another whole sequence she's dressed in a kilt and is defending herself against God knows what with a dirk and shield.

Many cards date of course from the First War: there's 'Dreaming of my boy at the Front' and 'Hope you'll soon be Home' as well as a whole maternal/domestic sequence showing G surrounded by children, some of them hers, and on one occasion Buck himself. Then there's Gladys playing with a dog, Gladys clutching a garden rake, and Gladys staring in some amazement at a horse: sometimes she appears to have been transported to the Alps and is seen in front of a singularly phoney backdrop winsomely removing skates.

Then again there are cards on which four different shots of her have been neatly arranged to form the petals of a rose in full bloom: on others the colours have been altered so that the same photograph reversed can be sold as an altogether different card. Gladys Cooper cards were not so much a craze as an industry, and to this day, as attics and cellars are cleared out and scrapbooks rediscovered, her relatives still regularly get sets of them sent back through the post. G herself took in later life to using them as Christmas cards: not reprinting them, but simply gathering up the first hundred or so that came to hand each year and sending them out again to friends and relatives with 'Love G' scrawled across the original message. It is some tribute to her popularity that nobody ever seemed to get the same card twice.

New ones are still coming to light: G staring out of a roseclad cottage window (in reality I suspect another backdrop), G poring over a script while a cat nibbles her ankles, G entirely dwarfed by a vase of marigolds, G and her first two children as three lockets on a necklace inscribed 'Thinking of You, Dear' and then G relegated to the bottom right-hand corner while her children take over the central space themselves. Later cards show her sitting at the wheel of a sportscar, paying a bill and 'thinking of her little Joan' who is depicted in a sort of bubble above her head. If by about 1914 Gladys Cooper wasn't the biggest star in the country, it was certainly no fault of Messrs Foulsham and Banfield.

Back in the live theatre *Havana* was the first of the Edwardes shows in which Gladys had any chance at all of making her mark: she was 'a touring newspaper beauty' with a line or two of her own. Buck recalled an already ambitious lady:

> When she was earning £5 a week (in *Havana*) she would say in all seriousness 'When I am earning £100 a week'. And we used to say 'Yes, dear', humouring her like a stupid child – but she accomplished it. In later years when she was earning £200 a week she would frequently say, also quite seriously, 'When I have a theatre of my own'. And again we'd humour her by saying 'Yes, dear' – but she accomplished that, too.

Havana ran through the whole of 1908 at the Gaiety, and it was during that summer that G became unofficially engaged to Buck. Her sister Doris was once again called on for help:

> We were still girls living at home, and father didn't approve at all of Buck, who was a gambling man and considered rather a rake at the time. He and Gladys used to have to go out on the sly, and I was forever covering up for them. Father indeed once forbade Gladys ever to see her young man again, but Gladys of course just ignored him and they went on meeting all through that year. Then in December they decided to get married, but they didn't tell my parents because Gladys was only just about to have her twentieth birthday. And I was the one who had to keep the secret.

Towards the end of her life, G took the view that if her father had not forbidden her to marry Buck the affair would have blown over without a marriage at all; as it was, family opposition made her all the more determined to become Mrs Buckmaster and get a home of her own. The wedding was set for St George's, Hanover Square, on the last day of the *Havana* run: Buck, a confirmed   27 young sport, viewed the secrecy of his forthcoming alliance as yet one more lark in a life that had already been decidedly larky. G took it all rather more seriously:

> Bit by bit I smuggled clothes and various belongings from home, sneaking out with suitcases when no one was looking . . . how I ever had the courage to do any such thing I do not know. I was not only fond of my home (and was, on the whole, very happy there) but I was afraid of my father. He could be, when angry, very cold and stern. He belonged to that period when fathers disliked every young man on principle – and often on sight – who came a-wooing unless of course the young man had been chosen and picked out by himself, and I really cannot imagine him contemplating or choosing a husband for any of us. Nor was it as if I had knocked about a lot on my own, or was thoroughly emancipated and independent. On the contrary I was Edwardianly dutiful, and still 'minded' what was said to me.

Came the Saturday, December 12th, 1908, and the wedding went off according to plan: Gladys had lied that she was twenty-one in order to get the licence and Doris was a witness, though there was of course no one else there from G's family. Buck filled the church with young men about town and ex-brother officers from South Africa, and after the service they all drove off in a coach-and-four to Richmond for the wedding breakfast. Buck claimed that he narrowly escaped serious injury when two of his heartier friends, unable to find dry rice to hurl over the happy couple, used instead a ready-cooked rice pudding. Apart from that, the day seems to have passed without other incident, and Gladys returned to the Gaiety to play the last performance of *Havana* and join in a champagne celebration backstage after the show. The happy couple then set off for a honeymoon in Eastbourne, leaving the unfortunate Doris to go home and break the news to her parents before they had time to read it in the morning papers. By all accounts they were a great deal less than ecstatic. 'My father,' said Gladys, 'refused to speak to me for nearly a year, and I had to creep home to see mother on days when I knew he'd be out of the house.'

chapter four

1908=1912

THE honeymoon was not a success. On the morning of December 13th, 1908 Buck and G awoke in an Eastbourne hotel to find themselves married but in considerable parental trouble: clearly they could not go home to either set of relatives, but on the other hand there was no real idea of where they would live or how they would support themselves, since Buck's salary from Ladbrokes was still going to pay off his old gambling debts and G's salary from the Gaiety was scarcely enough to support anyone but a girl living at home with parents (as G had been) or one under noble or at any rate wealthy male patronage (as many others still were).

They were thus a honeymoon couple under considerable strain, and the stay at Eastbourne was not much helped by the fact that, within a day or two of their arrival at the Hotel Metropole there, Buck developed mumps and G promptly went down with shingles. Their fortnight over, two semi-invalids returned to London and began to consider a marital future which looked decidedly unrosy.

G immediately went to see George Edwardes in an attempt to redraft her contract: by now she'd realized that she was never going to be a leading lady in musical comedy, and that she didn't anyway much want to be. What she wanted was the freedom to try her luck in the legitimate theatre as a straight actress, and to get away from chorus or 'Young Lady' work once and for all. 29

Not that she yet wanted to leave the Gaiety altogether: she merely wanted the freedom to come and go, working for Edwardes when he had a decent part for her and for other managements when he had not.

There were indeed already signs that other managements were beginning to show an interest in her, as Somerset Maugham recalled forty years later:

> I am rather vague about dates, but I think it must have been early in the year 1910 [in fact 1909] that Charles Hawtrey [one of the foremost actor-managers of the day] called me up one morning and asked me to come to the Royalty Theatre in Dean Street where he was producing plays, I believe in partnership with Vedrenne, to see an actress he wanted me to meet. He was about to put on a light comedy which at his request I had translated from the French for him. I forget what it was originally called, but I gave it the name of *The Noble Spaniard*, and as there was nothing much to it, in order to make it more picturesque I turned it into a period piece in the hope that the pretty clothes would make up for the thinness of the intrigue. There was a good part for Hawtrey, but he hadn't yet found an actress for the chief female part.
>
> 'I've asked a girl to come here who might do for us,' he said when I had shaken hands with him. 'She's at the Gaiety just now, in the chorus, but she wants to get on the legitimate stage. She's as pretty as a picture.'
>
> 'Can she act?' I asked.
>
> 'I shouldn't think so,' he answered cheerily. 'But you wait till you see her. She's a knock-out.'
>
> The words were hardly out of his mouth when a young woman was ushered in. Hawtrey got up and took both her hands in his.
>
> 'Darling. This is Mr Maugham. I've just been telling him you're the most beautiful girl in the world.'
>
> She smiled and shook hands with me. She was very simply dressed in a coat and skirt, and singularly composed considering that she was being thought of for her first speaking part and that if I approved of her she would have the chance of playing opposite the most popular comedian of the day. All that Hawtrey had said of her was true. Her beauty was fresh,

healthy and spring-like. Perhaps because notwithstanding the calmness of her demeanour she was inwardly a trifle nervous, she had a pensive look which reminded me of that beautiful Greek statue, no more than a fragment alas, of a girl in the museum at Naples which bears the name of Psyche. She had the same delicate features and the same virginal air. I was surprised when Hawtrey said, 'She's married to Buck, you know.'

After a few minutes conversation she left us and Hawtrey asked me what I thought of her.

'She's the loveliest thing I've ever seen in my life,' I answered. 'But how d'you know she can act?'

'It's not a difficult part and I can teach her.'

'All right then. By the way, what is her name?'

'Didn't I mention it? Cooper. Gladys Cooper.'

Edwardes however made it clear when they next met that she was not to be released: G, unperturbed as ever in the face of a crisis, announced that in her view marriage broke all other contracts and that she was off to Hawtrey. Edwardes then announced that he would sue, the Hawtrey management took fright, and as a result G did not work anywhere until the end of 1909 by which time she was three months pregnant.

Buck's attitude to G's career was, both now and later, faintly ambiguous: like many of his brother officers and men about town he was proud to have married a girl from the chorus, albeit an unusually ambitious and dedicated one. The money she would bring in, though little enough, might prove useful: on the other hand, what gentleman could admit at that time to having a working wife? And in any case, where the ambitions of most chorus girls ended at a 'good marriage', G's ambitions were only just beginning. What she wanted was a career in the theatre. What he wanted was a wife.

At first this created no great problems: they were sexually a very attractive and mutually attracted couple, and G in 1909 had a career locked in legal troubles and was thus able to devote most of her time to Buck, who was slowly beginning to get his finances back on to something approximating the firm foundation on which to build a family.

They took a small flat first in Baker Street, and Buck left Ladbrokes to start work as a freelance bookmaker, picking up   31

Mr and Mrs Herbert Buckmaster

what he could off the turf and occasional other jobs in the sporting world while 'looking around' for something more permanently reliable.

Still officially 'imprisoned' by her Gaiety contract, G had no alternative but to sit back in Baker Street and wait for Edwardes either to take pity and release her, or else make her the offer of a decent speaking role in one of his musicals. The latter he did, and in *Our Miss Gibbs* and *The Dollar Princess*, the last two shows she was to do under her Edwardes contract at Daly's and the Gaiety, her parts were considerably improved.

That, however, was that: by now her first daughter Joan was well on the way, and Gladys was resolved that if marriage could not in fact break all other contracts, then motherhood certainly could. She left Mr Edwardes and his world of musical comedy with some relief and virtually forever: the next musical she was to do was at the Saville fifty years later. Her departure from the Gaiety did not however go unnoticed or unmourned. 'Bow down your heads, O Lovers of Musical Comedy,' wrote one critic at the time, 'for beautiful, charming, fair-haired Miss Cooper has forsaken you. No more will she trip divinely down the stage and say, with her admirable smile, as she did in *Havana*, "Hello, people – people hello".'

Gladys herself was by now only too glad to be rid of a world to which she never felt she truly belonged, and which as early as 1906 she'd described to a student paper in Cambridge as 'not what suited her best'. Years and years later she and another ex-Gaiety Girl, her one-time understudy Ruby Millar, were together on a television quiz show during which panellists had to guess what the two veterans had in common. Their link was of course the Gaiety itself and Miss Millar recalled the glamour of it all – drinking champagne from slippers and getting home to find her entire bed filled with gardenias. The chairman turned to G: 'all I ever found in my bed', she told him acidly, 'was the hot-water bottle mother used to put in there every night'.

In some ways, thought G, Buck enjoyed his wife being at the Gaiety much more than she ever did: 'He would sit in the front row of the stalls, always in full evening dress because he wanted to be noticed, and of course everyone knew who he was – dashing and very handsome, always with a gardenia. We were a rather scandalous couple at that time, you know: Buck had always been the black sheep of the family and after the marriage so was I.'

But by now G was about to have a child of her own: Joan was born on July 5th, 1910 and for the rest of that year Gladys stayed out of work, helping a nanny to look after the new baby and going down occasionally to Foulsham and Banfield to earn a little money from the postcards. By Christmas however she was more than eager to get back to real work; with the baby and a nanny to accommodate they'd moved to a slightly larger flat in Clarence Gate Gardens, and money was still very tight. Work was not all that easy for her to come by: having abandoned musical comedies, she found other London managements unwilling to give her parts in the straight theatre because she was still branded as a Gaiety Girl and a postcard beauty. Though the postcard contract was now worth nearly £200 a year and she had no intention of giving it up the way she'd given up the Gaiety, G was now at the beginning of a twelve-year struggle to get herself taken seriously as a dramatic actress in the London theatre.

Her first break came from the Vedrenne-Eadie management, who put her into a comedy called *Half-a-Crown* at the old Royalty Theatre: Dennis Eadie himself headed the cast, but only for three nights which was as long as the run lasted. His management was however sufficiently impressed with Gladys to offer her a three-year contract which she gladly accepted, though almost at once

33

Gladys with her daughter Joan

they loaned her out to George Alexander at the St James's who was directing his annual summer-holiday revival of Oscar Wilde's *The Importance of Being Earnest*. G was cast as Cecily Cardew:

> I don't think I realised then quite how lucky I was to be at the St James's directed by Sir George in a marvellous part like that. A. E. Matthews was also in the company and one rehearsal I remember complaining about my costume, which had been worn by a good many other Cecilys in previous revivals: Matty hauled me over the coals and told me nothing mattered as much as being at that theatre. Still, the costume was terrible: in the end I got some scissors and slit it down the back and then the management had to make me a decent one.

Moreover she took a dim view of all the Alexander-worship that was still going on at the St James's: a boisterous girl, inclined to sing backstage and race down the stairs from the dressing-room when she heard her cue, she found it difficult to creep around in the cathedral-like atmosphere:

> Why there was this atmosphere I never really understood, for George Alexander seemed to me quite a pleasant sort of man: true he was enormously good-looking, a matinee darling, and his clothes were immaculate—the crease of his trousers being famous all over London. But he never struck me as a person who wanted to be treated as a demi-god, so I didn't.

And, at least in the glossy magazines, G herself was already something of a star: a full-page photograph in *The Throne and Country* that year showed her again dressed for ice-skating with a patently unreal snow-capped mountain in the background and a caption reading 'the popular young actress Gladys Cooper, well-known on both the musical and the light comedy stage'. But now, for the first time, she was also beginning to attract decent reviews from the more serious papers: A. E. Matthews remembered 'an audible gasp at her beauty' when she first went on stage in *The Importance*, and one critic added 'though no man in possession of his optical faculties could deny Miss Gladys Cooper the gift of beauty, the sceptical might have doubted her acting   35 abilities. Her performance as Cecily has swept away all such unworthy thoughts: she gave evidence of the possession of a delightful sense of humour and a keen appreciation of the author's sparkling wit. She was the personification of dainty archness, and had the remainder of the cast reached her level of success, the success of the revival would have been ensured.'

As they presumably didn't, it wasn't, and *The Importance* closed after a few summer weeks, but G herself always said that her best pre-1939 review had read simply 'Gladys Cooper surprised us by acting' and from now on her notices were never to lose that air of faint astonishment that anyone who looked so good could perform even adequately.

Nevertheless, the theatre was her life, to the exclusion of almost everything else: Gladys's total lack of political involvement or interest was such that she could write in her diary of this time: 'one afternoon the King and Queen attended an all-star matinee we were doing for charity and I, taking a small part, spent most of the performance being thrilled by the strange sight of struggling women being thrown out of the theatre by perspiring policemen. One woman was so firmly chained to her seat that they had to take her out seat and all.' It took some time to explain to Gladys that they were suffragettes.

Following *The Importance*, she stayed at the St James's to do *The Ogre* by Henry Arthur Jones. The *Telegraph* thought her 'natural and pleasant', an opinion that was by no means shared by Robert Loraine, the actor-manager with whom G went to work next in a revival of *Man and Superman* at the Criterion. Loraine was in the habit of giving notes to his fellow players even after the first night, not a custom ever endorsed by G who once noted that acting was something one did, not something one thought or talked about: 'I got so sick of finding him in the dressing-room with constant suggestions that he took to leaving me little notes about what to do on the stage, and these I used just to tear up unread. One note instructed us to have rubber heels put on our shoes so that we should not make any noise and disturb him by walking about backstage while he was doing his big scene . . . ridiculous man!'

Loraine for his part thought they'd been unwise to engage 'a musical comedy girl' for a Shavian role, and his temper was not improved by the fact that they'd also engaged Pauline Chase whose background was similar to G's. 'What we need here,' 36 Loraine told the management sourly, 'are intellectuals.'

Still under contract to Dennis Eadie and the impresario J. E. Vendrenne at the Royalty, G then did a series of brief runs through the winter of 1911/12. Between seasons at the Royalty, where shows tended at the time to close within about a month despite, or perhaps because of, their billing as 'new worthwhile plays for discerning audiences', G also began to work with Seymour Hicks who'd taken a fancy to her in the old Gaiety days. Hicks however did not want her for her acting ability:

> My first memory of this beautiful woman was seeing her as almost a child, sitting in the Savoy Grill room at a time when she was rehearsing to play with a provincial company in my *Bluebell in Fairyland*. I did not speak to her, but some years later I happened to visit the Gaiety to see *The Girls of Gottenberg* and there singing in a sextet to my surprise I saw that Bluebell of a few summers before. What her capabilities as an actress might be I hadn't the faintest idea, but with such a face I knew if she couldn't do something she would have to be stupid to the last degree; and as this I was sure was most improbable, I wrote to her and asked her to come and see me.

Accordingly, Hicks put her into occasional sketches of his at the Coliseum as 'set-dressing' while G continued to regard her real work as that for Vedrenne–Eadie at the Royalty. It was there, in March 1912, that she had her first real success as a straight actress.

chapter five

1912-1913

THE play was *Milestones* by Arnold Bennett and Edward Knoblock: it ran for 607 performances and for almost every one of them G played the small but showy last-act part of the Hon. Muriel Pym. A distinguished cast led by Eadie himself, Mary Jerrold, Hubert Harben and Owen Nares worked their way through an elaborate *Upstairs Downstairs* kind of family saga which started in 1860 and had by the time of Gladys's entrance got as far as the 1912 present. It opened to rave reviews: 'Messrs Vedrenne and Eadie,' wrote Findon in *Play Pictorial*, 'have cast their bread upon the waters of the Royalty, a theatre hitherto given over to lost causes, and it is going to return to them not after many days but forthwith in the form of big loaves and, if I am not much mistaken, fat fishes.'

For G, the eighteen months of *Milestones* were among the best she'd ever known inside or outside the theatre: to be acting for the first time in a 'legitimate' West End hit, to have a daughter of two old enough to play with and young enough to be left uncomplainingly with nanny while mother went off to the theatre, all added up to an ideal domestic and working arrangement. Or almost ideal: true, Buck seemed to be coming home to Clarence Gate Gardens a little less often than at the very outset of their marriage, and seemed now when he was at home to be less
than jubilant about G's success. His own finances were now in

rather better shape and he found it perhaps hard to understand why G was not settling more readily into the routine of being a wife and mother and nothing more. But his concept of marriage was, even for its time, more than a little chauvinist: one of his favourite stories concerned a friend of his who one morning after breakfast lined up his entire household staff in the hall and gave them a month's notice. Turning to his wife in front of them all he then said, 'And you can take a month's notice too,' and, Buck would add in some glee, she did.

But if the marriage was cooling a little, it was still not in any kind of real trouble: even if it had been, G would not have had a great deal of spare time in which to consider the problem. The Vedrenne–Eadie management believed in getting their money's worth out of an actress in those days, and as G was only required for the closing thirty minutes of *Milestones*, they would loan her out to other theatres for first-act roles or special matinees or Sunday-night jobs:

> I worked harder at the Royalty than I have ever worked in my life, I think: in a year I played about twelve different parts. I used to depend on the dressers to tell me what I was playing and spent most of my time rushing between the theatres and Regent's Park to see if Joan and the dogs were all right ... one month they lent me out to Drury Lane (a theatre which I hated to act in – it's too big) to play an early scene as Beauty in *Everywoman*. There was just time to get from one theatre to the other and do the two parts. On the first night at Drury Lane, Vedrenne sat in the front row of the stalls and as I 'died' I saw him holding his watch in his hand, terrified lest I should be too long 'dying' and so too late to get back for the last act of *Milestones*.
>
> Actually that 'dying' scene did take rather a long time and when I got used to it I sometimes used to doze off on the stage. One night I did go right to sleep and when Alexandra Carlisle hurled a champagne bottle at a mirror, shattering it to bits, I woke with a start and called out, 'What's that?' thereby rather ruining the death scene.

Mr and Mrs Buckmaster were now living with Joan and the nanny on a combination of their salaries: Buck, having cleared his Ladbrokes' debts at last, was still a gambling man to the   39 horror of his family (and indeed G's) but had learnt enough not to trust his luck only to the horses: he would now wager on virtually anything, ranging from the Bombadier Wells heavyweight title fight to whether or not he could get his fist through a top hat at the first attempt (he could). Even G had taken to a little light gambling: for several weeks she won considerable sums off a bookmaker called Hutt of Balham until he wrote saying that regretfully he couldn't bet with her any more. 'If,' replied G, 'you doubt my financial stability, kindly check with Hoare's Bank who will reassure you.' 'Madam,' came the reply, 'I am not for one moment thinking of your financial position, but of my own.'

Buck still didn't feel that her career need be taken with too much seriousness, any more than that of countless other good-looking 'gels' who had married his friends after brief careers at the Gaiety. He himself must have been aware that he didn't have much of a job, but then with a working wife and one very small daughter and nannies at a going rate of sixty pounds a year, the financial demands on him were not great. Nor was there much indication that any of his friends were in search of serious work: this after all was still 1912, when a gentleman of reasonable leisure and considerable sporting and drinking interests could hardly have been expected to chain himself to an office desk five days a week.

By the end of 1912 G was so exhausted that Eadie agreed to release her for a brief holiday in France. She went with Buck to a hotel in Paris where, dining at the next table, they found Arnold Bennett.

'I am sure' (whispered one of the girls at his table), 'that's Gladys Cooper.' Bennett looked at her and in his high-pitched voice asserted, 'Oh no it isn't. Gladys Cooper is in my play in London.'

Presumably Mr Bennett was not a postcard man: pictures of G were still flooding through the posts and the combination of a certain amount of fame and legitimate theatre work made the immediately pre-war period the only one G was ever to look back on with much nostalgia: 'To be perfectly honest, I think I had the best time of my life then: everything was easy and very pleasant and not such a "dog-fight" as it has become. I was growing up and I went about to jolly parties with jolly people.'

That wasn't all G did: through a meeting with the airman Gustav Hamel she became one of the first women to fly regularly, and narrowly missed being the first woman ever to loop the loop:

40

(*opposite*) As '*Beauty*' in Everywoman

Hamel was actually strapping me into his plane for this adventure when there arrived at the airfield a Miss Trehawk-Davies who was a great flying enthusiast. She'd come to Hendon aerodrome from a sick-bed when she heard what Hamel was about to attempt, and she asked me if she could have the flight. Naturally I had to give way in the circumstances, and as I was driving away from the aerodrome I saw them climbing to loop. That night the papers were all full of 'First Woman Loops the Loop' and I felt I had missed a grand chance of going down to air history.

G didn't miss much else in 1913: the year started well for her at a New Year's Eve charity ball at the Albert Hall, where she and Buck first met the actor-manager who was to become her most frequent co-star and constant friend until his death in 1934, Gerald du Maurier:

'He took her on one side and said, "Seeing you here I have just had an idea. We have been trying to think of someone for the leading woman's part in *Diplomacy* and I believe you could do it."'

Even allowing for du Maurier's notoriously casual approach to the stage (and the fact that he failed to tell G she only got the part because Marie Lohr's pregnancy made her withdraw), this was an idea which bordered on the lunatic. *Diplomacy* was the English translation of Sardou's classic melodrama *Dora*: it had first been staged in London in 1878 with Mrs Kendal in G's part, and ever since that time the role had been played by a tragedienne of considerable dramatic stature and usually of a certain age. Du Maurier, acting on the curious instinctive feeling for the theatre which only in later life was ever to let him down, decided to cast against type and do it 'modern' even if that meant going with a girl who could politely best have been described as inexperienced for the role.

The model for Wilde's *An Ideal Husband, Diplomacy* had long been popular with English audiences despite Shaw's frequent dismissal of the play as 'Sardoodledum'; and in reviving it yet again, du Maurier knew that he had to either exorcise or live up to all the ghosts of prior productions. He chose the former alternative, cast an equally young and inexperienced Owen Nares opposite G, decided to play Henry himself and was much helped in the production by old Sir Squire Bancroft, the play's first producer and still owner of the rights.

Du Maurier put *Diplomacy* into Wyndham's in March 1913; it ran a year, more than a hundred performances longer than the first production, and G and Nares were to get another 350 performances out of it a decade later.

> When it became known [said Gladys] that I had been cast for Madge Kendal's part people told Gerald du Maurier that both he and 'Old B' were mad. The knowledge that this was being said only helped to spur me on, and Owen Nares and I spent hours in our dressing-rooms rehearsing together. We realised that the play gave each of us a very big chance and we did not spare ourselves.
>
> No one criticised us for some time; Sir Squire and Gerald just watching us day after day, till one afternoon it was suddenly said: 'All the company except Miss Cooper and Mr Nares may go now.' Terrified, Owen Nares and I were left alone on the stage to go through our big scene with 'Old B' and Gerald in the stalls. It is difficult to give a performance 'cold' in an empty theatre, and I always rehearse very badly . . . at the end there was not a sound. Had we failed?
>
> For what seemed a very long time we stood on the stage, waiting for someone to say something – to tell us that we were wrong and would not do, or that we were right. Then, very slowly, 'Old B' and Gerald came up on stage to us and said that we had made them cry so much that they were not able to face us sooner. I think that was one of the most marvellous moments of my life.

Though neither could have been expected to realize it at the time, G and Gerald were to become one of the great theatrical partnerships of the twenties and early thirties: Gerald was fifteen years older than Gladys and from an altogether more arts-oriented background, though it could perhaps have been argued that both their fathers were in a sense journalists. But much more important than that, or anything, was the fact that she and Gerald soon found they shared one simple theatrical belief – a belief in naturalism, in being on the stage more or less what you would be off it whenever the work allowed.

This may not seem a particularly amazing or unusual or important belief for an actress in the latter half of the twentieth century, since it is taken for granted that we now have in general terms a   43

With Seymour Hicks in Broadway Jones, *1913*

'naturalistic' theatre. In 1913, London had nothing of the kind: theatregoers were still living in the larger-than-life shadows of the actor-managers, the barnstormers, the ranting Shakespearians all of whom believed that to be an actor entailed being as little like an ordinary mortal as possible.

Du Maurier changed all that: he was the first actor to light a cigarette on stage, the first to wear his own street clothes, the first to look in fact much the same on Piccadilly as across the footlights. Charles Hawtrey, with whom Gladys was to work a year or two later, was another of the great naturalists and so too were Ronald Squire and A. E. Matthews to whom G had taken an immediate liking at the time of *The Importance.*

Instinctively, I believe, she knew she was never going to be a Shakespearian, nor did her particular style of bright efficiency on stage mark her out for Chekhov or Ibsen: she might perhaps have been a great Shavian had not first Mrs Patrick Campbell and then (in her own generation) Sybil Thorndike and Edith Evans used up most of those opportunities. But in the absence of any single writer at this stage of her career (Maugham was only to come many years later) G chose rather to ally herself to a style, and that style was above all du Maurier's.

Diplomacy opened on March 26th, 1913, and the drama critic of *The Times* approved: 'Miss Gladys Cooper has hitherto been a dainty player of dainty parts; last night the opportunity came to her of showing something bigger and she took that opportunity splendidly.' G herself was in no doubt about what made her right for the play: 'the parts had always been played in the past by immensely distinguished players far too old for them: we were less distinguished, but we were at least the right ages to make the plot work'.

For the first time in her theatrical career she was on what was for 1913 good money (£40 a week), and *Diplomacy* ran on at Wyndham's throughout the year: by now, she and the family, in search of a little more space, had moved from their flat to a maisonette in the Finchley Road. Peter Graves, son of one of Buck's greatest friends, was living downstairs: 'None of us had much money then but we seem to have been able to afford most of what we wanted (anyhow, most that was good for us) and we were very happy. When I was a little older, we used sometimes to go and stay with Seymour Hicks and his wife at Herne Bay where we'd bathe, have tea out of doors, sing and dance to a

45

grand piano. It was long before the days of cocktails and gramo-
phones and motor cars which were luxuries then, not necessities.'

Diplomacy also saw the beginning of G's lifelong friendship
with the du Maurier family; it's Angela, Sir Gerald's eldest
daughter, who here describes their first meeting:

> It was a very hot Sunday, and Daddy and I drove off in the
> Ford to Rickmansworth to meet the train off which a lady was
> coming to spend the day. We got to the station and 'Now, off
> you go to meet her.' I did not know who I'd come to meet.
> 'Just pick out the prettiest face you see,' said my father.
> Under the tunnel and up to the far platform went I, aged but
> seven, and out of the train poured a very large crowd of
> people. I went straight up to a very lovely person in a blue
> hat which matched her eyes, held out my hand, and Gladys
> and I went back to the car.

chapter six

1913-1915

1913 was also the year of G's first film: called *The Eleventh Commandment*, it was one in a series that Adolph Zukor was then making for his Famous Players company in Europe and America, many involving stage stars in their most famous roles. Thus Bernhardt had made *Queen Elizabeth*, James O'Neill (Eugene's father) had done his celebrated *Count of Monte Cristo*, and Mrs Fiske had played *Becky Sharp* again.

The Eleventh Commandment seems to have been rather less distinguished: '2-reeler' said the plot synopsis, 'in which a guardian spends his ward's inheritance and then tries to make her marry a cad.' G had no later recollection of the film whatsoever, and the chances are that her work on it would have occupied no more than a week while she was playing in the theatre every night. On cinema posters she was already billed above the title as 'Britain's Most Beautiful Actress'.

But her heart belonged as ever to the theatre, in so far as it ever belonged anywhere, and during the filming she'd never left *Diplomacy*: the extra money did however mean that she could afford to buy a little seaside cottage in Frinton and it was there that Joan and a nanny spent the summer with G joining them for weekends and Buck as often as he could.

She finished the run of *Diplomacy* more than ever determined to work with du Maurier again as soon as the occasion arose: his   47 ability to be precisely casual on stage, his belief in naturalism, and above all his tendency to make the theatre an extension of his social life rather than an interruption of it, all endeared him to G, for whom he was pre-eminently the perfect footlights partner. As he had nothing immediate on offer, however, she returned to the Royalty where she was still officially under contract to Vedrenne and Eadie and did two brief runs in *The Pursuit of Pamela* and *Peggy and Her Husband.*

Pamela was the account of a young girl married to an older man who decides to run away from him and roam the world alone. Scenes took place in Honolulu, Hong Kong and Alberta and one of especial abandon featured G drinking half a bottle of sherry: by now she was in pursuit of a lover because, said one review, 'Pamela has no more shame than a rosebud.' Theatre suppers were being advertised in the programme for 1/6d and on the back cover was G herself advertising Liberty silk scarves for £1.4.6d.

In her working life, Gladys was by now reasonably well established, but at home things were not quite so secure: Buck had spent Christmas 1913 with some Ladbrokes' friends in Egypt and the marriage, though still outwardly rock solid, was beginning to show one or two hairline cracks. Nothing was evident or definite (the trouble wasn't to break into print for another two years) but rumours of G's close attachment to Dennis Eadie at the Royalty were all over London, whilst on Buck's side not even his closest friends (who were many and remained loyal to him over half a century) would have described him as the soul of sexual fidelity at all times.

Still, G had her work and her daughter, and there were weekends in Frinton or at Frederick Lonsdale's open-house home at Birchington in Kent: she reacted to private unhappiness now the way she always would, by great bursts of sustained public activity.

A. E. Matthews, who'd been with her in the *Diplomacy* cast again, was organizing a film parody of *Macbeth* for which G was to play 'an American witch' and there was another film on the horizon as well – *Dandy Donovan the Gentleman Cracksman*, in which she was co-starred with Owen Nares, her *Diplomacy* leading man, and Thomas Meighan (later to become Gloria Swanson's screen lover). G did not care for the film: 'I have forgotten the story now, and who I was supposed to be, but I do remember that some of the scenes were taken at Bushey and that, all within a few minutes, I had to ride a galloping horse, be shot at, fall into water and be gallantly rescued. It was years before anyone offered me another engagement on the films.'

The Bioscope took a less jaundiced view: 'Miss Cooper,' it said, 'looks exquisitely beautiful in some very charming gowns.'

But within a week or two of *Dandy Donovan* came the best of all G's jobs for Vedrenne and Eadie at the Royalty, and indeed the best showcase she'd ever been offered as an actress:

'One day I had a message from Dennis Eadie to say that I was wanted at the theatre at once. Arrived there, I found great mystery afoot. Eadie whispered to me to come up to the managerial room and when I got there he locked the door.

"What on earth. . . ?" I said.

"Hush," he replied. "We have found a wonderful play which you must read."

"All right," I said. "Let me have it and I'll take it home at once."

"Oh no you don't," said Eadie. "The play does not go out of this room. It is going to be a tremendous secret. You must sit down and read it here and now."

I never quite knew why new plays were so often looked upon as such secrets and only mentioned with bated breath – I never heard of anyone listening at the keyhole and rushing round the corner to write a replica in five minutes – but it sounded so exciting that I naturally did as I was bid and sat down with *My Lady's Dress*.'

For the first time in the West End G achieved equal billing with Eadie over the title, and in a long and distinguished castlist she could count on the support in smaller roles of both Lynn Fontanne and Edith Evans:

'I would stand night after night in the wings,' Dame Edith told me sixty years later (she was nine months older than Gladys) 'just staring at your grandmother. She must have thought I was barmy, but I simply couldn't believe that anyone could be so beautiful. I'd seen anyone like her and I never did again either . . . her beauty was the real thing – straight out of the bath. Lovely golden hair and she always kept those extraordinary eyes, right up to the end. Oh, how I envied her.'

'A triumphant tour de force,' said *The Times*, 'for Miss Cooper – she has never played with more delicate feeling than as the weaver's woebegone wife or the poor little cripple of White-chapel.' Trocadero theatre suppers had gone up to 5/– in the programme ads.

Edward Knoblock (in those days he was still spelling it Knob-lauch) was the author of *My Lady's Dress*: to tell the story of the making of a single dress, through a dream sequence, he moved his plot from the first-act present back to 1650 and included scenes in Italy, France, Holland and Siberia. In a cast of twenty, most of whom had two or three roles, Gladys played no less than seven: Anne, Nina, Annette, Antje, Annie, Anna and Anita, all (it need hardly be added) intended to be reflections through time and space of the same woman.

'A thoroughly interesting evening,' wrote B. W. Findon, admitting that a coherent plot synopsis was however beyond him: photographs indicate G in a vast range of hats, cloaks and costumes, alternately cuddling, stabbing or simply addressing a large variety of men most of whom turn out to be Dennis Eadie in various disguises. Programme captions such as 'Gioann, in order to ruin Nina and her betrothed, schemes to destroy their crop of silkworms' do suggest a somewhat complex chain of events, but *My Lady's Dress* seems to have been just what London wanted in early 1914, and to have fulfilled much the same function as serialized sagas of upstairs-downstairs life on television half a century later.

Reviews again focussed on G's beauty and her talents as a clothes-horse, and it was left curiously enough to the London correspondent of the *New York Tribune* to publish, on April 16th, 1914, the first really detailed and serious critical assessment of G as a dramatic actress. Commenting on the number of roles she was playing, he wrote:

It is a task from which a much older and more experienced actress might well shrink. It is, indeed, her youth [she was twenty-five] and exuberant vitality which carry her success-fully through this ordeal. It is a demand upon physical ener-gies as well as upon technical skill. But into this rounded slenderness of body Nature has packed reserves of force so inexhaustible that her freshest and most convincing work is done in the last two scenes. Of economising her strength or

One of the seven roles she played in My Lady's Dress *at the Royalty in 1914*

reserving it for the critical moments, Miss Gladys Cooper has no notion. She pours it all out at all moments with a splendid prodigality. A little more experience will teach her restraint.

She has a true power of emotion; not always the best way of expressing it but, since the emotion is there, it is felt. She has an abundance of lighter touches. At her age she has necessarily much still to learn, but it is evident that she has escaped from her difficulties by a caressing charm of manner, by her youthful courage and by her genuine dramatic gifts.

With reviews like that, they looked all set for a long run at the Royalty: this however was 1914 and when war broke out on August 4th the Vedrenne–Eadie management, in common with most others, closed up their theatres – a thoroughly unnecessary precaution, thought Gladys. Events were however beyond her control: Buck was eager to get back into uniform as soon as possible, and G herself rapidly realized that it was the end if not of an era then at least of a way of life. In the nine years since her first stage appearance at Colchester she'd established herself on both stage and screen as a considerable beauty and an adequate actress. She'd married, had a daughter, bought a house and become a regular name in the gossip columns of the immediately pre-war months. She was even being given the credit for Frinton: 'not so long ago it was little more than a waste of sandhills to which trippers from Clacton made adventurous excursions. Now it is one of the most popular resorts on the coast. Frinton's progress began when some enterprising people laid out a golf-links . . . then Miss Gladys Cooper began to be photographed there and so Frinton was made.'

G stayed on at Frinton for a few August days in 1914 after the closing of *My Lady's Dress*, but very soon Buck wanted her back in London urgently. Being married and over thirty now, he'd been told that he was not eligible for the commission he'd been recommended at the end of his South African service fourteen years earlier. Not pleased, and determined to see active service as soon as possible, he sent G to see Lord Birkenhead whom he knew she'd met at one of Beerbohm Tree's parties in the dome of His Majesty's: 'Off I went to the War Office and found him seated in a huge room next to Winston Churchill whom I did not then know. "Please,' I said, "I've come for a job." They roared with laughter. "For yourself?" "No, for my husband," I told them. Churchill was then with his Royal Naval Division and said why did my husband not join that? He did so at once.'

Before he could start his training again, Buck however fell out of a taxi, thereby injuring his knee and making the R N V R commission impossible. Luckily, as it turned out: the battalion he was destined for crossed into Holland a few weeks later and was interned there for the duration of the war. Buck joined the Cavalry instead and got to France with the Royal Horse Guards early in the following year.

G, left alone in London with Joan and her devoted nanny, decided to evacuate them to Frinton and to do whatever war work she could. Buck was at Aldershot sending increasingly restive letters home about how they were keeping him away from the Front on purpose, but as there seemed little else going on G decided to return to her old friend Seymour Hicks, now valiantly doing music-hall sketches and other bits and pieces to occupy stages that otherwise would have been deserted in the general rush to mobilize. Hicks put her into something called *The Bridal Suite* (playing 'She') at the Coliseum and then, towards December, announced that in his view a visit to France was indicated.

Billing his tour as 'The National Theatre At The Front', Hicks made plans to take a company of seven led by himself and his wife (Ellaline Terriss) together with Gladys, Ivy St Helier and a cinema projectionist to show some short films. 'Soldiers!' read the posters, 'Fellow countrymen of whom we are so proud, and to whom we owe so much! By permission of Earl Kitchener of Khartoum and Field Marshal Sir John French we, your brothers and sisters, have come over from England to try and entertain and amuse you and bring you a message from home! It's a long way to Tipperary, but not too far for us! Bless You! Ellaline Terriss will sing more sweetly and act more charmingly than ever before! Seymour Hicks will perspire more freely! Ivy St Helier will delight you as she always has done! Gladys Cooper will act and look more like her postcards than they do! C O M E I N, S O L D I E R S. As many of you, and as often, as you like. You will confer a favour on us by letting us work for you and for those angels in disguise, the brave ladies who nurse you. G O D S A V E THE KING! GOD PROTECT YOU AND YOUR BRAVE ALLIES! LONG LIVE ENGLAND! VIVE LA FRANCE and BRAVO, BRAVE BELGIUM!'

Suitably inspired, Hicks and his little company set off to

become the first of the concert parties into France in World War I. Wrote Hicks later:

> It was bitterly cold, and listening to Miss Cooper reciting Kipling's *Gunga Din*, I became aware of a depth of power within her that she had never hitherto had an opportunity of showing while appearing in the trivial pre-war comedies with which she'd started to make a name . . . it was with the greatest admiration that I watched her untiring and successful efforts to bring a breath of home to the wounded and mud-covered men returning to rest camps from the trenches.

Gladys herself had less enthusiastic memories of the venture:

> It took us twenty-three hours to travel from Rouen to Havre, our antiquated French train being constantly side-tracked to allow Red Cross trains to go by. The moon shone brightly during part of our journey, and the French officer in charge of our train cheerfully told us that the line had been bombed by German aeroplanes the night before. This information put the wind well up me, and nearly all through the night I sat in utter darkness with my nose glued against the carriage window looking for hostile aircraft.

Nevertheless the concert party had a considerable success, as Ellaline Terriss wrote in her diary:

> We saw the New Year (1915) in at the Hotel de France in Rouen. There were many officers there, French, Belgian and British, who had all been in the very thick of the fighting since the outbreak of War. So we gave them a concert too, our smallest audience but one of our most grateful. As the bells tolled midnight we all linked hands and sang *Auld Lang Syne*, the French and Belgians doing the best they could with our, to them, outlandish words. Then a French officer sang *God Save the King*, a young English officer rendered his own *Marseillaise* and an Equerry to the King of the Belgians sang his own anthem.
>
> Other performances were of course always makeshift as far as stages were concerned. Planks were put across baskets to make a stage, dressing-rooms were unknown, and often we

54

With the Seymour Hicks concert party entertaining the troops in France, 1914

played in almost complete darkness. But the enjoyment of the men made that darkness light, and our own pride in being able to please them banished any shadows. Everywhere there was mud, mud, mud. In some places, I am told, the soldiers tossed up for the privilege of carrying the girls of the party across it. We did give one performance under somewhat normal conditions. That was at Le Havre; we were told that the Mayor had offered us the Grand Theatre, with a seating accommodation of 1800 free of all cost for two performances. The British commander in Le Havre advised acceptance on condition that the audience was composed of equal numbers of British and French soldiers. He also told us no mention had been made of the cost of lighting and heating, and that he had no funds available for that purpose. We did the shows all right – and nobody ever asked us for the money. Our visit was now nearing its close. We should dearly have loved to stay, but there were contracts and managements waiting for us at home.

Through all the mud and the chaos and the long train journeys of that concert party tour of the Front, there was just one thing Gladys had not told Hicks or any of the troupe: she was pregnant again.

chapter seven

1915

G SPENT 1915 in Frinton and in London: from the time of her return from the Front in January through the birth of her son John in July to a brief charity-matinee appearance in November, it was to be the one year of her adult life when she did virtually no acting of any kind. Buck, intensely jealous that she had got to the Front before him, was still in training at Aldershot. Joan was in the safe keeping of her devoted Nanny Aves, and Gladys was left to cope, more or less alone, with a libel suit which finally broke in the *Daily Mirror* of January 13th. A banner headline that morning read MISS GLADYS COOPER AWARDED HEAVY DAMAGES FOR LIBEL: BEAUTIFUL ACTRESS'S STORY OF DEFAMATORY RUMOURS; and some indication either of G's stardom at the time or else of the *Mirror*'s unique sense of news values can be gained by a very small sub-heading which ran 'French report heavy losses at Front'.

The report, told across two pages of pictures of Gladys, Buck, Joan and others involved, relayed a curious story. Seven months earlier, on June 11th, 1914, a paper called the *London Mail* had run an anonymous paragraph in their gossip-column under the headline 'Hush'.

Heaven and earth [it read] are being moved, in a popular phrase, to hold in check a scandal of theatreland which   57 looms daily more threatening. I cannot obviously say more at present than that you all know and admire the lady and the man in the case. A second name, that of a man since tragically gone, is also mentioned but will I earnestly hope be struck from the suit should it come on. Despite the publication of pictures showing complete domestic bliss, she was never really happily wed, which was entirely her own fault inasmuch as she rushed to the registry office against the advice of all. As to the prospective co-respondent, well, his marriage was ludicrous.

That had been the only reference in the *Mail* to this 'scandal of theatreland' and no other paper had taken it up during 1914; it had none the less become a considerable talking-point around Shaftesbury Avenue, largely because the characters were all so recognizable. Who but Gladys had in the last five years had such a well-publicized 'rush to the registry office' even if it had in fact been a church? Who but Gladys was constantly being photographed for postcards with her husband and daughter in 'complete domestic bliss'? And if she was the actress, and it was a scandal of theatreland, then the man in the case was obviously Eadie, known to have an unhappy marriage at the time. And what of the other man, 'since tragically gone'? G's friendship with the air ace Gustave Hamel, the man with whom she'd narrowly failed to loop the loop, was well known, as was his disappearance over the Channel in 1914 – an unsolved flying mystery heavily publicized at the time because it was thought Hamel might have been a German spy going into hiding rather than a courageous air pioneer whose plane went into the sea during a hailstorm.

By the end of that year, the rumours were therefore flying all over London: Buck was on the verge of divorcing Gladys because of her intimate friendships with Eadie and Hamel. This, in her view, called for action.

In court she was represented by Sir Frederick Low, who said the plaintiff was a young lady who had made very great and very dramatic progress in the acting profession. Such success always excited a good deal of jealousy and exposed the successful actress to attacks, and for some eighteen months now a person or persons had been circulating rumours of a defamatory nature regarding Miss Cooper, Mr Eadie and Mr Hamel. These rumours went from
58   mouth to mouth and had caused Miss Cooper the greatest anxiety

and suffering. In order to try and stop them she had herself photographed with her husband and child. Counsel handed a copy of this photograph to the Lord Chief Justice and the jury, and said that copies were circulated to show that she was living with her husband in the most amicable domestic relations.

G herself then gave evidence in the witness box, saying that she had acted with Mr Eadie and been friendly with the late Mr Hamel, and had lunched with both with her husband's knowledge. Counsel for the *Mail* then suggested that possibly none of the people mentioned in the paragraph were in court, but Buck was swiftly on the stand to say that in his view the paragraph definitely referred to his wife and had caused her much suffering. Eadie, taking the stand last, said there was not the slightest truth in any of the rumours. The defence called no other evidence, the jury retired, found in favour of Gladys, and the Lord Chief Justice awarded her damages of £1200, a not inconsiderable sum for the time. He added that if the writer of the paragraph wished to establish that he had not intended it to refer to Gladys, then he should appear in the witness box to say so. No one appeared and that was more or less that, though it is possible to argue that Gladys's image of youthful, almost childlike, innocence had received a public bashing from which, despite the outcome of the case, it never truly recovered. On the credit side, she was thereafter to be trusted with roles of a rather greater maturity.

Libel proceedings over, G retired to Frinton to await the birth of her son; Buck meanwhile had managed to get himself moved from Aldershot to the Royal Horse Guards barracks in Regent's Park, just behind where he and G now had their Cumberland Terrace house and a location he regarded as one step nearer to the Front. His gambling instincts had not deserted him at the outbreak of hostilities, however, and his correspondence early in 1915 indicates that he was writing to insurance companies to find out what the odds were on the war ending by a series of carefully selected dates. The arrival of John, and the imminence of Buck's departure for the Front, had done a lot to improve family life in Cumberland Terrace: Gladys's father had even brought himself to forgive them for the elopement. He wrote to Buck:

I hear from Gladys that you are off to the Front. I would have liked to have shaken hands with you before you go, but I am just writing a few lines to wish you God-speed with all my

59

heart and to assure you (if you need any assurance) that you take with you my own and my wife's affectionate good wishes and our earnest hope that you come back in safety to those whom we all love. Affectionately yours: Charles Cooper.

In a haze of goodwill immediately before the departure, Seymour Hicks had taken Buck out to lunch and offered to settle up any financial difficulties he was in 'up to two hundred pounds'. For once, Buck recalled later with some pride, he didn't actually need the money and he set off to France having just seen his newborn son, secure in the knowledge that the marriage was still all right. And so, for the duration of the war, it was: G's letters to him at the Front are those of a loving and dutiful wife. Admittedly they indicate an increasingly active professional and private life, and with the wisdom of sixty years' hindsight it's possible to find in them evidence that she and Buck were in fact drawing farther and farther apart as he settled back into the army routine he so loved and she became increasingly independent and high-powered around the theatres of London. But the letters are full of the children growing up and other domestic notes, they reflect a panorama of G's life between 1914 and 1918, yet they leave out the one truly important development in these years, which was her rapid rise from being one of several good-looking juvenile leads around the West End in 1914 to being by 1918 London's only actress-manager:

Write to me whenever you can [she implored Buck] even if it is only one line. I shall write every day, so that if the posts go wrong you will know it isn't because I haven't written . . . I got a car from the Austin people to take and fetch us from the theatre every night and they are charging me £12 a month which isn't bad . . . Joan and John have had colds but are getting much better . . . Joannie says an extra prayer for you every night . . . business seems to be good and I am getting flowers each night from unknown admirers! So I am getting off in my old age! . . . I am sending out the clean linen you asked for . . . I was thankful to hear from you but upset that you have been sent straight up to the trenches . . . it is quick work . . . John seems to be teething . . . I wonder if you are very cold and uncomfy at night . . . it is the first night of Somerset Maugham's new play tonight and he is

giving a little supper party afterwards, at his house so I think
I shall go on there when I have finished writing this letter. I
had a singing lesson this afternoon . . . another day gone and
still no letter from you. I can't understand it. I try not to
worry . . . yesterday I had my first ride for five years . . . what
joy this morning to get two letters from you. They came in the
middle of the morning and Joannie and I read them together
and when I read her out the bit where you said, 'Don't let
Joannie forget me,' she said, 'Well, that's funny.' She too
misses you awfully and in fact if we say very much about you
being away, she weeps . . . tonight they were firing off a lot
of guns for practice and the big one, in Regent's Park shook
the whole house. John loved it . . . I have bought a Dundee
cake and some chocolates and one or two other things from
Fortnum's which I thought you might like, also the papers
you asked for. I will ask Tom Schreiber to send you out some
cigars . . . I am going out to buy a map of France and try to
follow where you've been and where you are . . . have you
ever seen anything more dreadful than those photographs of
me in the *Sketch* and *Tatler*? I nearly wept when I saw them
. . . I lunched at the Carlton today with Gwennie Brogden-
Boyd-Rochfort and Minto and afterwards we went to a
matinee at the New Theatre. I have no other news I'm afraid.
I am so sorry you are feeling depressed. It is the misfortune
of war . . . went to a Mother's Meeting this afternoon . . . I
am writing this in the nursery: Joan is in the bath and an

*'The Inter-Theatre Mixed Foursome Golfing Competition for the
Ascar Asche Challenge Cup at Stoke Poges Club, Slough. Miss
Gladys Cooper approaching the first green.' 1914*

awful temper. She has just told Nannie she is worse than the Germans . . . I ordered your Kolynos and will write to your mother about the apples and pears . . . funny to hear of the men putting up my photo in the billets . . . Zeppelins came over again on Sunday night and went to eight counties but they didn't come here. I am just off to do a charity matinee which I think will be very funny: Diana Manners, Nancy Cunard etc are all in it . . . a compass or something has come for you from Negretti and Zambra so I passed it on . . . I rode this morning at 9.30 with Capt. Vaughan and he lent me a big black charger and told me to tell you he wouldn't have dared put you up on her, but I think he was only pulling my leg . . . I am riding with him again on Saturday . . . I sent off your gaiters, also two jam puddings from Fortnum's and some Devonshire cream . . . we are doing wonderful business still – crowded houses every night! I sent you two bottles of gin from Fortnum's . . . Joan and Doris came to my play and said they liked it better than *Peter Pan*! Have done nothing all day except take Joan to church. John gained ten ounces this week. I have paid my income tax – £134, isn't it awful? . . . *The Birth of a Nation* is wonderful – the best film I have ever seen . . . I am so sorry to hear your head has been bad. Doris and I are going down by train to Frinton for the week-end . . . the children are staying there for Easter . . . Muriel du Maurier is also looking for a French maid for the children so if you should hear of one do let me know . . . the children are looking splendid and very brown but they are awful down here about showing any lights so all ours are wrapped in brown paper – so depressing . . . tomorrow I make my debut in Shakespeare for a charity matinee at Stratford: all the 'nuts' of the stage are in it such as Ellen Terry, George Alexander, Irene Vanbrugh – and Gladys Cooper . . . we do it in the afternoon and get back in time for the evening performance at the Playhouse . . . there are lots of rumours about an invasion of the East Coast which are making me rather nervous about the children being at Frinton but I will find out at the weekend what they think of it there . . . I am sending you a Stilton cheese . . . they brought down a Zeppelin the other side of Chelmsford last night . . . I had a ripping ride in the Row this morning . . . Captain Vaughan said that women are much easier to teach than men.

2 The Playhouse

chapter eight

1916–1918

THOUGH the defiant, and indeed sometimes mindless, optimism of her letters to Buck at the front gives little indication of it, the war years were not altogether easy ones for G: now in her late twenties, with two children to support plus nanny and a couple of houses in London and Frinton while Buck's financial arrangements remained precarious, she was not one of those who could or would sit back and await the eventual return of her soldier.

Instead, within a few weeks of Johnnie's birth, she was back at work. There being no suitable plays around, she went first into A. E. Matthews' film parody of *Macbeth*. Called *The Real Thing At Last*, this was a distinctly curious venture: Matthews, in a moment of characteristic eccentricity, had bought a complete film studio, cameras and all, for £3500 and declared that his intention was 'to corner the film markets of the world'. To this end he approached his friend J. M. Barrie who in twenty-four hours, on two sheets of notepaper, came up with the outline for a *Macbeth*, 'as Hollywood would have made it'. Barrie himself was to direct, for a salary of £10 a week, and an immensely impressive cast (Irene Vanbrugh, Nelson Keys, Edmund Gwenn, Owen Nares, Marie Lohr, Leslie Henson and Godfrey Tearle) was engaged for ten shillings a day each. Some idea of the tone of the movie can be gathered from Leslie Henson, playing Shakespeare 65 himself, picking up a telephone and saying, 'Shakespeare here. How did they like my play in New York?'

This being the only screenplay Barrie ever wrote (and the film itself being also long since extinct) it has a certain fascination: three English witches were immediately followed on to the screen by three American witches (one played by Gladys) 'looking most glamorous and dancing round an enormous glittering metal cauldron'. Macbeth and Macduff had their climactic duel on top of a skyscraper, and the picture was made at Bushey very rapidly indeed. It did not however meet with much favour from the critics who took violent exception in particular to a scene where Lady Macbeth, played in drag, sent Macbeth a note reading, 'Dear Macbeth, the King has gotten old and silly. Slay him. Yours. Lady Macbeth.'

The Real Thing At Last was launched at a Royal Command Performance in aid of the British troops on March 7th, 1916 at the London Coliseum. Barrie himself designed an elaborate stage set through which the film cast 'disappeared' before reappearing on the screen, and the piano accompaniment was written and played by Frederick Morton, who six months later was to have a rather greater success with *Chu Chin Chow*. The film however died a rapid death: 'if this is the kind of entertainment provided for royalty and society in war time' despaired one critic, 'well! well!' 'Ill-considered sorry stuff,' groaned another. So much for G's Shakespearian debut on film: she was never to have much luck with the Bard.

The link with Barrie was however to prove useful, not only in terms of *Peter Pan* six years later, but also more immediately: in the November of 1915 she went to the Coliseum in his *Half-an-Hour*, a one-act melodrama which was later to become one of the world's first talking pictures.

It was a brief run on a variety bill, and by Christmas G was already in rehearsal for the first time at the theatre which, although she could hardly have known this at the time, was to become her semi-permanent home from 1916 to 1933.

The Playhouse on the corner of the Embankment and North-umberland Avenue by Charing Cross, had originally been constructed in 1882 by a property speculator who had bought the land in the hope that the railway people would have to expand Charing Cross station and he'd thus have a profitable resale: 66 when this failed to happen he grudgingly built a theatre in the site, one which opened in March 1882, was rebuilt in January 1907, and stands to this day. In 1915 the Playhouse had been taken over by Frank Curzon, and Curzon it was who offered G the lead opposite Charles Hawtrey in an H. M. Harwood comedy called *Please Help Emily*. In company with Noël Coward and many others, G was later to acknowledge Hawtrey as the greatest formative influence on her playing of comedy: a consummate comedian with a rare gift, among comedians, of being able to explain how it was done and instruct others in his art, Hawtrey was by now at the very height of his career and working with him was considered to be something of an honour.

'Hawtrey,' said Gladys later, 'was a joy to act with: he taught and helped me more than anybody. His own art was consummate – there was nobody to touch him for the absolutely perfect polish of his acting. To be with him was an education, and he was ever so generous with his help and praise. I have never known anyone who could convey so much by just the tilt of an eyebrow.'

Hawtrey himself was less effusive in his recollection of G: she rates only one reference in his 300-page autobiography (edited by Maugham) and it is to note that she was 'an experienced actress, excellent in the part'.

IIe was directing *Please Help Emily* himself, and their opening night in January 1916 drew some enthusiastic reviews: a farcical plot involved G (as Emily) awaking to find herself in the pyjamas, bed and flat of a man she has never met. 'A delightful Playhouse farce,' said the *Observer*, 'and Miss Cooper is a fascinating minx in all her costumes.' Owen Seaman for *Punch* thought that 'Miss Cooper's natural charm and ingenuous *espieglerie* were a perpetual delight' and offered his compliments to the author. A large ad. in the programme enquired, 'Are *you* being blackmailed or in other difficulties? If so go to William Pierrepoint, inquiry agent to the Nobility and Gentry. Entrusted with divorce and delicate negotiations in all parts of the world. 27 Chancery Lane.'

Emily ran on to virtual capacity through the summer of 1916 and as well as playing three regular matinees a week, G would also do charity performances of *The Admirable Crichton* and other shows on her afternoons off. Business however began to flag towards the 200th performance in the middle of August and Curzon, allowing G a few days to be with the children at Frinton, put her straight into rehearsal for another Playhouse comedy, this one to be called *The Misleading Lady*. A Broadway import,   67 which starred Gladys opposite Malcolm Cherry and Weedon Grossmith, it concerned a high-society girl getting chained up in a mountain cabin in the Adirondacks because she would not submit to marriage.

Playing a very minor role in *The Misleading Lady* was a nervous twenty-five-year-old Ronald Colman: 'such a handsome young man,' he heard G murmuring in the wings one night, 'but why does he have to be such a terrible actor? So very clumsy – and those feet!'

Reviews however were generally enthusiastic and *The Misleading Lady* became another big Playhouse success so rapidly that Curzon was prompted to make G a remarkable offer, one she referred to rather off-handedly in a letter to Buck at the Front:

> Frank Curzon wants me to go into management with him at the Playhouse on the same terms as Gerald du Maurier is at Wyndham's. I don't have to risk any money and would get a salary and a share of the profits. I told him I shall have to think it over.

Though G was seldom one to be much impressed by luck good or bad, this really was an extraordinary chance: it was one thing for Wyndham's to attempt to hold du Maurier on a similar deal – one of the leading actor-directors of his day, and at a time when glamorous leading men were in short supply, could presumably have named his theatre and his price. But for Curzon to take on Gladys purely for her name (since there was to be no financial deal involved), knowing that she was neither a director nor an author and therefore would simply continue to appear in the productions as a leading actress, was in pre-feminist 1916 a gesture of either intense prescience or immense generosity. Though there had been occasional other women in management around the West End (notably Lady Bancroft and Mary Moore) they were almost always there through a family connection with the owners of the theatre. G was taken into partnership by Curzon simply because she was G.

'All the theatrical world,' reported *The Sketch* on November 8th, 1916, 'should be interested in the news that Miss Gladys Cooper is going into management at a West End theatre in partnership with Mr Frank Curzon. "Remember please," she said, "that this is going to be an essentially business firm, simply Frank Curzon and Gladys Cooper, without any leavening Mr or Miss."'

The Sketch

No. 1241 —Vol. XCVI.   WEDNESDAY, NOVEMBER 8, 1916.   SIXPENCE.

AN ACTRESS WHO EVIDENTLY "MEANS BUSINESS," AND IS GOING INTO MANAGEMENT : MISS GLADYS COOPER.

All the theatrical world—and in that should be included playgoers as well as "the profession" itself—was interested in the news that Miss Gladys Cooper is going into management at a West End theatre, in partnership with Mr. Frank Curzon. We had better put the matter in her own words, as recently reported. "Remember, please," she said, "that this is to be an essentially business firm, simply Frank Curzon and Gladys Cooper, without any leavening Mr. or Miss." Leavened or unleavened, everybody will wish the popular young actress luck. She is here seen as Helen Steele, in "The Misleading Lady," at the Playhouse.—[*Photograph by Foulsham and Banfield, Ltd.*]

Sketch frontispiece, 1916

Curzon remained the sole licensee of the Playhouse but from now onwards the programme bore the legend 'Under the management of Frank Curzon and Gladys Cooper', an arrangement that was to run on into the mid-twenties. *The Misleading Lady* ran for 231 performances through the winter of 1916 and then she and Curzon put in a brisk revival of *The Passing of the Third Floor Back* with Johnston Forbes-Robertson, while they thought about what to do next. The play they settled on for 1917 was *Wanted, A Husband*: 'a purple tale of passion,' wrote Owen Seaman, 'so bad for the morals of the servants' hall'. 'A rag rather than a play,' noted *The Tatler*, adding acidly, 'Miss Cooper, like so many other actresses, is nowadays compelled by dramatists to adhere to only one kind of part, that of a wayward and extravagant queen who thinks it is her mission in life to put men in their place and give them as much audacity as she thinks they will stand.'

Rising above the reviews, the Curzon–Cooper management got another reasonable run (fifteen weeks) though this was only half as long as the previous comedies G had played there; by mid-summer 1917 they were therefore looking for something else and, with Buck still at the Front, G was keeping him informed of their financial situation: 'We did a big library [ticket-agency] deal so even if the play had failed we'd have got our expenses back before we opened. I had always looked on *Diplomacy* as my biggest first night but the Playhouse means another big step up and I wish you could be here . . . after the first night [of *Wanted A Husband*] I made a little speech and said the title was rather poignant as so many of our husbands were being so wonderful overseas.'

With a mixture of pride and faint embarrassment, Buck was discovering that he was married to an actress whose fame far outran whatever she happened to be doing at the Playhouse in 1917: half a century later I asked a Chelsea Pensioner for his memories of her:

In the regular army we all had our picture idols and Miss Cooper was certainly among them: you could see her not only stuck up on the walls of barrack rooms but also in the trenches and if you opened a packet of cigarettes she fell out of that too, on a cigarette card. She was the most beautiful woman in the British Isles: everybody knew that. When the Colonel came round to inspect us in the trenches I had to take her picture down from behind my bed because he wouldn't have pin-ups. Then somebody stole mine so I had to go round and pinch somebody else's. That was how it went. You just couldn't get away from her: she was pencilled out.

She was also determined, long before many of her contemporaries had realized the importance of the new medium, to make a success in films however much she might both dislike and despise the process of actually shooting them. The Samuelson company offered her the lead opposite Owen Nares in Marie Corelli's *The Sorrows of Satan*, a five-reel drama about a girl in love with a prince who is really the devil:

I have seldom been so miserable [wrote Gladys later]. It was snowy weather and for half a day I crouched over a horrible little fire, waiting to be called to do my bit in evening clothes. I have never been so cold; and I remember suddenly turning to Nares and demanding, 'Are you and I quite mad? What on earth makes us sit shivering here all this time when

Playhouse 1916: The Misleading Lady *with Malcolm Cherry*

we might be somewhere warm and comfortable? Do we actually need the money? We don't: we could do without it. The only excuse I can see for submitting to this horrible experience would be if our children were hungry and crying for bread in the gutter.' *The Sorrows of Satan* was an appropriate title. I have come to the conclusion that film-making puts me in a very bad temper.

Nevertheless she persevered with it, and *The Sorrows of Satan* was duly released to some respectful reviews. Back in the theatre, she and Curzon had decided that after three comedies in quick succession perhaps what the Playhouse next needed was a melodrama. While they were searching for the right script, G gritted her teeth and did two more 1917 films: the first, *Masks and Faces* was a charity venture in aid of the Royal Academy of Dramatic Art, then in dire need of two thousand pounds if it was to build its theatre. The second was another Samuelson project, this one a screen version of her pre-war Knoblock success *My Lady's Dress*. Her current Playhouse co-star Malcolm Cherry was cast in the old Dennis Eadie role, and a long feature in *The Bioscope* that August noted:

> That the Samuelson film version of this fantastic play aroused a great deal of interest was proved by the uncomfortably crowded state of the Shaftesbury Pavilion Theatre on the occasion of its first screening ... the representation of so many diverse characters makes considerable demands on the versatility of the stars, and it is inevitable that Miss Cooper and Mr Cherry should meet with greater success in some parts than others ... neither can be classed as character actors, and though they are admirable as a well-connected society couple they are a great deal less convincing as crippled cockneys, faithless Russian peasants, fur traders or silkworm breeders ... the film could do with some abbreviation, though the pianist rendered popular incidental music throughout the projection without apparent signs of fatigue.

Samuelson, never a man to mince words on his posters, put A SUPERLATIVE SUCCESS! and GREATER EVEN THAN MILESTONES!!

chapter nine

1917=1920

B Y the end of the summer, Curzon and G had found the
melodrama they were looking for: called *The Yellow Ticket* and
billed as 'a thrilling story of Imperialist Russia' it featured Allan
Aynesworth as an evil police chief, Arthur Wontner as a heroic
British journalist and G as 'Marya Varenka', a Jewess unable to
get a visa to see her dying father in St Petersburg – the visa
being the yellow ticket of the title. 'The trouble,' said *The Tatler*,
'is that Miss Cooper doesn't look like a Russian and still less like a
Jewess. It's a good old-fashioned pre-war melodrama played for
all it's worth: Miss Cooper has however still to learn the power
of reticence – her big scenes are somewhat ranting.' The *Daily
Telegraph* critic thought on the other hand that she had 'thrilling
force as she abandons herself to the wild emotions of the moment'
and they got a total of two hundred and thirty-four performances
out of it.

Aynesworth, cast as the lecherous chief of the Secret Police,
collected some rather good reviews but didn't endear himself to
G during the run:

> One night I found him crouching under the lintel of his
> dressing-room door during an air-raid with the idea, appar-
> ently, that he was taking cover. Being just a few yards away
> from Charing Cross we were an easy target, and there was a

Playhouse 1917: The Yellow Ticket *with Allan Aynesworth*

machine-gun almost opposite us on the Embankment and the
shrapnel used to sound a tattoo on our glass roof. Then I had
to threaten Aynesworth with the sack after he'd said he'd
lost his voice and I found him in a quite different theatre
directing another play . . . a dear old thing, really, but so
pompous. If there was a revolution in this country and he
wasn't put to death as one of the leading aristocrats he'd
die anyway . . . of a broken heart.

Backstage squabbles apart, *The Yellow Ticket* ran happily
through the spring of 1918, at which time the Curzon–Cooper
management got themselves the greatest success of all the twenty-
two plays that G was to do at the Playhouse, *The Naughty Wife.*
Not that it could have been accurately forecast: a mediocre
comedy by Fred Jackson 'revised and enlarged by Edgar
Selwyn', it dealt with a best-selling author (Charles Hawtrey,

renewing his hugely successful partnership with G) who allows his young wife (Gladys) to elope with another man (Stanley Logan) and then ruins their affair. A simple plot, but good enough to last out the war and achieve a remarkable total of 598 performances in an eighteen-month run: 'It says much for Miss Cooper's talent and perseverance,' said *Play Pictorial* and it was her longest-ever run.

At the time of the first night the war was still much in evidence: 'due to a shortage of male labour', said a programme note, 'the scene setting for Act Two will require an interval of twenty minutes. Should an air raid warning be received, an announcement will be made from the stage (if during an interval) or the Electric light will be turned up in the auditorium for the space of one minute (if during the play). This will allow any Naval or Military officers whose duty requires them at their posts the opportunity of getting there. The audience are invited at their own discretion to remain in the theatre if the All Clear has not been received before the end of the performance.'

G had by now learnt the importance that clothes were to play in her career on the stage: a prominent programme note announced that 'her gowns, coats and hats have been designed and executed by Mr Reville at 15 Hanover Square'. Moreover once she knew they were in for a long run, she made a point of having her costumes redesigned every six months and inviting the society papers back for another look.

It was during the run of *The Naughty Wife* that Buck came back from the war and tried, like so many others of his generation, to pick up the threads of a marriage which had been put on ice for the duration. It was not, he wrote, easy:

> For three and a half years my wife had been accustomed to do without me and to manage her own life. When war broke out she was earning £20 a week; when it ended she was earning £200 a week. In 1918 Gladys made a £5000 share of the profits with Frank Curzon and £4000 in salary – nine thousand in all. I came back to someone with an entirely different mentality and outlook on life; in addition, my nerves were frayed with three-and-a-half years in France. During my absence she had made an entirely new set of friends: I had done the same. We had written to each other practically every day of those three-and-a-half years, and in nearly every letter we said   **75**

'Never mind, we will make up for all this Hell of being parted when the war is over' but we never did, for our troubles began almost as soon as I got home.

With a three-year-old son he'd almost never met, and a now eight-year-old daughter to welcome him home to the house in Regent's Park, Buck thought for a while that the marriage might be going to work out; but G recognized more quickly that she had become 'a complete stranger' to him. Nor were their social lives any longer compatible. Buck's friends were those with whom he'd survived the war, and for whom he was shortly to open Buck's Club in Clifford Street, the enterprise to which he gave the rest of his life; G's friends were a cross-section of theatrical and international high society. A scroll bearing the headline GC: FRIENDS which Edward Knoblock made her put up on her dressing-room door at the Playhouse in 1917, had, by 1930, been signed by (among 200 others) the Prince of Wales, Stanley Baldwin, Groucho Marx, Nellie Melba, the Marquis of Queensberry, W. Somerset Maugham, Noël Coward, Ivor Novello,

On the beach at Frinton: Buck, G, John, Doris and Joan

George Grossmith, Clara Butt, John Barrymore, Basil Rathbone, Irving Berlin, Sybil Thorndike, Rudolph Valentino, George V and the King of Greece.

G was now no longer Mrs Buckmaster in anything but name, and there seemed to neither of them any point in prolonging a dead marriage: Buck noted sadly in his diary that he 'would have liked to see the children grow up' but in fact he did, as they all continued to live in and around London and to stay in reasonably close touch. Buck was henceforth to be found more often than not at his club, and G and the children at the house in Cumberland Terrace ('complete' remembers Doris 'with a large staff') until early in the Twenties' she began to rent the country house at Charlwood in Surrey which was to be her main home for the rest of that decade.

'Since the divorce,' added Buck, 'I have never for one moment regretted it and my advice to all and sundry is, should life become a continual bicker, make the clean cut and start afresh.'

In fact, such was the slow process of the law, their divorce did not become final until December 12th, 1921, the thirteenth anniversary of their wedding. Said Doris:

> They didn't really have a chance after the War. Buck came back to the house in Cumberland Terrace and it seemed no longer to be a part of him. He didn't feel anything belonged to him and he wasn't quite the same man who'd gone away to fight. They'd lived through so much, he and his friends in France, that when they got back they thought 'Hell, let's enjoy ourselves' and he used to come home tight, and those after-effects of War really infuriated Gladys. Before the divorce he'd also started his affair with Nellie Taylor, whom he later married, and Gladys was very good about not naming her in the action or being difficult the way many wives were. Nellie was much more what Buck really needed: she gave up the stage for him, and seemed far more docile around the house.

Fully a decade was to elapse before Gladys married again, though throughout the twenties her name was linked to a whole series of people ranging from Ivor Novello (improbably, since his affections lay largely with members of his own sex) through Raymond Massey to the then Duke of Westminster (more   77 plausibly, since His Grace bestowed upon G a priceless sapphire bracelet, later lost, and offered marriage, an offer she declined on the grounds that he'd leave her inside six months).

These were the years of the bright young things, the flappers and Coward's poor little rich girls, and though G could never bring herself to join such an idle existence (since their nightclub lifestyle failed to suit an industrious actress-manager with two children to support) there's no doubt that her celebrity kept her on the fringes of their world. And a good thing, too: widely hailed as the most beautiful woman in London, G drew a large proportion of her audiences from the ranks of those who simply wanted to sit and stare at her despite her constant attempts to prove to them that she could act well too. This particular audience was not one which eagerly studied theatre reviews in the highbrow press: instead, a good frontispiece in *The Tatler* or *The Sketch* was enough to remind them that there was 'a new Gladys Cooper' at the Playhouse. The society and fashion pages were G's territory, and she haunted it assiduously. Her customers were not renowned for their intellects or theatrical knowledge, and indeed the chances are that many of them saw her in the same play twice without noticing the fact: what they wanted was after-dinner entertainment and G had learnt the rules of that particular business better than most. Which, on balance, may well have been why Curzon took her into management at the Playhouse in the first place.

Early in 1919, during their sustained success with *The Naughty Wife*, Hawtrey and she were offered a new Somerset Maugham comedy, written in a sanatorium during the last winter of the war and originally entitled *Too Many Husbands* but now known as *Home and Beauty*. Though Alexander Woollcott described it as 'fragile, light of touch and untranslatably English' the play has in fact proved as durable and international as many of Coward's comedies and ended up in 1955 being turned into a Hollywood musical for Marge and Gower Champion called *Three For The Show*, before a National Theatre revival by Olivier in the middle sixties established proper respect for a minor classic of its kind.

The Playhouse put it straight into rehearsal at the end of the *Naughty Wife* run, bringing back Malcolm Cherry to play, with Hawtrey, the two husbands with whom G has to juggle when the one she thought killed in action also returns from the war. At a time in our island history when large numbers of wives were having to cope with the return of one husband from the war, the timely joke of a wife having to cope with two guaranteed *Home and Beauty* two hundred and thirty-four performances at the Playhouse, taking it through to the Easter of 1920.

This was to be the beginning of an immensely successful partnership between G and Maugham at the Playhouse: over the next ten years she was to do three more of his plays there (*The Letter, The Sacred Flame* and *The Painted Veil*) and more than any actress of her generation Gladys came to represent the archetypal cool Maugham lady. He himself remained a constant fan, writing in 1953:

> It's interesting to consider how Gladys Cooper has succeeded in turning herself from an indifferent actress into an extremely accomplished one. I have a notion that her beauty has been at once her greatest asset and her greatest handicap: an asset because she would never have gone on the stage without it, for she is not the born actress who, whatever she looks like, is impelled by her nature to act (she would have competently

In the car outside Charlwood with John in 1918

Her constant co-stars at the Playhouse: Charles Hawtrey (left) and Malcolm Cherry in Maugham's Home and Beauty, *1919*

run a business or, married to a landowner, managed an estate); a handicap because . . . there is a certain coldness in perfect beauty which is, not repellent, to say that would be an exaggeration, but not alluring. Some irregularity of features enables an actress to display emotion more effectively . . . if Miss Cooper has succeeded in overcoming the handicap of her startling beauty it is to be ascribed I think to her great common sense and to industry . . . she was prepared to leave nothing undone that could be done by hard work to make her

80

performance as good as she possibly could. And you could rely on her. She was not one of those tiresome creatures who may give a perfect performance one day and a poor one the next. These plays of mine had long runs and from my point of view as a dramatist, not the least of Miss Cooper's merits was that, however long the run was, her performance never varied.

She played in three plays of mine and one (*The Painted Veil*) that was dramatised by an American playwright from one of my novels. I did not write the plays for her, I wrote them for themselves: but I greatly admired her and it was inevitable that I should bear in mind the probability that she might care to act in them, with the result that the character I invented was more or less unconsciously coloured by this . . . I owe much to her.

'A screamingly funny play,' said *The Tatler* of *Home and Beauty*. 'Never has Miss Cooper given us so successful a characterisation,' and though several other critics thought the two-husbands-one-wife idea both cruel and heartless, their reviews did no lasting harm at the Playhouse box-office where customers were already getting in the habit of asking for tickets to 'the new Gladys Cooper play' whatever that play might be.

By now she herself was getting acclimatized to being an un-married lady again; she had the children (custody was, in the custom of the time, automatically granted to her; Buck, a devoted if rather distant father, was hardly likely to endure two small children racketing around his newly-formed military club) and the faithful Nanny Aves and an increasingly large staff and menagerie. To the hordes of dogs and cats, who were to accompany G from now until the end of her life half a century later, had recently been added a pony for Joan (presented to G on stage one night as a practical joke by Hawtrey during the run of *The Naughty Wife*) and some flying bats to which Gladys was curiously devoted though her sister Doris was not.

The home in Cumberland Terrace could now scarcely accom-modate the family plus their small personal zoo, so after a certain amount of house-hunting and one or two short summer seaside rentals Gladys took a long ten-year lease on The Manor House at Charlwood in Surrey, close by what is now Gatwick Airport, and it was there they were to live almost throughout the 1920s.   81

GLADYS COOPER

Dating back in part to the fourteenth century (and sold in 1977 for very nearly a hundred thousand pounds) Charlwood was mainly black-and-white timbering and had eight acres of grounds including a stable for the pony and a pond with an island in the middle. During her stay there Gladys also took in cows, sheep, wallabies, a snake and a pet monkey. Life at Charlwood for

With John and some members of their Charlwood menagerie, 1920

residents and guests alike was nothing if not eventful (du Maurier got bitten by the monkey and took understandable objection to the fact that most of the uglier animals seemed to have been named after various of his stage roles) but Gladys loved it and would commute daily to the theatre in an open sports car called a Storey driven by a Belgian chauffeur called Gurney whose favourite English expression was 'OmyGawd' as they narrowly avoided yet another collision.

Novello, staying the weekend at Charlwood as he often did, found himself shot through a hedge by the Storey – he was behind it at the time, attempting to push G up a hill when she decided to put the car into reverse. Then there was the time Gladys broke down and had to be rescued by the music-hall star Harry Tate, driving a van with his mother sitting bolt upright on a kitchen chair in the back, and the other time when she got a puncture on the top of Redhill at midnight, driving home after a performance. Gladys was at the wheel, Doris as usual perched in the back with the luggage and food from Fortnum's for the weekend, and there they sat for an eternity waiting for another car to pass so that they could beg a lift. An hour and a half later, recalled Gladys, one did:

> Two young men got out and asked if they could give us a lift. Of course we accepted at once, and climbed into the back with their mother. I've never been so frightened in my life. They drove like lunatics down into Redhill, straight towards a level crossing, without any headlights. Doris was hiding her face in her hands and praying. Then the mother turned to me and remarked quite casually, 'My son's done a lot of flying, you know; had a lot of crashes too.' Somehow by the grace of God we got home in the end, and as they were leaving the mother said, 'I wonder if I could ask who it is we've been giving a lift to?' Thinking how thrilled she'd be when she discovered, I said, 'Actually, I'm Gladys Cooper.' 'Oh,' she replied, 'and I'm Mrs Crisp. Good night.'

chapter ten

1920=1921

Uring the run of *Home and Beauty* G did a bit in another silent, *Unmarried* (starring Gerald du Maurier and Mary Glynne) which was a propagandist melodrama on behalf of unmarried mothers. 'Confused,' said *The Bioscope*, 'though Miss Cooper poses nicely for camera with other society beauties.' Her career in the cinema, and her love for the camera, were still more than a little tentative.

In the theatre, she was about to go through a rather haphazard time: Maugham's *Home and Beauty* ran through to the April of 1920 and then G went back with her good friend Malcolm Cherry to her old pre-war home at the Royalty to revive *My Lady's Dress*, the run which had been cut short by the outbreak of war. The play had lost much of its old appeal however for cast and audiences alike and by August she was back at the Playhouse rehearsing *Wedding Bells*, an American comedy. Owen Nares and Edith Evans were with her in what *The Times* described as 'an ultra-amusing account of a lady who decides to re-marry her divorced husband' and it added that 'a Pekingese dog and a Japanese house-boy are also important members of the cast' though curiously and untypically G seems to have taken neither of them home after the run.

But of all the shows that Gladys did at the Playhouse in the Twenties only one dropped below a hundred performances, and

84

this was it. *Wedding Bells* did just twelve weeks and failed to make it through Christmas.

Under Gladys's eminently favourable agreement with Curzon at the Playhouse she was allowed to take the occasional break from that theatre and, after the comparative failure of *Wedding Bells*, she decided to accept an offer to return briefly to the Gaiety – no longer the home of George Edwardes and his musical spectacles but now staging something almost equally ambitious, a sequel to Maeterlinck's *Blue Bird* to be called *The Betrothal*.

> It was quite the wrong theatre for that play, and originally I was cast in quite the wrong part: they wanted me to be Light and I wanted to be Joy which was a veiled part, and I wish I could play it again – she was a mother whom none of her children knew until the youngest unveiled her. I was so veiled I couldn't see a thing and my dresser Motty had to lead me around backstage. Granville Barker was producing, a very exact and exacting man who gave everyone every inflexion of every word in the play . . . he was a restless man who walked about a great deal and one day he suddenly tore off his coat in an outburst of exasperation at the way the rehearsal was going and called out, 'May God forgive this cast, for I never shall.'

Critics weren't all that enthusiastic either and a number of people were indignant at having paid to see Gladys and then not being able to see her through all the veils. Cecil Beaton however remembers being much impressed: 'The long-awaited unveiling of her face in the last act was for all who witnessed it such a supreme moment of beauty that a gasp went through the entire house. For me the emotion was so intense that the memory of it will remain with me until I die.'

But *The Betrothal* failed to live up to Maeterlinck's earlier fantasy success and within a couple of months G was at the Aldwych doing a series of special matinees of *Olivia*, the W. G. Wills adaptation of Goldsmith's 'Vicar of Wakefield'; Norman Forbes was playing the old Irving role and G, remembering the success Ellen Terry had always had in the title part, went along to her for some advice:

I called at her flat in Burleigh Mansions, Charing Cross Road.   85

She received me with that grace for which she was renowned, but I felt that she had only a very hazy idea of who I was. I told her what I wanted and suddenly, to my intense surprise, she got up from her chair and began to act the part for me. Goodness knows how many years it was since she'd played it herself [nearly forty], but she remembered it almost perfectly and, most wonderful of all, for ten minutes or so she really seemed to be a young girl again instead of the darling old woman that she was. It was one of the most remarkable experiences of my life.

After the first performance she came to see me in my dressing-room. 'I haven't been inside,' she said, 'I was too nervous, but I've been walking up and down outside the theatre thinking of you.'

'A play of eighteenth-century sentiment,' said *The Observer*, 'in nineteenth-century prose and acted in a twentieth-century manner . . . Miss Cooper is always good to look at, if not always good as an emotional actress. She suggests a modern Miss arrayed for a fancy dress ball, although an occasional note reminds us she is not without stage talent.'

With reviews like that it was soon time to move on again, and by the beginning of May she was rehearsing for her third major production of 1921, a 'fantastical comedy' by Lord Dunsany called *If* which Nigel Playfair was doing at the Ambassador's, and for which G found herself in thoroughly tiresome company, so unlike the people at her own dear Playhouse.

Playfair struck me as a strange sort of producer: all he ever did was sit in the stalls and watch; when I asked him whether I should play Miralda very common or very refined all he said was, 'Oh I don't know; do what you like.' But he was right to make me 'keep in' the munching of a lot of sweets from a paper bag: I did it one day by mistake at rehearsal and it gave us one of the best laughs of the play.

I didn't get many others, acting with Harry Ainley; whenever I had a funny line he would say his next one very fast so that mine was lost, or else he'd be standing right in front of me so the audience couldn't see who was speaking.

As for the author, Lord Dunsany was a rather peculiar person about the handling of what he had written, and didn't

86

like having his play tampered with in any way. Most authors don't, of course; but during the run he often brought me carnations of his own growing, lovely flowers which he wrapped up in bits of old newspaper.

By the autumn, G was about ready to get back to the Playhouse where Curzon was waiting for her with Channing Pollock's sensational crime drama *The Sign on the Door*.

This was the play which gave Gladys her first genuine triumph as an actress: 'Starting with her usual visualisation of the innocent and virtuous stage heroine,' said *The Times*, 'Gladys Cooper surprised all London by her gradual development in this piece: no one had considered her capable of such dramatic strength.'

While consolidating G's success at the Playhouse, *The Sign on the Door* was a useful pointer towards the way she could be shaping her career: backed by a strong male cast and working in other modern-dress thrillers, far away from the artificiality of 'period' which she could never really cope with, Gladys was to repeat *The Sign on the Door* in one way or another over and over again.

From now on Gladys had her own theatre and could do more or less what she liked in it: after *The Sign on the Door* she was over the next twelve years only to leave the Playhouse for *Peter Pan* or the occasional special engagement, and her unique situation there meant that she would virtually always be in work. In some ways, this could have been to her disadvantage: at a time when such contemporaries as Sybil Thorndike and Edith Evans were forced to test themselves against all kinds of stage texts simply because of their situation as freelance actresses, Gladys was able to do only the work she knew she was reasonably good at. The Playhouse was not a theatre for the classics, thus G never did the classics; and so when in the late 1930s, she turned her attention to Shakespeare it was already too late – she'd had neither the training nor the practice.

On the other hand, it is arguable that G would never have been a great classical actress in the first place, and that therefore being her own impresario for most of the first half of her star career simply meant that she could look after herself better than most.

The Sign on the Door ran three hundred performances through the winter and spring of 1921–2, and when it was over she went back into movies.

Ivor Novello had now become a close friend and frequent   87

Picture postcards

weekend visitor to Charlwood: throughout her life Gladys was deeply impressed by very good looks, and would forgive almost anything on their account. Her later heroes and friends ranged through Paul Newman to Dirk Bogarde and in any list of male virtues the importance of looking good was always paramount to her. Her special devotion she reserved, interestingly enough, for those actors who like her had started out as male or female pin-ups and then been able to prove that they were also capable of impressive stage or screen performances: as a general rule she would incline therefore towards Vivien Leigh and Kay Kendall rather than such classicists as Sybil Thorndike or Edith Evans whom she thought over-solemn in their approach to the business of being an actress.

Gladys's tolerance of ugliness was very nearly as low as her tolerance of illness or exhaustion or inefficiency: she regarded it as a sign of weakness, as something to be fixed as soon as possible. Making the best of yourself was another of her maxims and one which was, in her day, a rather more American than English belief. But then Gladys was in many ways an American long before she went to live and work there: not entirely coincidentally many of her early Playhouse successes were by Americans.

But it wasn't only Ivor Novello's looks which appealed to G. She loved his music, which she would whistle on a curious monotone and she was, in company with many others, bowled over by the boyish charm which he managed to preserve well into his middle years. Whereas the young Noël Coward seemed to G somewhat smug and 'too clever for his own good', Ivor was just right and there are many who reckon that she was for several years much in love with him and indeed wanted to marry him – believing, apparently, that she could 'cure' him of his lifelong bisexuality.

As for Noël Coward, G had first met him a few months earlier, over the Christmas of 1921, when she'd taken a few days off from the Playhouse and gone with a skiing party to Davos. Micheàl MacLiammòir was living there at the time and remembered being 'thunderstruck and tongue-tied by the glamour of Gladys and her party' but Noël, then just twenty-two and still two years away from his first real success with *The Vortex*, found the meeting even less encouraging:

In order of appearance rather than precedence, Ned Lathom's 89

Christmas guests at Davos that year consisted of Clifton Webb, Teddie Thompson, Gladys Cooper, Edward Molyneux, Elsa Maxwell and Maxine Elliott ... we went on tailing parties, strung out in a long line of sleds behind a large sleigh on which Elsa sat screaming like a banshee. We went on skating parties, Swedish Punch parties and lugeing parties ... Gladys Cooper took a marked dislike to me, and we had several acrid tussles, notably at a lunch party at the Kurhaus where she remarked in a tone of maddening superiority that it was ridiculous of me to go on writing plays that were never produced, and why on earth didn't I collaborate with somebody who really knew the job?

I replied that as Shaw, Barrie and Maugham didn't collaborate I saw no reason why I should. Whereupon she laughed, not without reason, and said that she had never heard of such conceit in her life, and that she might just as well compare herself to Duse or Bernhardt. I jumped in here quickly on cue and retorted that the difference was not quite as fantastic as that. After which the lunch continued amid slightly nervous hilarity. Oddly enough, after this preliminary blood-letting, Gladys and I parted glowing with mutual affection, and the glow strengthened through the years with never so much as a breath of disharmony.

Playhouse 1923: supported by Ivor Novello in Enter Kiki

chapter eleven

1922=1923

AT the time of the film *The Bohemian Girl* in 1922, Ivor Novello had only appeared on the stage in brief revue sketches, though his music had been familiar for half a dozen years, since *Keep The Home Fires Burning*, and his face was well-known to early cinemagoers from three earlier pictures. He was now twenty-nine, five years younger than Gladys, and for this their first production together he got £200 and she around £150, reflecting their current box-office values. There was a starry supporting cast which included Constance Collier (another good friend of Novello's) and the veteran Ellen Terry alongside such future Hollywood stalwarts as Gibb McLaughlin and C. Aubrey Smith who was later with Gladys to be a founding member of the British acting colony in Beverly Hills.

G played Arlene 'a gypsy girl who is really a Count's daughter' while Novello played 'a Polish officer posing as a gypsy' and a good romantic time was had by all during the filming. 'A faithful adaptation of Balfe's operetta,' said the *New York Times* later, 'in which Novello and Cooper distinguish themselves.'

The film coincided with the peak of Novello's celluloid fame as 'the Welsh Valentino', and topped the box-office polls in Britain for two solid years running. Unusually for an English film of the period, it also did very well in the USA.

When she returned from Bohemia to the Playhouse in June 1922, Gladys and Curzon decided to revive Pinero's 1893 classic *The Second Mrs Tanqueray*, somewhat courageously considering that the performance of Mrs Patrick Campbell in the title role was still well within the memory of most London theatregoers and that the legendary Mrs Campbell herself was still very much around.

Indeed the *Daily Mail*, not missing a trick, sent Mrs Campbell in place of their regular critic to review the first night:

> I did not recognise here [Mrs Campbell wrote] the Paula Tanqueray of my dreams, for this was another woman. Miss Cooper gives a splendidly consistent, human and sincere performance and her loveliness enchants. But there is not the child in her work, and artists should never be afraid of the child, for the kingdom of Art demands it.

Other critics were more enthusiastic. J. T. Grein, a severe reviewer never noted hitherto for his approval of Gladys, concluded: 'She was in aspect and in utterance and in mentality the woman of hazy antecedents, of unbridled passions, the wild bird that may be taught to live on a perch but never in a cage. For that achievement Gladys Cooper deserves unbounded praise, and there is no exaggeration in saying that in the English theatre she has attained her place among the leaders.'

Seventeen years after her Colchester debut, and five years after she'd joined Curzon at the Playhouse, Gladys at last had a full-blooded critical as well as social success there. The story of Mrs Tanqueray (a 'woman with a past' marrying into respectable society and eventually finding that her only way out is suicide) combined all the elements of snobbery and drama then demanded by Playhouse audiences, and G's decision to scrape her well-known hair back into a severe bun produced such headlines as 'Startling Change in Appearance of Well-Known Actress'. Cecil Beaton recalls:

> When Gladys decided on a revival of *The Second Mrs Tanqueray* it was a foregone conclusion that the cream-and-roses fluffy blonde would be inadequate in the name part that was considered to belong forever to its creator, the Beardsleyesque Mrs Campbell. But Gladys decided that she would chalk-

whiten her face, darken her stag-like eyes, wet her hair and drag it back into a huge tight chignon. In this startling disguise she had never looked more nobly beautiful; nor had she been acknowledged to possess such profound depths as an actress.

In later years critics and theatregoers alike would comment on the courage it must have taken to tackle so celebrated a role in the lifetime of its creator: I suspect though that it took no more courage than usual, for Gladys was not one to think twice about doing anything. The Playhouse needed a drama for the summer, the rights to *Mrs Tanqueray* were available, so why not? She was not a lady given to over-careful consideration of the pros and cons, nor did she worry or think much about anything that had happened in the theatre before last Monday. A sense of theatrical history, or an awareness of her own place in it, were matters for critics and outsiders to murmur about: her job was to act whatever came up and luckily at this moment in her fortunes what came up was Mrs Tanqueray. 'At a stroke,' wrote W. A. Darlington, 'she has made Pinero into a modern success and killed his meaning forever.'

The success that she and Dennis Eadie (that most faithful of her leading men) and Ernest Thesiger had in the revival confirmed G's tenure of the Playhouse. It was now her London home just as surely as Charlwood was her country home, and she knew the habits of her audience there better perhaps than almost any other manager in town. She knew for instance, instinctively and rightly, that hers was the kind of audience who could afford long country weekends. The Playhouse therefore, alone among central London theatres of the time, did not play Monday nights. Instead they would open up on Tuesday, do two shows Wednesday and Thursday, one on Friday and two on Saturday, thereby still achieving the requisite eight per week but allowing G and her company a good long break from Saturday night to Tuesday evening.

These weekends she herself would spend with the children at Charlwood: they were both now in schools nearby, and throughout the holidays and Sundays of the early twenties the Manor would be full of Gladys and her guests – Eadie and entire casts from the Playhouse, Novello and Coward and du Maurier and such distinguished American stage visitors as Barrymore and

93

Seaside snap with Joan and John

Tallulah Bankhead. There was the monkey that used to bite Novello, ducks and geese and cats and dogs and parrots and people, all gathered around Gladys as they would later gather around her in California and then at the last in Henley, grouped in a respectful mixture of admiration and amazement at the energy and variety of her life off-stage.

On stage, the triumph of *Tanqueray* continued: George V sent for du Maurier (who had directed it) and Gladys and told them that he much preferred G to Mrs Campbell in the role since she

(Mrs Pat) 'always seemed to me to speak with a slightly foreign voice'. Seymour Hicks told Gladys that she was 'the only Mrs Tanqueray for me,' adding as a postscript, 'some of your company ought however to be shot'. Gladys herself, thinking back on the production some years later, reckoned the real success ought to have been attributed to the designer Edward Molyneux:

> During rehearsals I did get rather nervous about whether or not I was going to be all right, and I decided to do the whole thing on looks. I took a break in rehearsal and rushed off to Paris where Molyneux put me into long clinging dresses and showed me how his mannequins were parting their hair in the middle and wearing those long ear-rings, and I thought then I'd seen how Paula should look. Luckily Pinero approved: he came to my dressing-room after the dress-rehearsal and was very encouraging, though he couldn't bear to stay for the first night – he just walked round and round the theatre waiting to see how it had worked.

When it was clear that the run was nearing the end of its six-month prime, Maugham offered Gladys a new play of his called *Our Betters*; feeling however that the role came too close to Mrs Tanqueray for comfort, she declined, and chose instead to make her first journey across the Atlantic. She went partly for a holiday, partly in search of a new play and partly to celebrate her new-found fame there, since *The Bohemian Girl* had made her if not a star in New York then at the very least a faintly familiar name. Aboard the SS *Olympic* in mid-ocean she received a cable from Gilbert Miller reading MEETING YOU AT DOCK WITH IVOR TWO PRESS AGENTS AND THE KEYS OF THE CITY but even that scarcely prepared her for the storm of publicity that was about to break over her head once she landed. Novello, billed as 'the handsomest star in Britain' had meanwhile signed a contract with D. W. Griffith whose Hollywood office was determined to publicize him as widely as possible. Inevitably, during an interview, the question of his marriage or rather non-marriage came up and as the great American public was scarcely ready in January 1923 for a film star then living with his male secretary, the word was spread that he was deeply in love with Gladys and possibly even secretly engaged to her.

95

'Will Love Find a Way?' screamed the *New York American* above a picture of Ivor greeting G off the boat, and countless fan magazines took up the question, thereby doing an untold amount of good to *The Bohemian Girl* at the box-office. G meanwhile had a happy if unromantic holiday with Ivor in New York, in the course of which they found a play called *Kiki* which they determined to do together at the Playhouse when Novello's film commitments permitted. All the New York papers interviewed G at length, published her 'beauty tips' and ran a hilariously inaccurate account of her first marriage ('Famous English Stage Queen Unable Overcome Husband's Instinctive Preference for Dark-Haired Women').

A fortnight of that was enough, and G then returned to discuss with her ever-loyal manager and partner Frank Curzon plans for the spring season at the Playhouse. Another revival seemed a good idea after the *Tanqueray* success, and they settled after some searching on yet another of Mrs Campbell's old triumphs – *Magda* by Herman Suderman. Again G decided to go for a 'new look' with which to surprise her audience and discourage them from making too careful comparisons with previous interpretations of the role. The result however was a muted re-run of *Tanqueray*: neither the play nor the performance seemed quite as welcome, but both were treated respectfully and they lasted at the Playhouse until the end of July 1923 by which time Ivor was back from America and it was time to think about doing *Kiki*. Despite the fact that Ivor Novello had never played a leading role in the West End, and that his stage experience was still negligible, Gladys was determined to work with him – so determined that she turned down the offer from Coward of the lead in his *Fallen Angels*. It says a good deal for Coward that, despite her rejection of his own work, he agreed to 'tinker' with *Kiki* for her and Novello in order to try and get it a bit better. Though a considerable Broadway success under Belasco's management, the play had originally been adapted from the French and was looking more than a little travel-stained by the time it got to the Playhouse, where not even Coward could do much to rescue a tacky little plot about a chorus girl who fakes a cataleptic fit in order to mislead her lover's wife. Bad taste apart, Playhouse audiences found it a little hard to take G as a French *gamine* so soon after her powerful appearances in the two Mrs Campbell roles, none of 96   which would have much mattered had Novello been stronger as

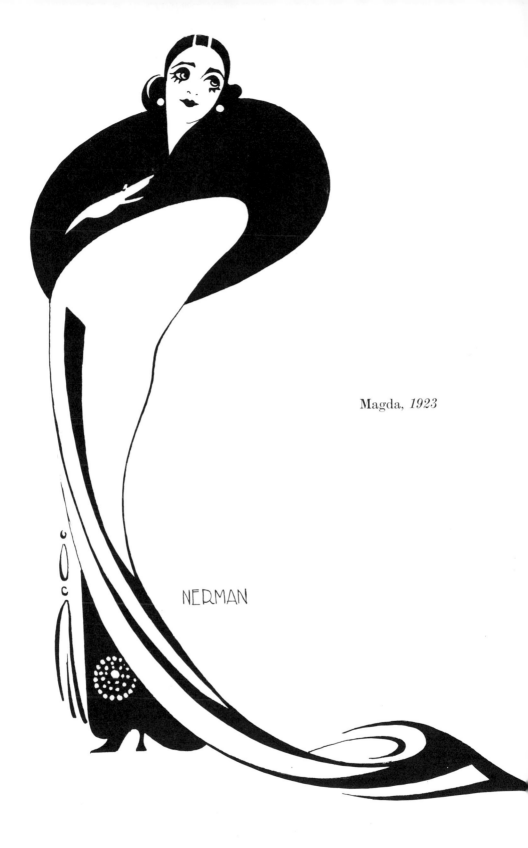

Magda, *1923*

NERMAN

the lover: 'Miss Cooper plays with spirit and intelligence,' said *Punch*, 'but Mr Novello works in a kind of dreamy trance, as if he'd rather be elsewhere.' Novello himself knew the trouble he was in:

> I was hopelessly miscast and the papers gave me hell – they described me as 'self-conscious' and 'amateurish' and I got it in the neck. I simply hadn't got the experience to play opposite Gladys at the Playhouse, and for years afterwards those reviews left me with an inferiority complex about the stage which I found it very hard to overcome. We played on for a few months, because people seemed eager to come along and look at Gladys and me in real life after seeing us on the screen; but I couldn't wait for the run to end, especially as I'd been offered £350 a week to play Bonnie Prince Charlie on the screen with Gladys as Flora MacDonald.

The play, now called *Enter Kiki*, ran on through August, September, October and November and every night at the stage door groups of fans would gather to collect the stars' autographs. G's fans were a smaller and more respectful group, waiting attentively to say 'Good Evening, Miss Cooper' as she passed. Ivor's, as befitted a new screen generation, were noisier and more numerous and inclined to shriek 'Hello Ivor!' as he appeared, thus infuriating Gladys's group who took to waiting for her on the other side of the street to avoid mixing with a crowd they regarded as socially inferior in every way.

Novello, always at his best in a crowd of unknown admirers, could never understand Gladys's attitude to her fans, which was one of irritable surprise that they hadn't got homes to go to or something better to do with their lives than hang around stage doors. She was never less than briskly polite to them as part of her professional duties, but she was never much more than that either. Gladys believed there was no fan like a distant fan: so long as they wrote to her, or kept themselves at a respectful distance, she had no hesitation in sending back polite, faintly regal, notes of acknowledgement for letters and flowers. She did not however approve of closer contact: my father, on tour once in Newcastle, took himself to tea with the legendary Gertie Taylor, a fan who had been sending Christmas presents and children's clothing to Gladys for her family for the best part of thirty years.

When they next met, Robert told G what he had done, only to

Flora Macdonald to Novello's Bonnie Prince Charlie (silent film, 1923)

receive the icy reply: 'You have ruined that woman. She was a perfectly good fan, and now she'll expect to be an acquaintance.'

The difference in their attitude to their fans nearly ruined the friendship between Gladys and Novello during the filming of *Bonnie Prince Charlie*: up on the Isle of Arran, in the depths of the 1923–4 winter, they were constantly surrounded by local admirers who made it impossible for G to leave the hotel without a full escort. Joan and John, staying with her, took an equal dislike to the crowds but Novello loved it all and, in G's view, went out of his way to encourage attention:

> One morning I woke up to discover he had become a flag-day seller in aid of some local charity. There he was in his make-up and film clothes, going about selling flags much to the admiration of the inhabitants and the trippers. We had a fierce exchange of remarks about the dignity, etcetera, etcetera, of publicity and ended up by not being on speaking terms with one another. We went back to the mainland at opposite ends of the boat, so mutually incensed were we.

chapter twelve

1923=1925

DESPITE the rows that developed on its location, *Bonnie Prince Charlie* was a considerable success at the box-office: though G had loathed 'plastering my face with silly green make-up' the general reckoning was that she looked lovely on the screen. Her reviews were equally glowing, but did her curiously little good as a screen actress: she wasn't offered another film for twelve years, and though she'd made a total of nine silents she was never really thought of in filmic terms until her Hollywood years – perhaps because until then she herself refused to take the cinema very seriously.

Her months of filming up in Scotland had however broken her links with the Playhouse for the time being: though she was to remain nominally in joint management with Curzon, she in fact did not work there as an actress between the end of the *Kiki* run in 1923 and the opening of *The Letter* in 1927. These years, the mid-twenties, were spent at other theatres doing a variety of other work including two consecutive Christmas seasons in the role G loved above almost all others – *Peter Pan.*

Her first chance came in 1923: Barrie's classic play had been in annual production since 1904 and such actresses as Nina Bouci-cault, Cissie Loftus, Pauline Chase, Madge Titheradge, Fay Compton and Edna Best had already left their mark on the boy who wouldn't grow up. G decided that it should be her part too 101 and was thus delighted to be approached by Gilbert Miller who had taken over the management of the play and was putting it into the Adelphi with a distinguished cast including Franklin Dyall as Hook and Stella Patrick Campbell as Mrs Darling.

Grein thought Gladys the best of all the Peters he'd seen: 'there is more hard-hearted cruelty and defiance in her, making us realize the aloofness of Peter from this world, yet the children love her and laugh at her still'. Others were less enthusiastic, regarding G as a somewhat revolutionary Peter because of her predictable determination not to play the part the way it had ever been played before:

> When I suggested various innovations to Tommy Vaughan [business manager for Miller, du Maurier and later Gladys herself] he said: 'Oh no you can't do that – it's never been done' so I inveigled Sir James Barrie out to lunch and got his permission to wear tennis shoes and a pair of du Maurier's old shorts. I also thought it was silly to go on using wooden swords, so Dyall and I had our fight on the pirate ship with real sabres. When I played the piece, it was the first time they'd done as good business with the adults in the evenings as with the children in the afternoons: we made it a really frightening play.

Barrie nevertheless was and remained a friend: when a decade later Gladys had her second daughter, Sally, J.M.B. became her godfather and sent a letter reading (from the play) 'One girl is worth twenty boys'.

The Times thought that 'confirmed and crusty Peterists' might find Gladys too 'modern' in the role, and another critic noted acidly: 'Peter Pan has grown up at last – into a pantomime principal boy.' G herself agreed that she was 'less than good' the first Christmas she played the role, but reckoned she improved greatly the second year when du Maurier was brought in to direct. Of that first season Arthur Marshall's fondest memory is of Wendy asking of the Lost Boys about Peter's age and hearing from the stalls a voice saying 'thirty-five'.

Back to earth after the first of her two *Peter Pan* seasons, and thrilled to have introduced two new cross-stage 'flights' into the role (she was the first to make Peter's initial entrance on a wire)

102   Gladys found the Playhouse still doing very well in her absence

To the Never-Never Land: Peter Pan *1924*

and decided therefore to stay at the Adelphi in response to an invitation from old Sir Squire Bancroft to revive *Diplomacy*, the Sardou standby she'd last played in 1913. But times had changed: a drama which managed to notch up more than a thousand pre-war performances now seemed to one critic the 'stagiest of plays: the characters are all wire-jointed marionettes without enough real life in them to vitalize a performing flea, and the structure of the play suggests a house of cards occupied by very distinguished and nice-dressed people – one breath of reality and the whole lot would topple over. *Diplomacy* contains many fine acting parts, but for the sake of one display of fireworks to have to watch Sardou's slow building up of the big scene is as dull as watching the carpenters building Wembley on a wet day.' *Diplomacy* however, now in its fourth major West End revival inside forty years, could withstand even the hatred of the *Daily Mail* and it ran on for yet another three hundred and fifty performances throughout 1924 despite the fact that in the middle of the summer G was severely bitten one weekend at Charlwood by Cuthbert, her beloved pet monkey, who'd taken a sharp dislike to yet another puppy being introduced into the Cooper menagerie there.

Then, towards Christmas, it was time to be thinking about *Peter Pan* again; this time du Maurier agreed to direct and they went into rehearsal with du Maurier's daughter Angela now playing Wendy:

> Clothes dreadfully shabby, ghastly shoes, no new wardrobe for a hardy annual like *Peter Pan* . . . but to watch the play shaping was like watching a child growing up . . . Madge Titheradge, Barrymore and Tallulah in front . . . Gladys was never better than when produced by my father, as she would have been the first to say. I think he taught her a great deal, and he believed in her capabilities as an actress more than in any other woman I remember . . . she always had immense intelligence, was a first-rate actress, and worked like a steam roller. Never sick or sorry, I have known Gladys play when other women would have been carted off to nursing homes in ambulances.

Angela's sister, Daphne du Maurier, also retains clear memories of the impression G made as *Peter Pan*:

104

It always made me think about what a marvellous *St Joan* she would have been (Sybil Thorndike created Shaw's role in that same year). There was a strength about Gladys, a vitality, a sense of courage on the stage that I'd never seen anywhere else and of course my father loved her, more deeply I think than any other actress he worked with regularly.

G's second and last *Peter Pan* did its usual run through to the end of January whereupon, the Adelphi being still available and the Playhouse still not in need of her services, she decided on yet another revival of a Pinero–Mrs Patrick Campbell classic. This one was to be *Iris*, and the play was to live for some time in the Cooper family memory not so much for the length of its run (a mere hundred and thirty performances, good by normal standards though not by G's at this time) as for yet another beloved pet monkey, bought to celebrate the first night and subsequently kidnapped by John Barrymore who, staying the weekend at Charlwood, decided his life would not be complete without Iris and took her back to Hollywood where she starred on his shoulder in several of his later silents.

Du Maurier was again directing, but (Pinero being still much in evidence) found it hard to get the play down to less than its old three-hour length, one acceptable to audiences of 1901 but not to those of 1925. Moreover du Maurier's directing style, one largely based on the 'do it like this' principle, did not suit the new romantic lead, an Irish actor called Anew McMaster, who was heard to mutter darkly in rehearsal that come the first night he'd be playing the part his way rather than Sir Gerald's. Came the first night, *Iris* still nearly an hour too long and McMaster changing his performance so drastically that the big love scene brought guffaws of uneasy laughter from the audience, and it was clear something would have to be done. G sent for the management and gave them a choice: either to keep the show as it was and to close on Saturday, or to allow her to take control and have a hope of lasting into the summer. The management chose the latter course and G promptly fired McMaster who returned to his native Ireland, built up a considerable and well-deserved reputation as a leading classical actor there, and almost never again played London in a long and otherwise successful career.

In his place G brought in Ivor Novello, remembering that though still something less than a good stage actor he was a considerable box-office draw, a theory borne out by the takings which rose abruptly from £900 in McMaster's last week to £2400 in Novello's first. He and Gladys were still considered a romantic team, indeed one of the first of its kind in British pictures, and though they were only to work together once more they remained close and loving friends up to the time of his death in 1951. Novello, in Hollywood several years before Gladys, was forever trying to entice her out there and on one occasion took to showing her photograph around the studios in the hope that her dazzling beauty would compel them to put her under contract. 'Who?' Sam Goldwyn is reported to have asked him. 'Gladys Cooper,' said Novello. 'She should come to the Coast,' said Goldwyn. 'She's the queen of the London stage,' replied Novello, 'you'd have to make her a good offer.' 'Is that so?' remarked Goldwyn and with that the conversation was closed for another ten years.

Other Americans were more enthusiastic about her: Karl Kitchen, asked to list the highlights of his recent European tour, concluded, 'The most impressive man: Von Hindenburg; most modest man: Franz Lehar; worst play in Europe: *Fallen Angels*; best acting: Gladys Cooper as Pinero's *Iris*.'

There were still the family summers at Charlwood: Joan, now at Heathfield in term-time, and John, at a prep school getting ready for Eton, would gather together with their faithful nannie and the innumerable animals and whatever guests G had staying at the weekends. Fairbanks and Bankhead and Barrymore from across the Atlantic, and du Maurier and Novello and Nares and Lonsdale and others from nearer home. Buck, too, was now a frequent visitor; the turmoil of his divorce and remarriage now safely in the past, he was determined to keep an eye on his rapidly growing children. Johnnie was already getting boxing lessons from friends of Buck's at his club, and Buck (who was himself a compulsive if eccentric sport) once rode down from London to Charlwood on a pony to visit his children. On another and more celebrated occasion he walked to Brighton in under twelve hours, the result of a challenge, and a few years after that he walked from the club to Land's End in ten days, averaging thirty miles a day.

But Buck's greatest sense of pride was reserved for his son's boxing: that summer, when John was only nine, he did a display and a cartoon appeared in the *Evening Standard*. By the following morning, the bemused cartoonist had received offers from both Buck and Gladys for the original; not knowing which of them should have it, he wrote in some confusion to Buck who replied, 'The answer, dear fellow, is perfectly simple: I shall purchase it and you shall then send it to Miss Cooper's dressing-room.'

With *Iris* looking highly unlikely to outlive August, despite Novello's credit at the box-office, G was in the market for a new play, as was du Maurier. She clearly couldn't go on doing revivals and *Peter Pan* forever, and one critic had already noted 'this actress, though icily efficient, will tackle any old thing provided Mrs Patrick Campbell has already made a success in it'.

The problem was in finding herself a playwright: Coward, still hurt over her rejection of *Fallen Angels*, had not bothered to send her anything else, Novello was turning towards musicals and none of the playwrights she'd found for the Playhouse seemed to have much on offer except Maugham whom she'd also recently turned down. Her work had largely been in revivals and adaptations from the French or the American. She had ruled herself out of the classical work then being undertaken by Thorndike and Evans, and there was a general critical feeling that, although Gladys was still far ahead on looks, in acting talent she'd recently been outstripped by the likes of Albanesi and Athene Seyler and Fay Compton. What G badly needed therefore was what she now got, an outstanding modern-dress success in a new play, and it came from the one playwright who apart from Maugham might have been considered made for her, though curiously they only ever worked together on this one occasion.

Frederick Lonsdale stood for, indeed immortalized, most of Gladys's seemingly casual virtues: the high-society playwright with a deep love of country-house weekends, he formed with du Maurier and G a unique three-cornered alliance constructed more of *The Tatler* and *Country Life* than *The Stage* but subtly professional for all that. This one occasion on which they came together was for one of the greatest successes any of them ever had, and it was perhaps just as well that circumstances never encouraged them to repeat it.

G had of course known Lonsdale for several years: one summer she and Doris and the children rented a summer cottage at Birchington where he lived, and shared it with Novello and Bobbie Andrews: P. G. Wodehouse was there that summer too, and there were frequent beach parties, to be followed in the subsequent **107**

Gladys in the early Twenties

winter by parties at the du Maurier home in Hampstead where G and Lonsdale were regular guests. Then, one evening in the summer of 1925, while G was still playing in *Iris*, Lonsdale went to dine with du Maurier at Cannon Hall. He was, recalled Daphne du Maurier:

> in high spirits, excited about a new play which he hoped would be produced by Gerald at Wyndham's. It may be that Mo [Lady du Maurier] provided too good a dinner, it may be that the port was too old a vintage and too strong for a man who was worried and depressed and over-tired. It may just be that it was an unfortunate example hitherto unknown, of damn bad manners, but the fact remained that when Freddie, seated before the fire in the library, looked up from his manuscript in eager anticipation, it was to discover a comatose Gerald with his head on a cushion and his feet up, not only sound asleep but snoring.

An understandably, indeed justifiably, outraged Lonsdale stormed out of the house taking his play with him, and promptly offered it to Gladys who rapidly formed a partnership with Gilbert Miller in order to present it at the St James's. They in turn approached du Maurier and offered him the chance to direct and play whichever of the two male leads most appealed to him; but he was now to be on a straightforward salary in an alien theatre whereas he could, had he not fallen into that fatal doze while Lonsdale was reading, have kept the play for his own management at Wyndham's and taken a percentage of the profits. It was to be the most expensive sleep of du Maurier's life, and one from which financially he never quite awoke.

He was none the less invaluable in rehearsal: du Maurier's instinctive knowledge of a Lonsdale play, and the retrieval of his friendship with the author, meant that Freddy could be encouraged to rewrite a potentially disastrous last act and turn the comedy from a near-miss into the greatest London theatrical triumph of 1925 – a year which also saw *Rose Marie* and *The Ghost Train* and *Lady Be Good*.

Briefly, *The Last of Mrs Cheyney* was *Raffles* by way of *Lady Windermere's Fan*: an infinitely elegant country-house comedy about a charmingly aristocratic burglar (G) and the man who falls in love with her (Sir Gerald). They opened on September 109

26th, 1925 and ran eighteen months for a total of 514 performances.

Reviews were ecstatic: 'Has there ever,' asked St John Ervine in the *Observer*, 'been a dramatist so audacious and daring as Mr Frederick Lonsdale? Name if you can (but you cannot!) an author who would do what Mr Lonsdale here does: begin his play as high comedy; abruptly change it in the middle of the first act to common crookery, return to high comedy in the second act, plunge headfirst into farce at the beginning of the third and end up amid the cheers of the audience with a charming piece of sentiment.' *Punch* was a bit less enthusiastic ('Miss Cooper was as usual effective and very nearly credible') but Grein thought she was 'dazzling' and the *Sketch* thought her clothes well justified the usual dash to Molyneux in Paris.

G was now at the very height of her London fame; not only had she a smash hit under her own management at the St James's, she'd also decided to grab, while the going remained good, an immensely lucrative offer to put her name on a brand of face creams and lotions which she would henceforth advertise in her programmes (and on huge posters in the windows of Selfridge's) as 'My Own Beauty Preparation'. The text here was a masterpiece of 1920s advertising copy:

> As many prominent people now lend their names to advertised products [it ran] I should like to explain that the preparations advertised here are my own – the result of nearly eight years' careful study and experimenting [quite untrue]. I have gone back to the days of Apothecaries and the Stillroom where, from Herbs and Flowers, such wonderful balms and lotions were compounded, and to those recipes I have added the knowledge that science has since given us.

There followed a sharp reminder that purchasing the kind of rival face creams advertised by other actresses could well lead to 'blackheads and enlarged pores', and then the reassurance that 'My cream is made only from the finest vegetable oils – oils from plants that grow in the sun . . . the same care has been taken with all my other preparations – they are made under my supervision at my own laboratories and in my opinion are as near to perfection as can be obtained. You can buy them in inexpensive sizes at the best stores, chemists and hairdressers everywhere price from 3/6d to 10/6d.'

I don't think Gladys ever discovered quite where 'her own laboratories' were supposed to be, but she worked hard at promoting the products at chemists and beauty counters around London and any other towns she happened to find herself touring through, and she was astute enough to make sure they did no lasting harm to those of her fans who were tempted to buy them on the strength of her almost poetic recommendation. In her later life I was always surprised that she never made television commercials, though if the right product and price had come along I suspect she'd have been in there pitching with the best of them.

chapter thirteen

1925=1927

he *Last of Mrs Cheyney* ran through the Christmas of
1925 and on into the spring and autumn of 1926, marking the
high point of G's West End social and professional life: by night
she'd be in the theatre, by day she'd be demonstrating her
Beauty Products in stores and exhibitions, where crowds would
collect to see, in the words of the *Daily Express* 'whether she
could be as good at selling lotions and creams and powders as at
acting'; needless to say she was, and the beauty business in
which she had a founding share ran profitably on into the late
twenties when she and Mrs Teddie Thompson, her partner in the
affair, came to a minor financial disagreement and decided to
wind the whole thing up.

The play also marked the high point in G's friendship with du
Maurier: they were a unique and ineffably elegant team, he still
the greatest and suavest actor-manager of the day but now less
than a decade away from his death and already haunted by inti-
mations of mortality, she at the height of her no-nonsense professional career. They were bound together by an alliance best
described by Sir Gerald's daughter Daphne:

> Gladys was probably the only woman in the world who had
> never flattered Gerald at any time and, though deeply appre-
> ciative of his genius, she never made any attempt to blind

112

herself to his faults. She met him on her own ground, as an equal, the most feminine of women with a face like Danae and eyes that will never be surpassed in our lifetime. She gave him what was probably the only genuine platonic friendship of his career. No wiles from her, no tantrums, no lamentations, no probings and interferings into his private life, no fifth-form jealousies, no undignified intrigues. Every matinee during the run of *Cheyney* they met for lunch like two men at a club, silent, shoulder to shoulder, Gerald with his cold beef and Gladys with a chop; now and then discussing the affairs of the day, brief and matter-of-fact, or comparing notes about each other's children. No lingering over coffee for her, no long stories, no confessions, no declaration of private misery, no mysterious revelations. No hammering down her great reserve: no indirect questioning, no sudden suggestions, penetrated the wall she had so wisely built around herself. What lay at the back of her mind, what remembrances, what past endeavours and what future goals only God and Gladys ever knew.

Possessing great physical and moral courage herself, she had little sympathy for the weak or temperamental, no patience with moods, no psychological insight. With her firm chin and wide nostrils she strode through life brushing obstacles from her path, her eyes on the horizon, an intolerant and rather gallant figure. Her common sense and her abrupt, matter-of-fact manners made her a very good companion for Gerald; she had the effect on him that a practical, thoroughly normal nursery governess has on a spoilt and pampered child.

The success of their play put Gladys back at the top of the popularity polls (a *Bystander* chart that year showed her at number one, hotly followed by Fay Compton, Jose Collins, Marie Lohr, Irene Vanbrugh, Sybil Thorndike and Phyllis Dare). She was the toast of London; Valentino and the Duke of Windsor (then Prince of Wales) paid court at her dressing-room after *Cheyney*, but outside the theatre her private life was anyone's guess. She herself would have been surprised and faintly indignant if you'd suggested that all through the Twenties there was a hole where the middle of her life should have been. She'd have pointed out, rightly, that for a divorcee with two school-age 113 children to bring up and a theatre and a house and a career to run, there couldn't have been a lot of time for self-examination, and that every hour of the day seemed to fill itself without encouragement or pause for thought. All true; true too, there were occasional lovers in this period, none of whom she'd discuss and all of whom preserved to their graves the tactful silence which was expected of lovers of the period.

That there may have been a kind of inner loneliness about G, now as later, did not have much to do with there not being a husband around; it had to do with that impenetrable wall the du Mauriers had come up against, and over which only Buck at the very beginning of her adult life and Philip Merivale towards the end of it could reckon to have successfully clambered.

The 'den mother', as Gerald described his beloved G, could now afford, thanks to *Mrs Cheyney*, to think about having a permanent London home again as well as the country house at Charl-

The Last of Mrs Cheyney as drawn by Punch, 1925

HASELDEN.

THE ROPE OF PEARLS.
(Enough to hang herself with).
Lord Dilling . . SIR GERALD DU MAURIER.
Mrs. Cheyney . . MISS GLADYS COOPER.

wood, and in Mount Row, just off Berkeley Square, she found some old stables and had them converted into Mount Cottage. But the organization of that, the running of the family at Charlwood and the run of *Cheyney*, though enough for some people, left Gladys with a certain amount of spare time which she decided to fill by going to work for the Play Actors' Society.

This was a Sunday night group, formed to try out plays which for some reason or other had failed to reach an immediate commercial home and G was often to be found alleviating the boredom of a sustained run by doing other shows for them. Now she went into rehearsal for *L'Ecole des Cocottes*, a French drama then banned by the Lord Chamberlain because it showed G's character, Ginette, climbing to wealth and good fortune over the bodies of a series of increasingly powerful lovers.

With her in the club performance of *L'Ecole des Cocottes* for its Sunday night premiere in December 1925 was a young John Gielgud:

> Leslie Faber first introduced me to Gladys, whom I'd only seen from the upper circle at the Playhouse which had the steepest slope in London. I was twenty-one and highly nervous, and Gladys would never give me the same cue more than once, partly because she'd never really learnt the part. I had an embarrassing love scene to play with her and was terrified throughout, and when she finally did the play for a run she gave my part to Denys Blakelock. Like all the great stars of the time she had a rather truculent manager and I never really got past him, though she did once let me audition as the understudy to Ivor in *Enter Kiki* before turning me down. She and du Maurier didn't really care for my sort of acting – they thought it was all too intellectual and serious, and that I took myself far too seriously which was probably true, though I didn't really approve of all their larking around backstage.

During the run of *Cheyney* Frank Curzon was taken very ill, and it gradually and sadly became clear to G that he would never be able to carry on running the Playhouse; under the terms of their informal partnership, one which had now lasted the best part of a decade, if he gave up the Playhouse then she would no longer be affiliated to it either. There was, however, nothing in   115 their agreement to stop her taking full control herself and that, at the end of the *Cheyney* run, is precisely what she did.

Curzon knew it was G who had given his theatre its character and sense of identity in the early twenties, she who had prevented it becoming just another London theatre taking in a stream of hits and misses and made it instead a definable place to visit. He was therefore more than a little delighted when she showed signs of wishing to return, and to return moreover in a new Somerset Maugham drama. In an effort to persuade her to do *Our Betters*, (a part G never played, largely because the producer, Anthony Prinsce, wanted his wife Margaret Bannerman in the role) Maugham had offered her the option on his next six plays and the first of these was *The Letter*.

Destined to become one of the hardy perennial melodramas of the twentieth century (Jeanne Eagels made the silent film version, Bette Davis made the talkie and as recently as 1977 the plot turned up on the screen again, this time thinly disguised as *East of Elephant Rock*), *The Letter* was based on a Maugham short story. Set on a plantation in the Malay Peninsula and then in Singapore, it has the best opening of any of Maugham's plays: as the curtain rises a shot is fired and a man staggers on to the veranda, closely followed by Leslie Crosbie (G) emptying the remaining bullets of her revolver into his crumpled body. From there on we're away in a drama of marital infidelity and miscegenation, strong on Chinese mistresses and unfaithful Colonial wives and stiff upper lips and torrid passions set amid the confounded heat.

Of the four Maugham plays that G did at the Playhouse, this was the one that ran longest (338 performances plus another hundred and fifty on the post-London tour) and G made the part of Leslie Crosbie so much her own that she was more than a little irritated to find it being filmed during her first year in Hollywood by Bette Davis instead. In the theatre, it was to remain all hers: neither subsequent revivals nor the Broadway production ever shook the memory of that first production; under du Maurier's direction, G had assembled a strong cast (S. J. Warmington as her lover on stage and just possibly off, Nigel Bruce as the husband, Leslie Faber as the defence counsel) and the reviews, though somewhat mixed, were clearly 'selling' notices since they had to reveal parts of what sounded like an intriguing plot.

116 The general consensus was that here was 'a feat of stage dex-

The opening shot as the curtain rose on Maugham's The Letter, *Playhouse 1927, her first venture into solo management. S. J. Warmington as the unlucky lover*

terity' which would fill the Playhouse for many months to come and so it did, getting Gladys's solo management there off to a flying start.

The first night programmes read 'Gladys Cooper presents, by arrangement with Frank Curzon' but Curzon was already a sick man and he died within five months of the premiere, having lived just long enough to see his beloved theatre safely and successfully into the hands of the actress he'd invited almost a decade earlier to join him in management there.

As for G, she positively thrived on the life of an actress-manager: when it came to *The Letter* she invested half her total capital, then £800, in the project. The other £400 she left in the bank for herself and the children in case of failure. When the curtain went up on the first night there was still nearly £200 left in the 'theatre account' which gives some indication of production costs at the time. But in its first full week after the reviews *The Letter* took £200, and when, some sixty weeks later, the tour finally drew to its close she had made a profit of forty thousand from the original four hundred she'd invested. Financially and theatrically it was the finest hour of her life, and it taught her a number of lessons (notably that she could rise even above such reviews as 'Miss Cooper plays her part like a Victorian duenna at a croquet party') as long as she kept a few powerful allies by her side – on this occasion the crime writer Edgar Wallace, who took his whole Sunday column the week after the opening to announce that 'Posterity will endorse my view, which is that Gladys Cooper's performance in *The Letter* will be remembered and acclaimed from generation to generation.'

The fact that even after the long and triumphant run of *Cheyney* Gladys had only found £800 in her account needs some explanation, at least to those who never knew her. G was not exactly careless about money; true she lived as well as she could, at the top rather than in the midst of her income, and was not averse to the occasional weekend in Paris or a winter fortnight with the children in St Moritz. Like almost all actors she was in near-constant tax troubles of one kind or another but money was not something she ever thought very deeply about until, in the closing years of her life, the need to continue supporting her born-deaf sister Grace and her by then mentally afflicted son John made her go on working in material most of her septuagenarian contemporaries would probably have thought twice about.

In these her middle years money was there, like water or electricity, to be used as needed: not to be wasted, certainly, but not to be hoarded either. As far as the taxman was concerned, he was reasonably welcome to what he could get from her: she saw it as no part of her duties to make his life any easier than it would otherwise have been, and on any list of priorities he came a good deal lower than the children and the animals and her staff at home and at the theatre.

Actors who worked for Gladys and with her at the Playhouse over the next seven years found her briskly efficient and a generally very fair employer, inclined to be over-generous in some of her early contracts (a fault she corrected by veering sharply the other way when times got harder) and all the better

118

for being an actress and therefore having, unlike most managers, to be around the building and indeed on its stage every evening.

In *The Letter* [wrote Maugham some years later] in order to get a crucial dramatic effect Miss Cooper had on a sudden to fall to the floor in a dead faint. This is not an easy thing to do in a natural manner without hurting oneself. For fear of this, the first time she rehearsed it, Miss Cooper did it with some hesitation, whereupon Gerald du Maurier by doing it himself, which was his useful way of directing, showed her how it could be done with effect and without danger. She tried it perhaps half a dozen times till he cried, 'That's right!' and ever afterwards she did it exactly as he had shown her.

It was Herbert Farjeon, writing a profile of Gladys a year or two later, who caught something of the essence of her success with the Maugham plays of this period:

Even as she discharges the contents of her six-shooter into the body of Mr S. J. Warmington, Miss Cooper remains to the backbone a typically tennis-clubbable English girl . . . and this is a great asset, since it enables her to present romance not as a wild, unattainable dream but as actually something within the reach of the typically English girls in the auditorium.

Looking back [said Gladys later] I think of Maugham as the easiest and most delightful author I ever had to work with. After we'd been rehearsing *The Letter* for some days both Gerald and I felt uncertain about the dramatic value of a 'blackout' in it. I rang up Maugham to tell him this, and all he said was 'If you don't feel it's right, change it'. I can't think of another playwright who would be so accommodating as that. Sometimes he even came to rehearsal with a blue pencil ready to cut out anything we felt would be wrong. He said so many of his lines had been cut that he would collect them together and make a whole play of them someday.

Another time Ernest Thesiger asked why he never wrote him a part. 'Oh but I do,' Maugham replied, 'only Gladys Cooper always plays them.'

chapter fourteen

1927=1928

The *Letter* ran throughout 1927 at the Playhouse, and Gladys settled happily into the routine of a theatre manager: a couple of days a week would be spent at the theatre with her general and box-office managers and the stage director, an efficient and devoted trio of men who took most of the day-to-day business off her shoulders and left her free to plan the forth-coming tour and correspond with Edgar Wallace over a play he was promising to write for her, though one that was never in fact delivered.

Maugham was by no means regarded as the house dramatist: two of his subsequent plays (*The Constant Wife* and *The Bread-winner*) were turned down by Gladys, and of the ten plays she produced subsequently at the Playhouse only another two (*The Sacred Flame* and *The Painted Veil*) were to be by him, and the latter of those an adaptation at that. Sadly, she was never again to repeat the financial success of *The Letter*, and her management started rather better than it was ever able to continue.

Her beauty business was at this time also thriving: there were full-page ads in the Playhouse programmes informing patrons of 'Some Facts About The Cooper Beauty Business', facts which still needed to be taken with a light pinch of salt:

1. This is entirely my own personal business and all the Beauty Preparations I sell are made to my own recipes in my own laboratories and under my own personal supervision.

2. All the preparations are exactly the same as I use now and in most cases have used for years.

3. I am therefore in a position to guarantee that if you will use them faithfully, good results will follow. It is my definite opinion that each is the finest of its kind that can possibly be obtained.

4. So wonderful has been their reception by the public that although less than two years ago some half-dozen shops sold these creams, shampoos and rouges, they can now be obtained from nearly every Chemist, Hairdresser and Store in the country.

To make sure of (4), Gladys arranged personal appearances in all the large chemists of the towns through which she was to tour in *The Letter*, and even did a deal with *Picturegoer* magazine whereby in return for an article from her about 'hair care' they would give away free packets of the Gladys Cooper shampoo with every issue of their March 1927 magazine.

So much for her professional life at this time; privately, Gladys was beginning to think she needed a change. The Playhouse had settled into a routine, Joan was about to leave Heathfield and go on to a finishing school in Paris, John was already at Eton and showing less sign of needing her only faintly maternal presence, and she was suddenly and for the first time in her adult life very lonely.

I had always thought that after my first divorce I would never marry again: I had my work, and well-paid work it was, and that made me a free and independent woman at a time when there were not so many of us around. I had my children, a beautiful home with all the animals I loved, and I was happy and contented. But as the children grew up I knew that, dearly as they loved me, the time was coming when they would choose their own friends and occupations, grow away from me and marry. It was bound to happen and I would not have had it otherwise. I despise the mother whose selfish affection will keep her child tied to her apron strings all her days, but I knew that I was now very lonely and how good   **121** it would be to have someone who thinks you alone are the one person in the world for him. My ideas of never marrying again gradually faded away . . .

But who? Even G had at long last realized the truth of Novello's private life, and there were precious few other actors about whom she cared strongly enough to contemplate marriage. Most of her closest friends such as du Maurier were already more or less happily married to other people, and few young actors would consider in those chauvinist days marrying an actress who already had one family and a theatre which she had proved herself entirely capable of running without their help. A marriage in the theatre seemed impossible: her leading men there were either too married or too young or too interested in their own sex, and outside the theatre she now knew precious few others, the Duke of Westminster having finally accepted her lack of enthusiasm for him and turned his affections elsewhere.

On the verge of her fortieth birthday, Gladys was no longer (in so far as she ever had been) a bright young thing capable of being swept off her feet by intense glamour or wealth or aristocracy, as so many of her theatrical contemporaries had been at least once and usually twice already. Instead she was an eminently well-established theatrical manager with a twenty-year career in the theatre already behind her and a working life which left remarkably little time for home-making or foreign travel or any of the other occupations then considered part of a wife's duties in even the wealthiest homes.

One of the tragedies of G's life was that she and Liberation missed each other by about thirty years: though she came of the first immediately post-Pankhurst generation, the code of her world still called for marriage wherever possible. There were other considerations, too: Gladys badly wanted another child, and knew that her time for having one was now running out. It was against this background that she met the man who was to be for nearly six years her second husband.

Sir Neville Pearson was ten years younger than Gladys, and at the time of their first meeting in the mid-twenties he was just extricating himself from a disastrous first marriage to a daughter of the first Baron Melchett. That they were both divorcees, at a time when that was still a faintly risqué thing to be, gave them something in common, as did the fact that G had often done charity work for St Dunstan's, the hospital for the blind created and run for many years by his father Sir Arthur Pearson whose title he'd inherited in 1921.

Pearson also inherited from his father a place in the family's publishing firm, C. Arthur Pearson, which subsequently merged with Newnes and ended up as a major part of the giant present-day IPC magazine empire. A handsome and titled baronet, bowled over by Gladys's beauty and for a while deeply in love with her, Neville Pearson was one of the few people around London at this time actually in a position to marry Gladys and even help support her while being strong enough in his own profession and social position not to feel threatened or overshadowed by hers. These considerations were important, at the time, and must have been enough to overcome whatever doubts either may have had about their real suitability for each other.

Their courtship was a comparatively rapid affair, and broke into print rather too quickly while Gladys was on tour in Cardiff with *The Letter* (Robert Newton now playing the part of the lover) and Sir Neville on holiday in Kenya. Both rapidly denied reports that they were to be engaged, possibly because his divorce had only just become finalized. On his return to Britain, Sir Neville issued a splendidly high-handed statement to the press:

> There is no truth at all in the report of Miss Gladys Cooper's engagement to me, published in an evening paper. Miss Cooper shares with me the deepest resentment at the impertinence and impropriety of papers issuing completely unauthorised statements of this nature. Speaking as one who is intimately connected with the Press, I am disgusted with this type of journalism which savours more of the cheap and sensational methods employed in another continent [could he have meant America?] than of the courtesy and accuracy which we are accustomed to expect from the Press of this country.

Nevertheless there was no smoke without fire, and a headline a few weeks later in the *Dorking Echo* for June 15th, 1928 announced:

MISS GLADYS COOPER MARRIED: BRIDE AND BRIDEGROOM SCRAMBLE OVER FENCE TO OUTWIT DORKING CROWD: Miss Gladys Cooper, that   **123**

well-known actress, was married to Sir Neville Pearson, Bart.,
of Pixholme Court, at Dorking yesterday. Every possible
effort was made to keep the wedding secret. It had been fixed
to take place at nine o'clock so as to avoid publicity, but
rumours had spread round the town like wildfire and crowds of
young girls and men waited for more than an hour outside the
building in the main street. Just before nine o'clock a big
closed car dashed up to the side of the register office and the
crowds immediately swarmed around it to gain a glimpse of
Miss Cooper who, looking radiant in a beautiful yellow frock
dotted with black flowers and a big yellow and black picture
hat, was seated in the back of the car trying to hide her face
behind her bag.

Sir Neville was seated in the front. He wore a well-cut
brown lounge suit and a trilby hat and smiled when he saw
there was no means of getting into the register office from the
side turning. The car was then driven to the main entrance,
scattering the crowd as it turned into the main street. Miss
Cooper was assisted from the car by Sir Neville, and she ran
up the stairs through the crowds who swarmed around. The
ceremony took place in a little sunlit room and Miss Cooper
replied to the registrar's questions in a clear low-pitched
voice . . .

After the ceremony a clever ruse was carried out: Lady
Ethel Pearson (the groom's mother) and Miss Cooper's two
children walked boldly out of the front entrance, and the
waiting crowd fully expected to see the newly-married couple
follow suit. Meanwhile however their car had driven round to
the side of the register office and the couple, scrambling over
the broken-down fence in the garden, made their way into the
side street and drove away to the Fresh Air Fund's open day
for children in Epping Forest where they were given a
bouquet . . . the new Lady Pearson said that if any of her
friends wished to recognise the occasion of her marriage they
could send a small donation to the Fresh Air Fund.

By early September, after having spent a brief honeymoon at
Maxine Elliott's villa in the South of France, Gladys was back at
the Playhouse in *Excelsior*, the H. M. Harwood adaptation from
the French which she'd originally done for a Sunday night with
Gielgud as *L'Ecole des Cocottes*. Harwood had now revised the

Sir Neville Pearson, Gladys's second husband

play, cut some of the more blatantly immoral moments which the Lord Chamberlain had originally objected to, and thus managed to obtain a regular licence for it. A sort of female rake's progress, *Excelsior* concerned the transition of Ginette (played by Gladys in a series of increasingly exotic gowns) from an impoverished Montmartre girl to the mistress of an impressive mansion and a less impressive corset manufacturer played by Athole Stewart.

Others in the supporting cast included Denys Blakelock (in the old Gielgud role of the young lover giving, in Sir John's view, a rather better performance), Hermione Baddeley, Ernest Thesiger, Nigel Bruce and Doris, G's sister, in her now habitual Playhouse role of the maid. Making her brief appearances in this character, Doris was alarmed to notice a regular hiss emanating from the stalls on several evenings and, deciding she really couldn't be quite as immediately unlikeable or bad on stage as this seemed to suggest, she sent a friend out front one matinee to investigate the 125 cause. 'It's all right,' the friend returned to report, 'they're not actually hissing you: it's just the noise made by a lot of people whispering to each other, "That's Gladys Cooper's sister!".'

For Denys Blakelock, the chance to act at the Playhouse with G was important, and one he later wrote about at some length:

> I could hardly believe that I was actually going to play an intimate scene with this untouchable Goddess whom I had worshipped at a distance for so many years. My great fear was that I might lose the part through lack of inches, as Gladys Cooper had always appeared to me to be rather tall. So into my shoes I put some elevators as a precaution, but by the time I got to London they were so uncomfortable that I was forced to jettison them by the roadside. I need have had no fear. When I came to stand by Gladys Cooper I found her less tall than I had imagined; and in the first scene, when the height question mattered most, she wore flat-heeled slippers and that difficulty was smoothed away. Without high heels she was well below me in height.
>
> How lovely she looked during those rehearsals . . . her golden hair, her delicately sun-tanned skin, and those enormous blue eyes set so perfectly in relation to the nose were something to remember for ever. I was never disillusioned by meeting Gladys Cooper. She has always remained glamorous to me, and of her beauty one could never tire. I was a little in awe of her during that first engagement; but I soon discovered that, as with all people in her position, she liked to be treated as a human being and not as a celebrity. She liked to talk about her house and garden, her home life and of course about her children. The maternal element in her was strong, and her acting at its best when that side of her nature was brought into play . . . to act with Gladys Cooper was an experience I had never expected to have in those days when I had sent her postcard photographs for her to sign and had stood waiting to see her outside that same stage door that I was now using as a matter of course . . . an interesting and rather admirable character, honest, forthright, strong-minded, courageous and, like so many beautiful women, completely lacking in vanity . . . once, as a young chorus girl, she was riding in a bus and she saw one of the 'kept' Gaiety actresses bowling down the Bayswater Road in her carriage,

wrapped in her rich furs. 'Yes,' thought Gladys Cooper, 'I'm going to have those one day. But I'm going to pay for them myself.'

Though financially it couldn't match *The Letter, Excelsior* brought Gladys a net profit of just over five thousand pounds thanks to thirteen weeks at the Playhouse and then an extremely profitable pre-Christmas fortnight at the Hippodrome in Golders Green which, with a seating capacity of over two thousand, could often be used at the end of a West End run to boost the final takings.

G decided to follow *Excelsior* with another Maugham, this one the most controversial in its time of all his plays: *The Sacred Flame.* It was to be Maugham's last major work for the stage and one which dealt simply and formally with the right of a mother to allow her son to die when his life becomes no longer feasible. Finding himself, as a playwright, the middleman trapped between the elegant artificiality of Oscar Wilde and the semi-colloquial 'reality' of Noël Coward, Maugham had decided to abandon playwriting but, before doing so, to have one last attempt at a rather different style of dialogue:

> I thought I would try to make my characters speak in a more formal manner, using the phrases they would have used if they had been able to prepare them beforehand . . . during rehearsals I found that the actors, no longer used to speeches of this sort, had an uncomfortable feeling that they were delivering a recitation, and I had to simplify and break up my sentences . . . my dialogue was, in some quarters, blamed because it was 'literary'. I was told that people did not speak like that. I never thought they did. But I did not insist. I was in the position of a man in a rented house whose lease is expiring; it is not worth his while to make structural alterations. In my last two plays I reverted to naturalistic dialogue.

Undeterred by the play's initial Broadway failure in the previous season, Gladys went into rehearsal of *The Sacred Flame* early in 1929 with an immensely strong Playhouse cast under the direction of Raymond Massey, a good and close friend who (like Maugham and du Maurier) was to stand by Gladys in her management years providing whatever support was most needed at the 127 time. G herself was playing Stella, the dead man's unfaithful wife, with Mary Jerrold as the mother and Clare Eames as the nurse who suspects murder. Also in the cast, playing the rather thankless role of the brother, was a young Sebastian Shaw who almost exactly fifty years later was to find himself a few hundred yards farther along the Thames Embankment, at the Mermaid Theatre, playing in a remarkably similar life-or-death drama called *Whose Life Is It Anyway*? I asked him then to think back to *The Sacred Flame*:

I'd already been working with Raymond Massey, and when he suggested me for the part I was summoned to the Playhouse where I remember a rather serene, totally unflappable lady surrounded by very efficient administrators. The whole theatre was run by Gladys with great style – I suppose the nearest equivalent nowadays would be the Theatre Royal Haymarket. I was highly nervous but also rather annoyed because just after signing *The Sacred Flame* contract I'd been offered a much better part in *Rope*. Gladys thought I looked altogether too young for the part, especially as we were supposed to be having an affair in the play. 'I shall be accused of baby-snatching,' she said, 'so make yourself look a bit older.' I had a lot of terrible wooden lines like 'I am the father, Major Liconda' and at the dress-rehearsal after I'd stood around on stage for hours watching these three great ladies (Mary Jerrold, Gladys and Clare Eames) acting away, Maugham came over to me and said, 'I'm sorry yours is such a c-c-cardboard c-c-character, but we have to have him there for the p-p-plot, you see,' so there I was, night after night, hanging around. One night in the wings Clare Eames told me she was soon going to die, and she used to faint on the stage occasionally because she was already very ill.

Another night one of the lights fused and we thought there was going to be a fire in the circle but Gladys went down to the footlights and said SIT DOWN AND STAY CALM and the entire audience did so while we carried on with the play. I was terrified they'd all be burnt to a frazzle, but she seemed to know instinctively that there was no real danger.

Normally she never really issued any orders, and all the business was done through a manager, but you were left in no doubt about who was ultimately in charge. Backstage we used to run a poker school in the green room, and if she had an unusually good hand she'd hold the curtain for a minute or two. She was marvellously friendly with her company, and the first star who ever really treated me like a human being in the theatre; but I don't go along with the theory that she had no nerves on stage. She always carried a handkerchief, you know, and she'd twist it around her fingers a lot.

I think I knew her in her prime: I'd never known such beauty, such dazzling efficiency, but we very seldom met outside the theatre – one wasn't encouraged to visit her at home or anything like that. In the profession at this time I think she was generally regarded as a woman without a natural gift for acting but with a will of steel and a determination to surround herself with the best available talent as a kind of protection against her own areas of inadequacy.

Writing in *The Times* on February 9th, 1929, the morning after the first night of *The Sacred Flame*, Charles Morgan thought that 'Gladys Cooper plays with more freedom and grace than we have yet known in her' but other critics were less happy. Here after all was a play about euthanasia some years before that became an acceptable talking point; it is also a play about suppressed sexuality, since the unspoken truth about the dead man was that he was impotent, and that again was a subject critics were not prepared to confront despite the fact that Maugham treated it in his usual clipped and tight-lipped fashion. Still, Agate and Grein, the two most powerful reviewers in town both thought it 'a fine play' and *Punch* alone managed to recall that it all began with Coleridge:

> *All thoughts, all passions, all delights,*
> *Whatever stirs this mortal frame*
> *Are but ministers of Love*
> *And feed his sacred flame.*

The flame showed signs of going out early in the run, however; first-night reviews had mentioned 'a problem play' which was not specifically what Playhouse audiences demanded for their evenings on the town, and the fact that the three leading roles were all played by women also proved a box-office deterrent since the customers were used to seeing Gladys 'paired' with a handsome male star.

Miraculously, albeit unintentionally, the Bishop of London came to their rescue; though he had not seen the play personally, he gave an interview describing it as 'one of the most immoral dramas in London', and within days they were playing to capacity. *The Sacred Flame* is in fact an extremely moral play, and one whose peculiar misfortune was to be out of its time, thought daring and sensational in the 1920s, it had become stylized and dated by the sixties when, for the only time in her subsequent career, Gladys revived a Playhouse success. She did it again in 1967, now of course playing the old Mary Jerrold part of the mother while Lana Morris played hers, and after a brief Guildford season they came into the Duke of York's where, despite a strong cast including Wendy Hiller in the Clare Eames role, they only survived seven weeks. 'No play,' wrote Irving Wardle of that revival, 'better illustrates Shaw's description of British life as a moral gymnasium.'

chapter fifteen

1928-1931

The *Sacred Flame* had been running for just over two hundred performances and was showing a profit of £10,800 when, in the August of 1928, it was announced that 'Miss Gladys Cooper will be leaving the stage for some considerable time'. The statement, a model of discretion as befitted the times, also gave the date of her marriage to Sir Neville Pearson in the previous year but declined to add that the reason she was leaving the stage was of course that she was soon to have her third (and last) child. In her absence, which lasted a little less than a year, Gerald du Maurier took over the theatre and staged a revival of *Dear Brutus* which ran until Christmas. But he was tiring now, weary of his profession and of the inroads on it made by the coming of talking pictures and a generation for whom Barrie was no longer quite so magical. 'It was a poor affair,' wrote his daughter, 'compared with the original play of twelve years before; everyone was miscast and Gerald seemed to make no effort with the production . . . what remained of *Dear Brutus* was given a decent burial after a hundred and eight performances which was just about a hundred too many for an admirer of Barrie.'

Away from the Playhouse, G had given up the Charlwood lease and up on the heights of Highgate the Pearsons had bought an old girls' school and were turning it into an elegant residence later known as 1 and 2 The Grove (a fashionable address whose 131 subsequent residents included the actress Adrianne Allen and the violinist Yehudi Menuhin); there Gladys awaited the birth of Sally and kept a kind of remote control over the affairs of the Playhouse which, after *Dear Brutus*, went into a steep decline during the early months of 1930. Whatever goodwill she had built up in the first three profitable years of her management there evaporated in her absence, as Barry Jackson ran a disastrous six-month season which cost Gladys just over six thousand pounds.

To make up for it, there was the joy now of Sally: G hadn't had a baby since John, who was now nearly fifteen, and was amazed to find that she seemed to be giving birth to an entirely new generation: 'babies now seem so adult,' she told a woman's magazine in 1930, 'and Sally looked about three months old at birth – I don't remember the others looking nearly so intelligent'. The Pearson marriage was still in good shape, if a picture of slightly less than total familial bliss: Joan, now on the verge of her twentieth birthday and leading an independent life around

Gracious living at the Pearsons' Highgate home, The Grove, 1931

London, was well able to cope with the advent of a new step-father although she remained of course infinitely closer to Buck and took to going on foreign travels with him. But for John, at Eton, the second marriage was much more difficult to accept, especially as his mother, in her usual Pied Piper fashion, seemed to have no trouble in taking on various Pearson stepchildren as her own.

An active private life now revolved around Highgate and there's no doubt that Gladys enjoyed the social stability of being Lady Pearson while being able, unlike so many of her contemporaries who had 'married well', to retain an independent working life as Gladys Cooper. Sir Neville seems not to have objected greatly to this, and those who worked at the Playhouse indeed remember him dropping in from his office during rehearsals to see what was going on. 'A rather outdoor man,' one recalled, 'very good on the tennis court but seemed to have difficulty making conversation in the living-room: obviously very much in love with Gladys, and for a while anything that was good enough for her was all right by him. His friends weren't really theatre people, though, and I think he found it hard to care terribly about the success or failure of a single play. He just wanted Gladys to be happy and for the home to be run as smoothly as possible. He had his own business to run, after all, and it wasn't as though he lived the same kind of life as Gladys's friends, so inevitably there used to be two groups of people up at The Grove on a Sunday . . . his and hers.'

Few people took to Gladys's second marriage so enthusiastically as her first husband: 'now that she is a Lady,' wrote Buck in his diary, 'I wonder if I become a courtesy Lord?' His club had just celebrated its tenth anniversary and despite a disastrous attempt to repeat its success by purchasing a second (which immediately folded up under him) Buck's financial affairs were in good enough shape to allow him to buy a steam yacht, a 65-ton teak and copper affair on which he and his second wife Nellie Taylor would spend much of their time until her sudden and sad death of leukaemia in 1932 put an end to the few years he spent with her, ones which were almost certainly the happiest of his life.

As for Gladys, she'd realized from the weekly box-office returns reaching her from the Playhouse that she'd have to get back there promptly if the theatre was to avoid total bankruptcy. Remembering the success of their last joint venture on 133 stage, *The Last of Mrs Cheyney*, she persuaded du Maurier to join her in *Cynara*, a stage adaptation of the novel which had in its turn been based on Ernest Dowson's classic poem 'I have been faithful to thee, Cynara, in my fashion'. 'An odd little piece,' wrote Agate, 'which can never quite make up its mind between exquisiteness and banality.' Briefly it was the story of a happily married man (du Maurier) who meets a girl at a beauty competition only to have her kill herself when she realizes she cannot break up his marriage. The surprise here was to find Gladys in the comparatively minor role of the wife. One critic indeed lectured her severely on the duties of an actor-manager: duties which apparently included always playing the largest part because that was what the customers paid to see. Here however the best part was that of the girl, and it was the one in which Celia Johnson fully established her West End reputation. Ann Todd was also in a large cast, and the critics, having got over Gladys's comparatively brief appearances, complained mainly about the 'cinematic' use of many short scenes being changed rapidly on stage. Despite them, *Cynara* lasted two hundred and fifty performances and was to be the last real success Gladys had there. They ran thirty-two weeks for a profit of £5500. These figures are almost exactly the same as those for *Excelsior* two years earlier at the Playhouse, but there was now an ominous difference: where *Excelsior* made its money in fifteen weeks with generally unfavourable reviews, it took *Cynara* twice that time on generally good ones to make the same amount of money. Times were changing, and changing fast.

The Twenties had come to an end and with them, almost too neatly, a whole way of life which included the Playhouse. True, Gladys's management there was to survive another three years, but they were to be ones of slow decline in which none of the remaining seven productions achieved a run of more than a hundred and thirty performances, and some did less than half that. The Depression, the coming of talking pictures and the increase of labour costs all contributed to the decline which set in immediately after *Cynara*, as – perhaps above all – did the nature of Gladys's own audiences. She, now close to forty-five though still in remarkably youthful shape, could not help but be a reminder to the ex-bright young things among her audiences that they were none of them getting any younger, and it was after all on youth and beauty rather than great dramatic strength that she had built up her following. Other audiences in other theatres may have been prepared to grow old along with Sybil Thorndike or Edith Evans: Gladys's audiences were different.

Nor was all entirely well in her private life: though she was delighted to have Sally, and determined to take rather more active interest in her upbringing than she'd managed in that of Joan and John, born in an earlier time when the demands of her career were more exclusive, it must have been clear to her by now that the Pearson marriage really wasn't going to work out. She and Sir Neville had been joined by a strong and dynamic sexual bond and precious little else; they had no social or professional interests in common, and if G had ever thought her second marriage was going to mean a relief from financial head-aches she was very soon disabused of that notion too, since much of the money for redecorating the Highgate house had come in fact from her account.

Like many outwardly rather chilly and even aloof ladies, G had I believe a strong sexual drive and it was one which for a while kept the Pearson marriage going, since there was almost nothing else there; but even that began to founder soon after Sally's birth and when Gladys went back to the Playhouse it was to pick up the pieces of another kind of life. 'Every night salad and cold ham after the play,' Pearson was once heard to complain, 'do you wonder she's such an acid lady?'

When the London run of *Cynara* came to a close Gladys took it out on a brief but profitable tour, arriving in Liverpool one Sunday night to find that due to a slight confusion at the local printers' her posters all read 'I have been faithful to thee, Cynara, in my fashion by arrangement with Gladys Cooper'.

Then, back at the Playhouse, she and du Maurier decided to make one more stage appearance together. He was now within three years of his death and tiring rapidly of the whole business of acting and living. She, on the contrary, was fully prepared to try anything which might keep her management of the theatre alive, and thought their old *Cheyney* magic might still be worth a few pounds at the box-office. Sadly it wasn't, at least not in the play she chose this time, which was a revival of Harwood's *The Pelican*, last seen in London in 1924 and all about an Australian lady who gives up the love of her life to go back to her husband so that her son can be declared legitimate and therefore eligible for Sandhurst. Not, as Agate said in his review, an alto- **135**

'I have been faithful to thee, Cynara, in my fashion': with *Gerald du Maurier at the height of their long partnership, Playhouse 1930*

gether gripping plot. Du Maurier played the French lover ('his moustache is a pity' wrote Darlington in total summary of the performance) and *The Pelican* staggered on for a mere seventy-two performances, an all-time low for G's management though not alas a record that was to stay unbroken for very long.

By the autumn of 1931 Gladys was back at the Playhouse and raring to go; the writing may perhaps have been on the walls there but she was never one to read that kind of message and there was always the old rule of thumb: when in doubt, send for Somerset Maugham. It was to work just once more. By now, Maugham had lost all interest in playwriting. He was finding novel-writing definitely more satisfying, but there was miraculously lying around the stage adaptation by Bartlett Cormack of his best-selling novel *The Painted Veil*, one which was about to be filmed in Hollywood by Garbo herself.

Under some pressure from Gladys, Maugham agreed personally to retouch those scenes in the Cormack adaptation which didn't seem quite right to her in rehearsal, and with a strong supporting cast (Lewis Casson, who also directed, and Arthur Margetson) she opened as Kitty Fane on September 19th, 1931. This was in fact to be her last really distinguished leading role until she took on Coward's Countess of Marshwood in *Relative Values* fully twenty years later, and of her Desmond McCarthy wrote in the *New Statesman*:

> The popularity of *The Painted Veil* is likely to depend upon the readiness with which people will go for the sake of the acting of the principal actress. Miss Gladys Cooper is as successful as Miss Gertrude Lawrence elsewhere in London, only she is here playing a much larger part, for in this play Kitty Fane is never off the stage. She is excellent.

This is the only moment in any of her several thousand reviews that the Gertrude Lawrence comparison shows up in print, and it is I think an intriguing one. Though 'Gertie' was ten years younger than Gladys, and never more than a casual acquaintance, they had a great deal in common both on stage and off, not least a kind of professional insouciance and the (comparatively rarely awarded) admiration of Noël Coward. True, Gladys couldn't sing, but there were many critics who claimed that Miss Lawrence didn't sing much either; both were often the despair of their   137 fellow players on account of a working attitude which seemed more casual than in fact it was. Both above all were determined not to be caught taking themselves or their chosen profession too seriously, and I'm inclined to believe that had Gladys been lucky enough to have Coward writing for her as regularly as he wrote for Miss Lawrence, her career might have taken a very different turn, one which would not have entailed spending the latter half of it abroad.

As it was, her own writers and fellow players were beginning to desert her; Maugham no longer interested in the theatre, du Maurier similarly disengaged, Lonsdale never at the best of times a prolific scribbler, Novello off into musicals and films, Owen Nares and Dennis Eadie and Charles Hawtrey and Seymour Hicks all figures from her theatrical past. The future to anyone but Gladys in her position would have looked exceedingly bleak; to Gladys it looked, as the future always did, neither bleak nor rosy. The future was just there.

Not even *The Painted Veil* could save her management now: she got generally glowing personal reviews for playing a part very nearly as long as Hamlet, and one which entailed never leaving the stage, but the play left a lot to be desired and many critics believed that the name 'Bartlett Cormack' was an alias to hide Maugham's own failure to lift his book off the page and on to the stage. 'Lady Pearson as wife of Murderous Bacteriologist' headlined one review, followed by the sub-heading 'long and boring evening'. In fact *The Painted Veil* offered infidelity, a Chinese cholera epidemic, and all kinds of adventure but the critics seemed determined not to like it as a play and it ran a bare hundred and twenty performances – a third as long a time as *The Letter* and half as long as *The Sacred Flame*.

G used what little spare time she had during the run to work with a ghost writer on *Gladys Cooper by Gladys Cooper*, a gossipy and oddly uninformative though lengthy volume of memoirs in which there were only five references to her present husband, the last of which read simply if a trifle abruptly:

> My second marriage is very happy. I have but one fault to find with my husband, and that is that he is so passionately devoted to his garden that he is invariably late for every meal we have, and on the occasions when we are dining out or going to a party I get into such a state of nerves that I give

strict orders that 'all garden tools are to be locked up before Sir Neville returns from his office'. That is the only fault I have to find in a man to whom I have been married nearly four years.

Others were beginning to tell a different story; the actor Peter Graves, a frequent visitor to Highgate, noticed a distinct chill in the air around The Grove:

Everything was all right as long as we stayed on the tennis court, but once we got back indoors for a drink there'd be strange icy silences or rather tight-lipped conversations about what time they'd either of them be home for dinner, if at all.

Una Venning, then regularly understudying Gladys at the Playhouse, recalls Pearson dropping in to the occasional rehearsal still:

He'd slip into the stalls after his own work was over for the day and sit next to me. 'Gladys should never play a really bad woman,' he told me once, 'her disgust shows through too much.' Another time he noticed a mistake on stage and asked me to tell Gladys about it. 'What me?' I asked, 'an understudy? No, you tell her.' 'What me?' replied Pearson, 'a husband?'

Doris, Gladys's sister, was now about to start a turbulent family life of her own but took a thoroughly dim view of the Pearson marriage:

Gladys had several male 'admirers' in the twenties who I didn't much care for, fortune hunters mostly, but Naps Pearson I cared for even less, though you couldn't accuse him of fortune hunting because their finances seemed about equal. Mind you, I don't think he cared for me much either; Gladys and I only ever used to meet at the theatre during that marriage.

The press were given a more cheerful story: at Sally's christening the two godfathers had been du Maurier and Barrie and there were, over the next two years or so, frequent pictures of them all at The Grove; 'baby Sally' became as frequently photographed as John and Joan had once been, and even the Bishop of London, having now presumably forgiven Gladys for the scandal of *The Sacred Flame*, was photographed taking tea with the little girl he'd christened. Lady Pearson's 'home notes' were frequently published by the glossy women's weeklies, offering advice on how to bring up 'healthy outdoor children', even in Highgate, though no longer concentrating much on the selling of beauty products now that she'd given up her interest in the Gladys Cooper face cream business.

G and Sally made the covers of *The Queen* and *The Lady's Companion* in a single week, and when the Pearsons went for their summer holiday at Frinton there appear to have been photographers hiding behind every sandcastle. The *Sunday Graphic* reported that 'neither Joan nor John Buckmaster seem unduly jealous of their new little half-sister Sally', not perhaps entirely surprisingly given that they were now twenty-one and sixteen respectively.

The living at The Grove was nothing if not gracious: there was a household staff of six, provisions were bought by G in bulk and then stored in the basement, Sally and her new half-brother Nigel Pearson were taught by a governess who, so spacious was the nursery wing, was also able to teach other children of the neighbourhood, and a good time seems to have been had by all except perhaps G and Pearson himself. Appearances were however kept up for several months, indeed years, to come, and such distinguished neighbours as the Ainleys and the Drinkwaters were not given much inkling, during the elegant Sunday lunches and the tennis parties, that anything was adrift.

Gladys was still an immensely sporting lady: true it had been a year or two now since she had fielded her own cricket team, the Gladys Cooper XI, to challenge a rival team from her ex-husband Buck's club, but she was still hunting in the winters and now tennis-playing all summer in the time left over from the administration of the Playhouse and The Grove.

Sally's nursery at The Grove was worth two entire pages in *Homes and Gardens*, and *Woman's Journal*, desperate for Pearson snaps, even took to reprinting still frames from Gladys's early home movies. G herself took to an increasingly eccentric range of charitable works, including the promotion of home-grown wines **140** and the organizing of actresses-versus-authoresses cricket matches on Hampstead Heath and there seems to have been a certain air of frenzied activity about her life at this time, as if she was trying to keep herself too busy to notice her slowly failing theatre and marriage.

At the theatre there was still a family of regular allies: Doris, Una Venning, a cockney stage manager called Waller, a tough business manager called William Patrick who would fight tooth and nail to keep Gladys financially above water and made himself fairly unpopular with others in the process, and Una Venning's second husband Gordon Hamilton-Gay who came in towards the end as a designer and stage director. Gladys (like her daughter Joan) was now a keen hunting woman, and Una would find herself playing the occasional performance on the rare days when the horse had thrown her:

> Gladys was concentrated rather than dedicated as an actress; when I played for her I was surprised to find that the parts really weren't often very good, but she could give them a kind of intensity. Then she'd come off the stage and play poker in the green room with the same kind of intensity. On her way back to the stage she'd sweep past old Dawson Milward in the wings, waiting for her entrance and usually nursing a cold. 'Another cold?' she'd query, 'you should have gone out for a long walk today.' 'But it was raining all day,' Milward would reply. 'Was it? I wore a mackintosh,' said Gladys and as she started the scene you could hear her muttering rather too audibly, 'Silly old fool.' Tolerance was never one of her great virtues, but by heaven she was fun to work for.

141

chapter sixteen

1931=1933

U NLIKE many of her theatrical contemporaries, Gladys was never much of a star-turn offstage; despite constant 'family' publicity she'd seldom be photographed away from the stage or the children, though there was one historic night at Ciro's when she got a glass of champagne poured over her head by Tallulah Bankhead. As a result of keeping herself fairly carefully out of the gossip columns, G was able to persuade large numbers of fashionable women to part with good money at the box-office in order to see what Molyneux had designed for her that season.

Yet public interest in the Pearson marriage was intense. Via the postcards and then a decade of publicity stills, the British and specifically London public had been living with G now for the best part of twenty years; they had watched her first two children grow from 'little Joan and John' through their teens and they had followed this new marriage through to the toddling of Sally. It was still a source of intense fascination: Pearson was after all ten years younger than Gladys, and there were many who 'knew' the marriage was doomed even before it was. With G at the Playhouse most nights, Sir Neville would often be seen escorting Joan to other theatres thereby giving rise to the inevitable uneasy rumours that having married the mother, he was now in love with the daughter.

Unperturbed, another of the words that should appear on her

memorial, Gladys continued to struggle with the Playhouse and with daily Highgate life: most of the animals had gone now, the marmoset and the macaw being thought unsuited to London life, and she was not to reassemble a full menagerie again until she reached California at the other end of this decade

For the moment there was a staff to handle and Sally to cope with and John to worry about, quite apart from whatever people were thinking about her husband and elder daughter. John was proving, at Eton, a 'difficult' teenager: a sensitive, highly-strung, extremely handsome and wittily talented young man, he had taken an intense dislike to Pearson and it was reciprocal. The two had very little in common, and of G's three children it was John who was perhaps most deeply and adversely affected by his mother's changing marital arrangements. He was emotionally very close to her and took in later life to blaming his eventual mental collapse on to her inability to cope with him, though in all fairness to Gladys it should perhaps be added that there are many non-working mothers who would have found that an equally difficult task.

Professionally, things were going from bad to worse at the Playhouse, where she followed *The Painted Veil* with a uniquely disastrous drama called *King, Queen, Knave*, one which staggered on for a mere twenty performances. A romantic saga of exiled royalty on the Riviera, it was the kind of plot, ironically, that Novello could have retrieved with a halfway good score but which, without it, sank with all hands.

The combined losses on *King, Queen, Knave* and *The Painted Veil* were now up over the five-thousand-pound line, and the total Playhouse loss account for 1931–2 stood at £12,000; a sum so large, in its time, that G wrote to her landlords pleading unsuccessfully for a reduction in the theatre's rent and noting that she'd had to pledge The Grove (or at any rate her share in it) as security for bank accounts overdrawn.

Deciding that she had to keep her theatre open at all costs, she threw into immediate rehearsal a curious comedy called *Doctor Pygmalion* which Ronald Squire had bought from the author, seeing himself well-suited to the title role, and for which he was now in search of a stage.

She and Squire (who like her had been on a percentage of *Cheyney* seven short but infinitely more successful years earlier) thus co-presented *Dr Pygmalion* under du Maurier's direction: **143** the old trio were back in action but the author here, Harrison Owen, was some way from being another Lonsdale and they survived a mere three months despite some remarkably generous reviews. One of the more curious aspects of the Playhouse in these last two years of G's management was that it began to be deserted by everyone but the critics, who still wrote of it and her in terms of considerable respect and enthusiasm even where this was scarcely deserved.

Now however, for the first time, a new note was creeping into the reviews, one which was to haunt G for the rest of her days: it turns up first in the unsigned review of *Dr Pygmalion* in the *Yorkshire Post*, whose critic, after praising Ronald Squire's immaculate comic timing, added a warning note about Gladys: 'Miss Cooper did not seem at ease all evening, and appeared desperately unsure of her lines in the last act.' From now till the end of her days, with rare exceptions, Gladys was never to be entirely sure of the lines on a first night: what began, I believe, as a subconscious protest at the amount of rubbish she was given to speak in her closing months at the Playhouse, ended as a genuine reluctance to learn the lines until the last possible moment, which was usually several days after the opening, by which time she could decide whether or not they were for a long run, and if they were she'd settle down to the dialogue.

Not that she ever dried up on the stage, or expected to be rescued by a prompter. She would always keep talking, though not about much that had to do with the play. In the end, it became an eccentricity and often an endearing one, since for the latter half of her career she was seldom to find herself in plays with distinctly memorable dialogue: it did however cause more irritation within the profession than anything else about her either on stage or off. Unfairly, her refusal to memorize labelled her a fundamental amateur in a world of professionals, and nothing could have been further from the truth. Gladys was as much a professional as Thorndike or Evans in Britain or Hayes or Fontanne in America; when the chips were down, as they often were, she could carry a show and several lesser performers on her indomitable shoulders. But her conditioning was not in the diehard classics: it had been, and was still, in a curious and now extinct form of light comedy which depended on the playing rather than the writing. Gladys's Playhouse scripts were, with the obvious exception of Maugham's, almost never published and

A Playhouse flop: Doctor Pygmalion, 1932 (with Ronald Squire)

with some reason: the idea that anybody had ever actually written them down was often hard to accept, let alone that they could be read afterwards. Her plays existed in performance, usually her performance, and not often anywhere else except the most desperate of weekly repertory companies. Like du Maurier and A. E. Matthews and Ronald Squire and their founding father, Charles Hawtrey (but precious few other players), Gladys was a sort of stage conjuror who worked, instinctively, with an audience rather than a director or a playwright. An intuitive gift for stylish light comedy was here, one which I believe could later be seen to some extent in such different performers as Kay Kendall and Maggie Smith, but it wasn't one which could be taught or transmitted or adequately described in print. You had to be there when she was working.

She was now entering her last full year at the Playhouse, and there were still three shows to do. The first was a thriller called *Firebird*, adapted by Jeffrey Dell from the Hungarian of Lajos Zilahy. The plot concerned a murder and a cover-up involving Gladys as the mother of a sixteen-year-old girl who is finally revealed as both the lover and the killer of the dead man. An unusually large cast included a young actor whom Gladys took closely to her offstage heart: he was Hugh Williams, and at the end of their lives some forty years later he was the only one still to be found writing plays for her.

Firebird opened to some ecstatic reviews, and though *The Times* found it hard to accept Gladys in the role of the Hungarian mother, with a sixteen-year-old child, yet almost every other paper took the view that the Playhouse had at last another smash hit on its hands.

Not so: though they ran just over a hundred and twenty performances and did another thirty on the road, *Firebird* proved an impossibly big-cast show for a small-auditorium theatre (the Playhouse had a seating capacity of less than seven hundred) and the profit after expenses was only just over two thousand pounds – a healthy change from the recent figures, but nowhere near enough to get the theatre out of its mounting debts.

Moreover the entire *Firebird* profits were swallowed up in the disaster that was Gladys's penultimate Playhouse venture. Looking around for a success with which to follow *Firebird* she settled on an appallingly self-indulgent tragi-comedy of the idle rich by Ivor Novello, written principally one suspects to provide

146

himself with the role of the film star known as King of the Lovers. Coming as it did a couple of years after *Private Lives* and fully eight years after *The Vortex*, in which Coward had said virtually all that needed saying about the bittersweet loves and lives of the hopelessly rich and theatrical, *Flies in the Sun* was bound to seem more than a little flyblown.

Written in the language of a *Woman's Own* serial, full of characters like G's Jane Marquis, the 'rich but heartless beauty of the Riviera', *Flies in the Sun* opened on January 18th, 1933 to some of the worst reviews that G or her beloved theatre had ever had: 'as boring as the people it is written about' snarled Ivor Brown, and even Agate thought it was a little tasteless to build a comic idea around the idea of a silent film star with a bad voice being ruined by the advent of sound, when this in truth had so recently been the fate of John Gilbert. A few fans were glad to see Ivor with Gladys again eight years after they'd last appeared on a stage together, but this was, sadly, to be their last professional partnership though they remained good if geographically distant friends until Novello's death twenty years later. *Flies in the Sun* ran for ten weeks only.

By now Gladys must have known that the end was in sight for her management; yet, still in the midst of a long lease, there was no easy way she could pull out. Nor was there much advice to be found: Tommy Vaughan and Frank Curzon, the business managers on whom she and du Maurier always relied, had both been dead the best part of five years now, Pearson's business knowledge did not extend to the theatre, and she had nobody around her on whom to rely. All she could hope for was a script that would get her out of trouble and early in 1933, amid the ruins of *Flies in the Sun*, she thought she'd found one.

It came from a comparatively untried playwright called Keith Winter, whose reputation lay mainly as a novelist and who'd been discovered by the actor Raymond Massey. He, Massey, had first read *The Rats of Norway* as a book and when Winter made it into a play he took it to G with the suggestion that they should both present and appear in it at the Playhouse with Massey himself directing. Raymond Massey was already, in 1933, an established leading man with experience in management, and he and his actress wife Adrianne Allen were already friends of the Pearsons: a few months later G and Noël Coward would be godparents at the christening of their son Daniel.

147

G was beginning now to feel that there was a conspiracy of critics determined to drive her out of the theatre: she'd already banned the critic Hannen Swaffer from the Playhouse for being regularly less than enthusiastic about her in his column and now, with the welcome financial and moral support of Massey, she was determined to put together a cast and a production that would restore her to favour and fortune.

The cast for *The Rats of Norway* was probably the most impressive she'd assembled at the Playhouse since *The Letter*: it featured not only herself and Massey but also Cecil Parker, Griffith Jones and a young Laurence Olivier in a story of two contrasting love affairs in a Northumberland boys' prep school (the rats of the title were lemmings, whose suicidal conduct on the Norwegian shores Mr Winter took as a metaphor for his story).

They went into rehearsal during the death throes of *Flies in the Sun* and opened on April 6th, 1933 to a generally ecstatic press; Agate was surprised to find 'a Northumberland schoolmaster's wife dressed by Molyneux' but Darlington thought 'it will pack the Playhouse for months to come' and there was a feeling that Gladys had at last discovered a genuinely exciting new dramatic talent in Mr Winter. Sir Harold Hobson recalls:

> The first play I saw in London that made on me an unforgettable impression was Keith Winter's *The Rats of Norway*. This was in April 1933. Its stars were Gladys Cooper and Raymond Massey. My recollections of it are vague, but I remember that its scene was a school, a place in which the raging passion was that of self-destruction. It was a place in which all love, all affection, had died; after beginning with great hopes, tremendous ambitions, and high ideals, those who ran it, played by Miss Cooper and Mr Massey, had seen their happiness shrivel and their future disappear. The tragedy which Keith Winter poignantly presented was that it was largely their own fault; like the suicidal lemmings something urged them irresistibly to rush towards the sea and drown themselves.
>
> As a matter of fact there is one thing which I do remember about *The Rats of Norway*, and I remember it vividly so that all the years I was a practising critic I used it as one of the touchstones of the plays I saw. If there was anything in a new

149

play or a new performance, or in an old play that could move me as Laurence Olivier, then at the very beginning of his London career, moved me in *The Rats of Norway*, I gave the production in which it occurred an enthusiastic notice. Olivier's moment came when, as a young schoolmaster, he stood looking out through a great window on to a cheerless lawn, and murmured to himself, in memory of a vanished world in which kindness and that charity which is love, still existed and even perhaps Parthenophil was not lost, these simple and heartbreaking words:

> *Four ducks on a pond,*
> *A grass bank beyond,*
> *A blue sky of spring,*
> *White clouds on the wing:*
> *What a little thing,*
> *To remember for years –*
> *To remember with tears!*

I saw Olivier twice in *The Rats of Norway*. Raymond Massey and Gladys Cooper, as the headmaster, a great man *manqué* as Buckley described him, and his wife, in their gradual downfall and collapse, were very impressive, but what remained with me when the play was over was less the tragedy of defeat than the sheer, sad beauty of the regret in Olivier's voice that the fine, untroubled peace of morning should descend to the ruin and destruction of night. I thought it a play to which, in spite of its grimness, the adjective lovely might legitimately be applied. I went round to Gladys Cooper's dressing-room and told her so. Whether she was taken aback by the grotesqueness of my appearance or, as is equally probable, she thought my description of the play totally untenable, I do not know. Anyway, she looked amazed.

C. B. Purdom, writing in *Everyman*, came up with one of the best definitions ever published of Gladys as an actress at this point in her career:

With her, acting is simply an art – something made. Every gesture, movement and tone is deliberately thought out, calculated to its single end. There is nothing spontaneous, or that even pretends to be. She walks according to a pattern, and when she leans against a door, or puts out her arms, or sits, or embraces her lover, the action can be analysed, each part of the movement noted and criticised, and when it is complete we get the satisfaction of having watched a job well done. She is cold and detached, as though her mind were in some other place. We do not get a glimpse of the real woman, only of the actress, and we know nothing of her except what can be displayed in her actions. There is no soul in her playing, nothing but a figure, a form, a perfect piece of mechanics; I admire it because there is no humbug. In her own line there is no one to approach her, and those who want to see the elements of acting fully exhibited cannot do better than to visit a play in which she is performing.

Olivier and she were to make two later films together, but this was their one and only joint stage appearance and I asked him many years later what he remembered of Gladys at the time of *The Rats of Norway*:

Well, she was a very big star then, still: I remember being on the top of a bus during my drama school days a few years earlier and hearing two women discussing who was the biggest star in London and they came to the conclusion that it was Gladys. I never forgot that, nor her kindness to me when we were doing *The Rats of Norway*. I was then just twenty-six and still very nervous, and she seemed to me to have an extraordinary coolness as an actress, I remember going in to wish her good luck on the first night and she was amazed. 'Luck? Luck?' she repeated, as if she didn't really understand the word. There can't have been more than about five minutes to go, but she was only just beginning to make up her face. She was a great hurdler, you know: she'd leap over people and productions and marriages when they went wrong, and she took the hurdles with extraordinary grace and simplicity and charm. But she was a brisk lady; there wasn't much sentimentality or softness there.

The Rats of Norway should by rights have been a smash hit on those reviews and with that cast; curiously, it wasn't. At the end of 123 performances the books showed a loss of £497, and though Olivier was glad to be getting out (since he'd been offered the chance to test with Garbo in Hollywood for *Queen Christina*) it   151 was with considerable sadness that Gladys and Massey put up the notice. With *The Rats of Norway* went G's last hopes of staying in management.

She was now in considerable debt, added to which was the £8000 that the Playhouse landlord (Frank Curzon's young daughter) was demanding in return for releasing G from the remainder of her lease. There was a very real danger of bankruptcy, and many people advised her to take that comparatively easy way out of trouble. G, conscious perhaps of being Lady Pearson but even more conscious than ever of being Gladys Cooper, decided that the more honourable thing to do would be to pay it all off, something she eventually achieved by selling a certain amount of personal belongings and luckily landing herself a lucrative if brief film job with George Arliss in *The Iron Duke.*

With Raymond Massey and a young Laurence Olivier in The Rats of Norway, *which closed her management of the Playhouse in 1933*

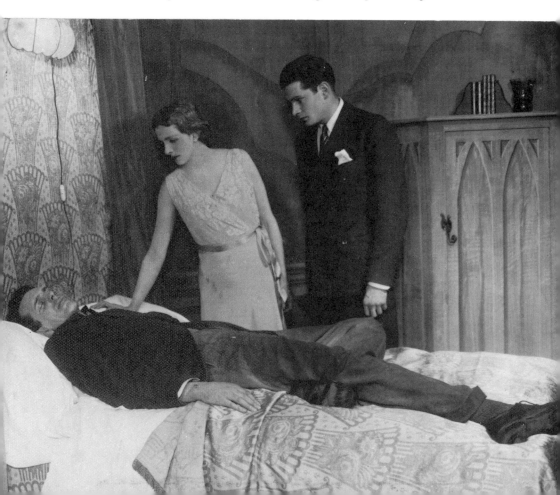

But this was the end of an era, the most important era in Gladys's professional life. For seven years she had run the Playhouse, made it her working home and achieved if not financial success then at least survival which for a woman in and of her time must surely be considered a remarkable feat. From being the postcard pin-up of World War I, she had set up a management which lasted as long as her contemporaries Tom Walls at the Aldwych or Nigel Playfair at the Lyric Hammersmith and was no less intriguing for all its many failures. She had created the nearest thing Maugham ever had to a permanent company for his work, she had started a number of young actors on their careers, and she had given du Maurier a comfortable background against which to go into his gentle decline: no mean achievements for an actress without professional training who was still a few months off her forty-fifth birthday.

But now it was all over, and on Gladys's last night at the Playhouse in July 1933 her old friend and understudy Una Venning went backstage, half expecting to have to commiserate with a rather depressed lady.

'Depressed?' said Gladys, 'What is there to be depressed about? We've had a few good runs but nowadays this kind of management surely isn't paying, so that's that, and I won't have to think about it any more.' And she didn't, either.

3 Hollywood

chapter seventeen

1933=1935

GLADYS'S was a cut-and-run philosophy, but on this occasion she didn't run quite far enough: though it was financially less than ideal, she had much enjoyed her closing partnership with Raymond Massey at the Playhouse, and the two of them therefore decided to keep the partnership going for the West End production of a Robert Sherwood play called *Acropolis* in the November of 1933. It was a brave, not to say lunatic choice: Sherwood was a distinguished American playwright (*Reunion in Vienna, Idiot's Delight, Abe Lincoln in Illinois*) with a somewhat dire penchant for historical rewrites of which *Acropolis* was one of his least successful.

Set in the Athens of Pericles' time, it was essentially about the building of the Parthenon and the struggle there between the men of peace and the men of war. An ambitious topic at the best of times, and one which a classical Shakespearian company such as the one then existing at the Old Vic might just have managed to tackle in a strong season. Massey of course did have a kind of craggy classical grandeur on stage (he was later to immortalize Sherwood's Abe Lincoln, at which time Coward was reputed to have muttered 'Ray will never be happy now until someone assassinates him') but the rest of the *Acropolis* company were relentlessly modern and the result was an eccentric mixture of styles and purpose.

157

Reviews were however extremely respectful, though all the papers made it clear that the evening, though undoubtedly worthy, was also wordy and hardly a barrel of laughs; as a result they were off within twelve performances, Gladys having reached yet another all-time low in her London theatrical fortunes.

Christmas 1933 was to be the last the Pearsons spent as an ostensibly happily-married couple; but though neither had yet started being unfaithful to the other with any regularity, there can't have been much doubt that they were still together only because of Sally and The Grove, and there was very little now, either emotionally or theatrically, to keep Gladys in London.

When therefore, early in 1934, her joint management with Massey was offered a second Keith Winter play, and when Massey saw the chance to open it in his native Canada and then play Broadway before reaching London again, it seemed a natural thing to do. Gladys had, in twenty-nine years in the theatre, never played outside Britain and the thought of New York was thus an extremely attractive one.

The play was *The Shining Hour*, and it opened at the Royal Alexandra Theatre in Toronto during the first week of February 1934: the company, led by herself and Raymond Massey and his then wife Adrianne Allen, sailed from Southampton on the *Aquitania* and during the crossing most developed acute seasickness, leaving the perennially indomitable Gladys to cope with Sally and the Masseys' young Daniel until the others recovered, at which point she opened her usual poker school – one that was to last the best part of a year through the Toronto, New York and London productions and only to close on the train back from Brighton to London after the very last performance of their post-London tour, by which time Gladys was very nearly three pounds up.

The outside world was still being given no inkling that things were badly wrong with the Pearson marriage: interviewed as she boarded the *Aquitania*, Gladys told journalists that, yes, she was much looking forward to visiting the New World, yes, she had been having a rather 'bumpy' time lately (a reference, curiously, not to her marriage nor to the failure of *Acropolis* but to the fact that both she and Joan had recently been in minor car collisions – Gladys's driving was not even in those days her strongest suit) and yes, she was taking her little Sally with her to the United

Daniel Massey's christening. Geoffrey and Daniel Massey,
Adrianne Allen, Marie Tempest, Noël Coward, Sally, G. Gertie
Millar and Raymond Massey

States 'because I just can't bear to be parted from her – besides,
it'll do her good to travel young, people are far too insular'.

'Queer Goings-On at a Northumbrian Private School' was how
the *Daily Express* critic had summarized Keith Winter's *The
Rats of Norway* at the Playhouse, and by that token his *The
Shining Hour* could best be described as 'Queer Goings-On in a
Yorkshire Farmhouse': the six characters were all members of
the same family and the plot recounted how Mariella (G) fell in
love with her brother-in-law (Massey), thereby driving his wife
(Adrianne Allen) to an early suicide by walking into a blazing
barn ('there are other ways of leaving home' noted one Broadway
critic somewhat despairingly).

But *The Shining Hour* was what used to be described as a
rattling good yarn, and it gave Gladys the one genuine success of
her years with Massey.   159

True, they got off to a bad start as Derek Williams (who'd been with Gladys at the Playhouse and was again in her company now) recalls:

> There was to be a gala opening in Toronto with the Governor General there to witness Gladys's first appearance on North American soil: she was after all still a very fashionable figure (had she not once played golf at Le Touquet with the Prince of Wales?) and everything was going fine until my cue came and I tried to open the door to get on stage and found it had jammed. Gladys was standing just behind me and hissed 'Get in through the window' so I did. By the time of her entrance the stage manager had scurried round with a screw-driver and all was well, so that she got an enormous ovation for her entry into the New World and was visibly very moved. The door never had a knob in it again.

After a fortnight in Toronto they opened at the Booth on Broadway to generally very enthusiastic reviews from the New York press, who were glad to welcome Massey back and to be having their first real-life look at Gladys. True, some of the subtleties of the plot (such as G's ritzy Mariella arriving at the Yorkshire farmhouse to be confronted with high tea and mur-muring she'd no idea how people could be expected to eat so much before dinner) got a bit lost on American audiences, who could hardly have been expected to cope with such ineffably English domestic, social and geographic distinctions. Nevertheless the advance was good, and that together with the notices launched *The Shining Hour* on a run which they could have sustained into the 1934–5 Broadway season had they not already promised to play it in London that autumn.

Also playing on Broadway that year, at the Alvin, opposite Helen Hayes in *Mary of Scotland*, was the English actor who was within four years to become Gladys's third and last husband. Philip Merivale was then forty-seven, two years older than Gladys, and married to an actress called Viva Birkett by whom he'd had four children. An engineer's son, born in India, he'd started out in 1905 (the year also of Gladys's stage debut) with Frank Benson's Shakespeare company at the old Coronet Theatre in Notting Hill Gate. From there he'd graduated westwards to Tree's company at His Majesty's where he'd first made his name

With Adrianne Allen watching the burning of the barn in The
Shining Hour, *New York and London 1934*

as Pickering in the original Tree-Campbell *Pygmalion*. When Mrs Campbell had taken the play to New York he'd become her Henry Higgins, and since that time he'd carved out a distinctive and distinguished career, primarily in the New York theatre, as an elegant and faintly cadaverous leading man much in demand by the kind of star actresses of the period who wanted their male leads to be supportive rather than competitive.

Merivale asked his old friend, Derek Williams, if he'd introduce them as he wanted Gladys to play with him in a charity matinée that season. Derek Williams:

> Philip said she'd always been a great idol of his but that he was nervous of approaching her directly, so I told Gladys this and she said, 'How stupid of him, tell him to come round to the dressing-room,' and so I did and that was how it all started. Later I asked her how they'd got on together and she said, 'Such a handsome actor, most attractive!' and then ages later, when we were on tour in England, I noticed that she was driving his car so then I knew that something must be up. There was another thing I learned about Gladys on that tour, too; you know how in her curtain calls she always used to move one step forward as the curtain was falling? I asked her why she did it: 'Hawtrey taught me that,' she said, 'it makes the audience think there's more to come, and that makes them go on applauding. If you stand absolutely still the clapping stops as soon as the curtain falls.' Technically she was superb, and much less selfish than that might make her sound; she was good about letting other actors get their laughs, and so few of her generation were. She was also still a great beauty: one afternoon we went for a long walk in the rain and after it she looked at herself with dripping hair in the car mirror and said, 'Derek, I'm getting so grey,' and I thought to myself, 'with dripping hair and no make-up you've never looked so beautiful'.

Philip Merivale was equally bowled over by her. 'My father,' recalls his son Jack, 'fell in love with her the very first time they met in New York. He wrote to us that he'd been totally tongue-tied by her beauty, and there's no doubt that as far as he was concerned it was love at first sight – Philip was stunned by Gladys and was to remain so until the end of his days.'

There's no doubt either that Gladys, though a considerably less romantic character than Philip, also fell as deeply in love as her independence of spirit had ever allowed: after the uneasy and cold years of the Pearson marriage, here was an actor who understood her, loved her and was apparently willing to follow her to the ends of the earth. It was not, of course, quite as simple as that: Gladys may well have regarded herself as free in all but the technicalities of a divorce court but Philip had always been a devoted family man, the father of four now teenage children – and the husband of a dying wife. Just how ill Viva Birkett was during that last winter in New York may not have been totally clear to him: but when she and Philip and Gladys and the Masseys sailed back to England on the *Brittanic* at the end of the Broadway season in May she never left her cabin, and within a month of their arrival home she was dead. Her children believe that she went to her grave knowing she had lost Philip, and knowing whom she had lost him to: Gladys's decision to sail on that same boat must rate as one of the most tactless of a life not always renowned for its depth of sympathy or human understanding.

Within a few weeks of Viva Birkett's death (of cancer) in June, 1934, Gladys and Philip went to Cornwall to stay with the actor Nigel Bruce and his wife Bunny, who were later to become the most constant of their Californian friends; by the time that holiday was over they were living together, and Gladys had determined to get herself out of the Pearson marriage at last. It didn't prove easy: Pearson may not himself have been the soul of fidelity in these past months, but he took the somewhat unusual view that for him to be divorced would do irreparable damage to both his social life as a baronet and his professional life as a magazine publisher. He therefore insisted, against the custom and practice of the day, that if Gladys was to get custody of their daughter (which was he knew the one thing she still needed from him) he would have to divorce her. 'The man is a cad and a bounder,' wrote Buck in his diary when he heard the news, and G's other menfolk were equally appalled. People simply didn't do such things in 1934: it was a gentleman's duty and obligation to let his wife divorce him, whatever the circumstances, and Pearson's decision now to play the game by an altogether new and different set of rules was a source of continuing amazement for the three-year period that the divorce process then demanded. 163

Gladys herself took a less dramatic view : she knew now that what she wanted was to keep Sally and marry Philip, and if the price of that was allowing herself to be divorced by Pearson even in the knowledge that Sir Neville was perhaps not an altogether innocent injured party, then so be it. There were other things to be getting on with, not least the London production of *The Shining Hour* which (again under Massey's direction) opened at the St James's on September 4th, 1934 to a cautiously enthusiastic press. James Agate found Massey unconvincing as a piano-playing Yorkshire farmer, and thought the whole play rather too hysterical for its own good; Ivor Brown and others were however rather more enthusiastic, and all recognized the melodramatic plot for the moneymaker it undoubtedly was – *The Shining Hour* ran on at the St James's through the winter and spring and then set off on a lengthy tour, by the end of which they had been playing for the best part of eighteen months all told, thereby recouping all the earlier losses and getting Gladys back on her financial feet for the first time since the early Playhouse years.

In the meantime, to help the bank balance, she had also done a few days' filming with George Arliss on *The Iron Duke,* a film which opened during the run of *The Shining Hour* and for which Gladys collected some glowing reviews as the Duchesse d'Angoulême. The film did not however appeal to Dr Goebbels, who had it banned in Germany on the grounds that Marshal Blucher was given an altogether too small and insignificant role in the Battle of Waterloo. This was to be Gladys's only film of the 1930s, and *Picturegoer* thought her 'altogether too static for the screen, though she does seem to have a good sense of tragedy'.

When *The Shining Hour* tour finally reached its end in Brighton in mid-1935, Gladys decided there was nothing to keep her in England: the terms on which she would allow herself to be divorced by Pearson had already been agreed, Philip was keen to get back to Broadway where his career was based, Sally could be kept with them and found a school in New York, Joannie was twenty-five and therefore well able to fend for herself, as were the four Merivale children, and Johnnie at twenty had that year made a start on his own stage career, playing with Cedric Hardwicke in *Tovarich.*

For the next thirty years Gladys was to be effectively an American resident: plays and films and family matters were to
164 bring her frequently back to Britain in all save the early war

Her first talking picture: The Iron Duke *with George Arliss, 1935*

years, but her base was now to be on the other side of the Atlantic where Philip's work and her own film future both lay. It was therefore with a sense of finality that she and Sally caught the boat train from Waterloo that summer. Buck was there to see them off, but of Pearson there was no sign and the press were not slow to comment on that. They too seemed to sense that it was a kind of final departure: 'Gladys Cooper's home in Highgate,' wrote the *Express*, 'is no more. The last of her belongings were taken out today and put into storage, and her son John has moved into a little flat in Chelsea.' The rest of the press were either too well-mannered or too ill-informed to speculate yet on a divorce; not so the New York papers who greeted her arrival off the boat with banner headlines reading COOPER TABOOS 165

ROMANCE TALK. 'Here to appear in a play with Philip Merivale,' said the *News*, 'Lady Pearson (Gladys Cooper on Broadway) dodged talk of a romance with the actor.'

The play was to be *Othello*, hotly followed by *Macbeth* in a season arranged by Philip to introduce Gladys to America as a classical actress, and a more disastrously over-ambitious introduction could scarcely have been imagined. Admittedly Merivale had a problem: a noble, poetic, courteous and rather Edwardian figure ('Oh, but she won't like that at all,' said Mrs Patrick Campbell when Gielgud told her Gladys was to marry Philip, 'he'll keep trying to read poetry to her in bed') he was already suffering considerable anxiety, not only over the recent death of his wife but also over the uprooting of G to New York and the ending of her Pearson marriage. True, Gladys had been more than willing to give that up anyway, but now that he had her in New York he felt somehow that she had to be encouraged to enter his world of classic Broadway revivals.

Her image there, in so far as she had one at all, was of a rather aristocratic visiting English lady who'd once been over and worked with Ray Massey in a drama of Yorkshire country-house life; now she was back, and to stay, but doing what? There was no way that the economy of Broadway would allow her to re-create anything like the Playhouse, nor was her conditioning in the Pinero–Barrie–Lonsdale–Maugham plays of much use in a city where none of those playwrights had ever been particularly successful. That whole area of light country-house drama and stiff-upper-lipped plays was never one in which Broadway had taken a great interest, and Philip decided that if Gladys was to have a New York stage career alongside his, then she had to be set up immediately in competition with Helen Hayes and Katherine Cornell and Eva La Gallienne and the other classical leading women of the period. Hence, within a few weeks of her disembarkation, she was to play Desdemona and Lady Macbeth in two of the most catastrophic productions either he or she were ever to find themselves caught up in: not a very auspicious start to Gladys's life in the New World.

chapter eighteen

1935=1939

I N so far as she ever bothered to blame anyone for failure, Gladys was on this occasion inclined to blame Shakespeare, whose lines she never quite managed to learn and whose plotting she thought frequently bordered on the ridiculous. Philip backed the productions with ten thousand dollars of his own money, virtually his entire savings, and he lost the lot. To his everlasting credit, he seems never to have blamed her, or even to have remarked that if she'd taken a little more trouble in rehearsal they might just possibly have avoided what the critic John Mason Brown was to describe in the *New York Post* as 'unbelievable ineptitude'.

Gladys herself thought the problem with *Macbeth* lay in what was missing from the text rather than what was there if only she could learn it: 'I rather think some of Lady Macbeth's best scenes have been lost over the years,' she confided to Sewell Stokes a couple of decades later, 'she starts out on much too high a note to begin with, and then fades out for far too long.' Not long enough for the New York critics, one of whom was heard to remark that Miss Cooper, 'was about as well-suited to Shakespeare as to walking on the water'.

For *Macbeth* the director was Henry Herbert, an ex-Bensonian like Philip but one determined to combine the old training with 'a modern interpretation' likely to appeal to New Yorkers of 1935.

PLYMOUTH THEATRE

OTHELLO and MACBETH

Philip Merivale · Gladys Cooper

In reality, here as for *Othello*, Philip did much of the production himself; they opened in Boston and then moved to the Ethel Barrymore on Broadway where they survived in repertoire for barely a month. 'I think,' said Laurence Olivier tactfully, 'Gladys was a little too practical, too modern, to have the patience to wrap herself up in Shakespeare's material.'

But Gladys was inclined to repeat rather than learn from her mistakes: less than three years later she and Philip were to be found back in London at the Open Air Theatre in Regent's Park running yet another disastrous Shakespearian season. One of the best things about G, albeit one of the most difficult for those who loved her, was that she genuinely never knew when she was beaten.

While in New York she and Philip had been struggling through the Shakespeares in the October of 1935, a Dodie Smith family comedy, *Call It a A Day*, had opened with great success in the West End – such success that a Broadway production was immediately planned, one for which the original cast would obviously not be available. Gladys and Philip thus took over for New York the roles recently created in London by Fay Compton and Owen Nares in this everyday story of St John's Wood folk, and G borrowed a trick from her old friend and colleague: where for London Nares had his son Geoffrey Nares playing his on-stage boy, for New York Gladys had her son John.

The director of the New York production was a young and somewhat amazed Tyrone Guthrie:

> I had never met Gladys Cooper, though I had often seen her act, and admired the way she had turned herself from a beautiful, pale-pink English rose into a well-equipped actress. She has never made the slightest pretence to being a dedicated artist, but is rather one of those people who have a living to earn and decided upon a career where her great physical beauty could be a legitimate capital asset ... at her own theatre in England there had been no great plays, not even ambitious ones, just a series of capably written, acted and managed hits ... her approach to rehearsals was briskly professional. Early in the morning she used to go out sliding on the ice in Central Park with her youngest daughter. She would arrive at the theatre, punctual and casual, and give the impression that, while moderately interested in her work and

169

(Opposite) New York 1935: a disastrous start to the Merivale stage partnership

entirely willing to do her best, her real interests were elsewhere. One thing was disconcerting: she never seemed to learn
the words. Gradually everyone put away the book and everyone seemed to have his part well under control – except
Gladys. She rehearsed in big horn-rimmed glasses, carried the
book everywhere and never lifted her nose out of it. In the
part she never stopped pouring tea, or putting on children's
overcoats or working with account books or making parcels,
so the omnipresent book was more than a bit of a bore. Madam
performed prodigies of one-handed dexterity, but nobody can
really tie up a parcel with one hand.

She saw I was getting worried: 'It's all right, dear. I always
do this. It'll be all right and I won't be a nuisance to the
others.' Even at the dress rehearsal she carried the book and
did not seem to know the words at all. We played in the
Morosco Theatre, which is very small and has no orchestra pit
and no footlights. A man in the front row of the stalls im-
pudently placed his derby hat right on the stage. Gladys,
making her first entrance when most players are half-paralysed
with fright, saw the hat, advanced upon it spouting her part a
mile a minute and, dead accurate, gave the hat a tremendous
kick and sent it flying over the heads of the audience into the
nethermost darkness of the pit. There was a laugh, and a
round of applause, and Madam proceeded with the business
of the play as cool as a cucumber.

This was more what New York audiences expected of Gladys:
a gracious English domestic comedy in which all her old Hawtrey–
du Maurier training could be shown off to best advantage in a
series of elegant gowns. She fairly blossomed in the role of
Dorothy Hilton, and played it to near-capacity houses at the
Morosco until the end of the 1935–6 Broadway season, at which
time G and Philip and Johnnie took it on a lengthy tour.

Where John was concerned, there was as yet no sign of the
clouds that were to descend a decade or so later; a handsome and
already accomplished young actor, he seemed to have inherited
all that was best in Buck and G and to be set fair for a thoroughly
successful stage career. Being Gladys's child was much less of a
problem for him on stage than it was later to prove for Sally,
since the comparisons were inevitably less direct, and now that
the Pearson marriage was safely a thing of the past, he was again

170

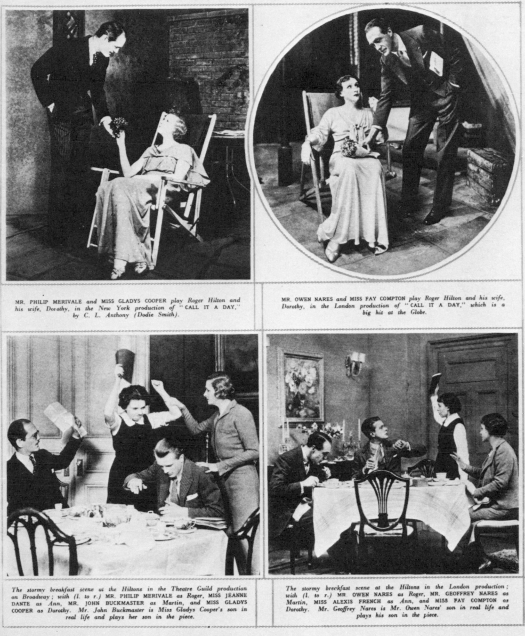

MR. PHILIP MERIVALE and MISS GLADYS COOPER play *Roger Hilton and his wife, Dorothy,* in the New York production of "CALL IT A DAY," by C. L. Anthony (Dodie Smith).

MR. OWEN NARES and MISS FAY COMPTON play *Roger Hilton and his wife, Dorothy,* in the London production of "CALL IT A DAY," which is a big hit at the Globe.

The stormy breakfast scene at the Hiltons in the Theatre Guild production on Broadway; with (l. to r.) MR. PHILIP MERIVALE as Roger, MISS JEANNE DANTE as Ann, MR. JOHN BUCKMASTER as Martin, and MISS GLADYS COOPER as Dorothy. Mr. John Buckmaster is Miss Gladys Cooper's son in real life and plays her son in the piece.

The stormy breakfast scene at the Hiltons in the London production; with (l. to r.) MR. OWEN NARES as Roger, MR. GEOFFREY NARES as Martin, MISS ALEXIS FRENCH as Ann, and MISS FAY COMPTON as Dorothy. Mr. Geoffrey Nares is Mr. Owen Nares' son in real life and plays his son in the piece.

"CALL IT A DAY" IN LONDON AND ON BROADWAY.

PHOTOGRAPHS BY VANDAMM STUDIO AND STAGE PHOTO. CO.

getting on well with his mother. He also took kindly to Philip who desperately wanted there to be a fusion of the two families and was already working towards the day when he would be able to gather the Merivales and the Coopers and the Buckmasters all together under one roof, an ambition delayed by the war and sadly not realized by the time of his death in 1946. Says his son Jack:

> Phil was a romantic and an idealist almost totally emasculated by Gladys, to the point where entire days of his life could be made or broken by a look or a word from her. She was in some ways a very cold lady, and I wonder if at first she really understood the extent of Philip's love for her; I think it was far deeper than anything she herself could really experience. For us, his children, it wasn't altogether easy; we'd been used to my mother's almost Victorian respect for my father, and here suddenly was a very modern lady who treated my father as, at best, an equal. Philip always said his position in the household was a little above that of his children but a long way below hers, and there was a lot of truth in that. It was suddenly Gladys who, for instance, would do the carving at lunch, and that typified the whole change which overtook my father with his love for her.
>
> It was as though he lost that part of his manhood which had made him a great matinée star, and he began to wilt away – mainly I believe because he couldn't bear a row, so at the first sign of any trouble he always gave in. He was determined that he and Gladys should survive as a couple, whatever the cost to his own dignity or pride; he felt that they'd been through too much, broken up too many other homes, for it to be allowed to go wrong now.

And of course it never did go wrong: despite many separations over the next ten years, caused by his work in the theatre and hers in Hollywood, they were and remained the Merivales, and Gladys kept Phil's name until the very end of her life, signing herself Gladys Cooper Merivale even twenty years after she'd watched him die. In her own special and admittedly sometimes chilly way, she did I believe love him more deeply than she had ever loved even Buck.

Philip was a prolific writer of letters, poems, diaries and even plays: one of the latter was called *Chevaleresque*, and when the *Call It A Day* tour closed in midsummer 1936 he and Gladys decided to try it out in stock at Locust Valley on Long Island. Even when given a more accessible title, *White Christmas*, this was some way from being a Broadway possibility and after it closed the two of them returned to England, since the Pearson divorce plans demanded they should provide Sir Neville's lawyers with actual evidence of their co-habitation.

This proved an expensive way of getting divorced, since in order to be caught in bed with Gladys in a Lake District hotel, Philip had been forced to turn down an offer of five thousand dollars to play in *Everyman* at the Hollywood Bowl: greater love had no man than Philip, and fortunately the publicity surrounding G's divorce in the autumn of 1936 was rapidly driven off the front pages by a more interesting scandal involving Edward VIII and a Mrs Simpson.

By Christmas, G and Philip were back in America and they decided to tour a curious two-handed thriller called *Close Quarters* which Oscar Homolka and Flora Robson had done without much success at the Haymarket a couple of years previously: 'I wonder who that can be,' said Miss Robson when the doorbell rang during Act Two. 'Whoever it is,' came a voice from the stalls, 'let them in.' The American tour was less eventful but for one thing: in Chicago, on April 30th, 1937, G became Mrs Merivale, the Pearson divorce having at long last become final.

The following day Philip wrote to his younger son David:

Yesterday Gladys and I were married. Thank you for your share in the cablegram which expressed your acquiescence. I hope we may make a happy place in this distracted globe for the large group or small nation composed by our united offspring. If we could buy an island and live upon it by ourselves I think we should be wise to do so – making our own houses and furniture and producing our own food and wine. But we aren't wise! We want to be artists and scholars and idlers and so forth: and so we shall continue to compete in this world with the rest of mankind for the worthless prizes thereof.

And it wasn't even as though the competition was getting any easier: on Broadway there was no way the Merivales could turn themselves overnight into the Lunts, given Gladys's inability to 173 cope with the classics and the curious fact that though now very much a couple in real life, they still somehow didn't look like a couple on stage. Gladys's dominance of Philip might not much have mattered if she'd been a tragedienne, as so many of his previous leading ladies had been. But a dominating comedienne overshadowing a classical tragedian made for an uneasy professional partnership: together, Gladys and Philip had nothing but failures in their native London and their only one real success in New York, *Call It A Day*, was already behind them.

It was not, God knows, for want of trying. Immediately after their marriage they returned to England, where they still meant to have a permanent home; inside the next twelve months there they did seven shows and lived at four different addresses, consistently failing to find either success or permanence in anything they did together.

The first thing they tried was *Goodbye to Yesterday* by James Parish which Basil Dean was putting into the Phoenix; a dire psychological drama about a Brighton schoolmaster with a penchant for shutting his children up in cupboards. Business was so bad during the first week that on the Saturday night Dean announced they'd be closing there and then. Gladys was not pleased: 'It is very bad luck,' she told the *Daily Mail*, 'to return to the London stage after nearly three years and then have this disappointment. If we cannot find a suitable play for ourselves here we may well have to go back to America and work there.' This was, at four days, to be mercifully G's shortest-ever run, and it was Agate again who had the last word, in the *Sunday Times* the morning after they'd closed:

'Mr Parish,' he wrote, 'should either shilly with Henry Arthur Jones or shally with Pinero: a piece which dilly-dallies between the two makes the worst of both worlds.'

There were signs now of increasing desperation in the Merivales' search for something in which they could play together successfully; there were also unnerving signs that Gladys, suffering her usual delusion that she would rust over unless she kept moving, was now prepared to turn up on stage in more or less anything that had the faintest hope of a run. Acting, which had once been a profession to her, was becoming more and more frequently just a job to be undertaken for the money, or for Philip, or to keep her in England near the children. There was very little joy now in her approach to the theatre, and it was beginning to show.

174

Moreover she was acutely conscious of the rapid decline in her theatrical fortunes; it had after all been barely seven years since she was at the height of her Playhouse management. Now Gerald was dead, and Curzon, and Hawtrey, and all her old stalwart advisers. 'I find it very depressing,' she wrote to Joan in a rare moment of self-expression, 'meeting awful people like Gilbert Miller who now seems to be positively gloating at the failures Philip and I are having. The theatre really does seem to have been taken over by some rather terrible people now.'

Yet she had no alternative but to carry on with it: at forty-nine she was hardly of retiring age even if she had wanted to be, and such money as she and Philip had managed to save over the years had been entirely drained away by that disastrous Shakespeare season on Broadway and by the divorce proceedings. They were living from play to play, day to day, in a series of rented houses, feeling more than a little relieved that, apart from Sally, most of their children were now managing to fend for themselves as often as not; though Jack was told he'd have to give up his Oxford student career as he had not the seriousness of purpose, nor his father the money, for it to be carried on for the full three years.

In February 1938 they went back into rehearsal. Sinclair Lewis's novel *Dodsworth* had already been a bestseller and a film, neither of which had deterred Sidney Howard from turning it into an immense and sprawling stage epic demanding fourteen scene changes and a cast of fifty. The American impresario and director Lee Ephraim took Cochran's Palace Theatre on Shaftesbury Avenue and hired an impressive company led by Philip and Gladys. The first night was expensive, ambitious, and over-long; Herbert Farjeon, writing in *The Bystander*:

> This ritzy production disastrously commits many of the most elementary errors now characteristic of our West End theatre. To begin with, there are fourteen scenes. This means thirteen changes of scene which, in turn, means thirteen waits. Thirteen waits in an age which rightly regards itself as an age of speed. Thirteen waits in a play challenging comparison with a film version of the same story without any waits at all. The stage staff at the Palace responds nobly to the demands made upon it, but the stage staff is not enough ... though it may be pleasant for a few moments to regard the new scene

175

when revealed, what happens within it is apt to be very short, very sketchy and very episodic. Oh, for no scenery and a play that has a chance to get going! But if *Dodsworth* were presented without scenery then we should be flung back on the text and that would be fatal, for it is little more than a peep-show with captions . . .

The part of Mrs Dodsworth, who needs above all else to be American, is played by Miss Gladys Cooper who of all English actresses since the first English actress appeared upon our stage is just about the most typically and inflexibly English . . . in times of stress, she adopts the inaudible accent of West Kensington. Still, the scenery did not fall over and the actors did not forget their parts.

'She glitters like the Matterhorn at daybreak,' wrote Agate, as though he had seen both. But vacuous, episodic rapidity was the general critical consensus and though the stage management got consistent raves for their set-changing routines, they alone were not enough to save a catastrophically expensive evening and *Dodsworth* was off within six weeks, leaving the Merivales only grateful that for once it wasn't their money at stake.

What they did next was no better if a little more understand-able: Philip, in his deep and uncritical love for Gladys on stage and off, took the view that despite recent Broadway evidence to the contrary, and indeed despite the entire pattern of her thirty-year stage career, he could yet turn her into a Shakespearian actress given time and the right surroundings. Accordingly, as *Dodsworth* was falling about their ears at the Palace, they agreed to a suggestion from the critic and manager Sydney Carroll that they should spend the summer of 1938 in his Shakespeare season at the Open Air Theatre in Regent's Park.

The plan was nothing if not ambitious: within six weeks Gladys was to play Olivia to Philip's Malvolio, Rosalind to his Jacques, Oberon to his Theseus and the title role in *Lysistrata*. Only one critic, Philip Page in *The Sphere*, actually admitted in print that she 'seemed to be having a little trouble with the lines' and this, reckons her stepson Jack Merivale who was also in the company, was a considerable understatement:

She never knew a line of any of it and she'd paraphrase whole speeches, or else turn to Orlando and say, 'Oh hallo, you're late,

I've been waiting ages,' which wasn't what you might call extremely Shakespearian. But the curious thing was that nobody seemed to mind much; she still looked a million dollars in shorts, just as she must have looked in *Peter Pan* fifteen years earlier, and she had a sort of authority which carried her through. When she got to *Lysistrata* she used to read most of her part off a sort of scroll, and when they were doing *As You Like It* I played one of the gentlemen lying about that bloody damp Regent's Park greensward while father did his 'All The World's A Stage' speech. Finding myself just next to a ground microphone I used to click my fingers into it when he'd finished, which sounded just like applause starting up, so then the audience used to join in and he'd always go off to a round. One night I told him I was doing it all and he refused to believe that the applause wasn't genuine, so the next night I did nothing and sure enough at the end of his speech nobody clapped and he wasn't at all

The open-air Oberon:
A Midsummer Night's
Dream, *Regent's Park, 1938*

pleased, so the next night I went back to clicking my fingers again and that was how we finished the run.

At the end of that season in the Park it was clear to them both that their best chance of professional survival now lay in America. That the children were mainly on this side of the Atlantic was a pity, but there it was; John was now at the beginning of a stage career which had started better than it could possibly hope to go on, and was making regular appearances in all the best gossip columns as the 'escort' of such up-and-coming young actresses as Vivien Leigh and Jean Gillies, Joan was to be married within another eighteen months, the Merivales were entirely capable of looking after themselves and Sally was still under ten and therefore eminently transportable. Back therefore, to Broadway.

The play that took her there was John Perry's *Spring Meeting*, in which G's old friend Zena Dare had just had a considerable West End success; with Gielgud directing, and A. E. Matthews opposite her, Gladys was to open on tour in England and then take it straight to Broadway. Gielgud, working with her for the first time since *L'Ecole des Cocottes* thirteen years earlier, was alarmed to find that she no longer troubled to learn the words very carefully, but the tour went well: clothed still by Molyneux, and looked after still by her ever-loyal dresser Motty, Gladys could persuade herself briefly that maybe things hadn't changed so drastically since the days of the old Playhouse tours. At the weekends she was still able to hunt (now with Sally rather than Joan or John) and to act and live as though the clock had been set back ten years. Then however came a stormy Atlantic crossing and a disappointing Broadway run: *Spring Meeting* opened to some glowing reviews for G, Matthews and Robert Flemyng but its first few weeks coincided with the usual pre-Christmas slump there, and though they held on over the New Year, by February they were taking salary cuts and by March they'd closed. Gladys had however spent a happy three months running her backstage poker school with Matty and keeping an eye on her son John, who was playing Lord Alfred Douglas that season on Broadway to the Oscar Wilde of Robert Morley.

'Morley really is surprisingly good in the part,' Gladys wrote to her daughter Joan back in London, little suspecting that within a year he'd also be her son-in-law.

chapter nineteen

1939

THINGS were, once again, not good: during the closing
weeks of *Spring Meeting* in January 1939 Philip (having already
had one failure that winter in *Lorelei*) went out on the road in a
Sinclair Lewis play called *Angela is Twenty-two* in which he took
over a leading role from the author himself but failed to improve
the business. Money was still very tight, so tight that when soon
after *Spring Meeting* Gladys got the news that her father had
been taken seriously ill and moved to a nursing home, there was
real doubt about whether she could raise the fare home.

She did however, and Charles Cooper lived just long enough to
see his most celebrated daughter once again, dying in her arms
on March 24th at the age of ninety-four after a long and generally
splendid life.

Gladys then sailed straight back to join Philip and Sally in New
York, and spent most of the rest of 1939 trying in vain to set up a
play. Separated again by the Atlantic from her elder children,
just as Philip was separated from his, this was a nervous and
worrying year for Gladys; rumours of a European war grew daily
stronger, and half the time they felt they should be back in
London with their families. On the other hand they could see no
sign of any work there, nor did there appear to be any real need
for them either privately or professionally in London; so long as
they stayed in New York there was just a chance that something   179

would show up, something which would get them out of trouble again and back into a position where they could make a sensible decision about their lives instead of about just the next few days.

Nothing showed up, however, and after a few weeks hanging about New York they decided to take *Spring Meeting* on a brisk tour, with Philip now cast in the A. E. Matthews role since Matty himself had long since gone home. Even that proved a loser, and in October 1939, by which time they'd reached Washington, Philip was writing home to England in some anguish about their financial situation:

> I have strong aspirations towards saving enough for a small house in New York State or Connecticut – such as I might have bought last year – only I had no money. *Lorelei* was a complete flop and Gladys was in England and I couldn't buy anything without consulting her. Then when she came out we lost more money over *Spring Meeting* and so far from buying a house it became all we could do just to keep a roof over our heads from January until now . . . we've been working like tramp steamers, picking up a week's job here and there in stock companies, and finally touring our *Spring Meeting* all over the East Coast for money that only just paid the household bills and gasoline for the car.

It was not, to put it bluntly, quite the life they'd planned for themselves and Gladys (though she was not given to expressing herself as openly as Philip in her letters home to Joan) was as close to desperation as she'd ever allowed herself to travel. Help was however at hand and it arrived, suddenly and surprisingly if indirectly, from the source of so much of Gladys's help in the past. It came from a du Maurier.

Sir Gerald had now been dead for more than five years, but his daughter Daphne had in the interim written a bestseller called *Rebecca*, one that was now about to be filmed in Hollywood by the English director Alfred Hitchcock who, despite his journey to California, was determined to keep the whole thing as English as he possibly could. Laurence Olivier was cast as Maxim de Winter, Judith Anderson was to be Mrs Danvers and the key role of Maxim's second wife was to be played by Joan Fontaine, Selznick (the producer) having declined to offer it to Vivien Leigh despite Olivier's urging. Hitchcock was determined to cast   181 as distinctively as he could within the budget (the supporting cast was eventually to include not only Gladys but Nigel Bruce, George Sanders, Reginald Denny, C. Aubrey Smith, Melville Cooper and Leo G. Carroll, a sort of checklist of the British acting community then living in America) though a letter written by Gladys to Joan three days after war broke out in September 1939 indicates that she'd had to test for the role:

Now that this ghastly tragedy of the world has taken place all my news must seem pretty silly to you in England, but here it is anyway: do for heavens' sake stay with Granny AWAY from London until this whole thing is over, and make sure Gracie is all right . . . we can't tell yet how the war is going to affect theatre business here but Philip has got a job in the new Helen Hayes play and I am going out to Hollywood to play Beatrice in *Rebecca*. They say it is a very nice part though I can't remember much about her in the book . . . Hitchcock made me do a test in New York in the worst possible conditions: my hair was in an awful state after the *Spring Meeting* tour and I had the most terrible toothache and could hardly open my mouth but Hitchcock said I looked lovely so I am thinking of adopting the cameraman who made the test. I am to get a guarantee of 3500 dollars for three weeks work, more if they go over which they are almost certain to, and they say that is *very* good money for a first film in Hollywood these days – apparently the place is already full of English actresses! As I have no prospect of a play at present this is very good news: I am taking Sally, and also Val (Philip's daughter) who will help look after her and also teach her while we are there, but we shall leave the dogs behind . . . John and Jack are thinking of joining up in Canada . . . John has been writing some awfully good songs lately and is making quite a name for himself in cabaret . . . poor old England: when I think of all we went through last time there was a war, and there you are back in the middle of it all again, I feel I should be there too though God knows what on earth I could do: I have to keep reminding Philip he's fifty-two now, not a lad about to go to the Front wherever the Front may be . . . really, sometimes he's just like Buck . . . Morally I really don't know where we're all supposed to be, and though I feel so terribly selfish about being here away from it all I'm afraid I really don't have much of a feeling about 'doing my bit' this time or sending my men to do theirs . . . it all seems to be such a terrible muddle but perhaps that's just because we're so far away now . . .

Soon she was to be even farther away: within a week she'd left the East Coast for California and her next letter to Joan, written from Santa Monica on October 3rd, 1939, goes some way towards explaining the complete and utter transformation that overtook G once she reached the Pacific. Seldom since Cortez can anyone have been quite so impressed with that ocean and its coastline; all her life Gladys had lived in cold and rainy climates and now, abruptly, for the first time in her fifty years, she was introduced to the sun. Its effect on her was electric: in the language of a later age she quite simply dropped out, having decided that anything – even beachcombing – would be preferable to having to leave this extraordinary paradise she'd just belatedly discovered:

I long for you all to be out here with me [she wrote to Joan] as you would adore the sun: you can get burnt here all the year round and when all the present troubles are over I am sure this will be the place to stay . . . you can live in the greatest comfort for less expense than anywhere else on earth! I have rented a charming little house right on the ocean with three bedrooms, two bathrooms, two showers, one large living-room and a long verandah where you can sunbathe all day long: they call it a beach house and there are avocado and orange trees in the garden and it only costs a hundred and fifty dollars a month which means that a week's filming would pay for about three months' living . . . Sally and Val and the dogs arrive from the East tomorrow . . . Philip's play seems to be in trouble and he can't wait to join us here as soon as it closes: Jack and John are still working in New York waiting to hear if they'll have to join up or what . . . David (Niven) is out here having just finished *Raffles* only he's on the Reserve so of course he'll be going back to fight . . . we work in the studio from 7 in the morning till 8 at night wearing heavy tweed clothes as it's supposed to be Cornwall in the winter! Some days they call me and don't use me at all which is very irritating, as I could be in the ocean . . . Nigel and Bunny Bruce have been awfully sweet to me: I play his wife   183

and Larry's sister in the film ... I have been asked to tea at
Myrna Loy's and they say she has the most lovely house up in
the hills ... people do seem to live awfully well out here and
it's all so different from London and New York: nobody
seems to take their acting very seriously and they all seem to
be on long-term contracts and half the time they don't even
know which film they're doing but they are apparently never
out of work and they don't have to keep looking for plays the
way Phil and I do ... all the young English here are talking
about going back but nobody seems to want to be the first to
leave ... Ronnie Colman is very nice to me and seems to have
forgotten about my being awful to him in that play we did ...
Robert Montgomery doesn't seem to understand how the war
can be going on without him ... I forgot to tell you I had a
wonderful flight out here: we left New York at 6.30 in the
evening and arrived in Los Angeles at 7.30 the next morning:
we came down to refuel at a little airport in Arizona just as
dawn was breaking and then we flew low over the desert and
between the mountains and it really was very exciting and
not a bit bumpy! The news reaches us from Europe every
day but we feel that we're living on another planet ... when
they have a film premiere here they erect grandstands each
side of the road where people sit and watch the 'stars' arrive:
you've never seen anything like it – just like a Coronation or
the Jubilee! ... they showed me what Hitchcock calls the
'rushes' of my first day's work on *Rebecca* and I look
GHASTLY but they say that Olivier looks very good in his
scenes: I don't know what it will be like, so difficult to tell
when they keep making you film it in little bits ... I don't
like the Joan Fontaine girl much, she is so 'cringing' in the
part but if they cut her right she may turn out good: oddly
enough she's quite like Daph du Maurier to look at and very
hearty off the screen, much like Evelyn Laye really ... Larry
is quite wrongly cast as Max de Winter but he is a big draw
here now since they saw him in *Wuthering Heights* so what
does it matter! The only real trouble I have is finding the
studios: I have rented a car but the roads all go very straight
and unless you turn off them at just the right moment, you
end up in the hills miles away from anywhere within a few
minutes! The English all stick together here: the Aubrey
Smiths and May Whitty and Constance Collier and Edna

Best and Herbert Marshall and his new wife . . . Nigel Bruce has just started a weekly radio series playing Dr Watson while Basil Rathbone is Sherlock Holmes: Willie (Bruce) gets 500 dollars and Rathbone gets 1500 for each half-hour they do. I seem to be writing about nothing but dollars but it really is fantastic what people make out here for doing comparatively little work . . . whether I shall ever do any good here remains to be seen, and probably depends on *Rebecca*.

California and Gladys were clearly made for each other, and Hollywood was now to be her main home for the best part of the next thirty years: it was as though on that first flight out from New York in 1939 she was leaving the whole first half of her life behind her and starting again, and the only pity was perhaps that she hadn't thought of it at the very beginning of her Merivale years. There was, after all, precious little to keep her in New York or London: her stage career had been in steady decline since the end of the Playhouse time, most of her theatrical friends seemed to have either died or reached California ahead of her, and once there she was a very long way away from her former life – a twelve-hour plane journey in those days even to reach New York, let alone London on wartime transport. To suggest that she was trapped in California for the duration gives no indication of how much she enjoyed being there: on the other hand, even had she hated it, the sensible thing might well have been to stay put and hope that the rest of the family might eventually be able to reach her, since Pearl Harbour was still two years into the future.

True, she wasn't at first getting the respect in California that might, on her track record, have been thought her due: her loyal and devoted friend Nigel Bruce wrote home in some disgust about the way in which Hollywood studio heads seemed to have not the remotest knowledge of who she was: badly lit, under-publicized, given appalling billing and generally treated as just another middle-range English character actress, G must indeed have felt that her professional life had changed a bit since, less than ten years earlier, she'd been in charge of one of the most elegant theatres in London.

But the sea and the sun made up for a lot, as did the memory of how poorly she'd recently been faring on Broadway; a month   185

In Rebecca *with Nigel Bruce*

after she'd finished filming on *Rebecca* she was, in another letter to Joan, still showing no sign of wanting to leave Santa Monica:

I am becoming a complete and utter beachcomber! The weather is still marvellous, still in the 90s this October week, and I bathe and sunbathe all day between feeding the dogs and wondering if there might be another film part for me anywhere . . . Val gives Sally her lessons on the verandah and we are all burnt quite black . . . I still feel terribly guilty about having all this while the people I love are fighting a war I still don't understand, but there it is . . . Philip and Helen Hayes are doing marvellous business and Gilbert Miller has offered me a Broadway play for January but I suspect it will be terrible and the whole idea of leaving here fills me with HORROR! One of the corgis has had some lovely puppies and we've called one Scarlett because she looks just like

186

Vivien and is very tempestuous! So far there have been no
more film offers but I must say I've been rather lazy about
searching for them, that's what this place does to one, but I
really must pull myself together now and get busy if I am to
stay . . .

By December, everything was getting rather colder: Warner's
casting office had told her there was a good chance of 'two or
three' English films being made there in the next year, but
hadn't specified which or whether there'd be work in them for
her. Meanwhile, she was getting faintly irritated at how well her
friends seemed to be doing:

Went to large dinner party at the Basil Rathbones last
Sunday: all rather too rich and overpowering with dinner on
a white terrace and servants! The next night I dined at
Roland Young's house and he only had Henry Daniell and
his wife, so Henry and I gossiped a lot about England and
Roly Young who'd been filming all day fell asleep at the table
and we had to wake him up as we were leaving to say good-
night and thank you . . . such a nice little man . . . Phil thinks
his play may last a year on Broadway and although it's
lovely for him to have a success again after so long, it's also
very depressing that we have to be so far apart: I could of
course go back to him but as the Miller play has fallen through
there seems to be nothing for me to do here, and now that
I've 'broken into' pictures I still think I ought to stay and
give them a proper try . . . if only we could both be working
then there'd be more money to send home to you all as I'm
sure you'll need it now more than ever before . . .

Though *Rebecca* was to prove in the end a considerable success
for all concerned, and certainly among the half-dozen best of the
thirty films G was subsequently to make in Hollywood, during
post-production there was considerable doubt about its chances:
Selznick himself noted that Joan Fontaine was being called 'the
wooden woman' and despite the fact that the novel had already
sold over three million in hardback in Britain and the USA, there
seems to have been real anxiety around the Selznick studio. The
film finally came in for just over a million dollars, but Hitchcock
and Selznick seldom saw eye to eye over it, and the latter fired **187**

off a stream of his celebrated memos: 'Fontaine's eyelashes compare with Dietrich's at her worst', 'for God's sake speed up
Larry's scenes . . . he plays as though he were deciding whether
or not to run for President instead of whether or not to give a
ball', and, most curt of all, 'I am disappointed in the fire'.

Despite Selznick's doubts, *Rebecca* was a winner: it picked up
the 1940 (and Hitchcock's only) Academy Award for 'best picture'
(thereby beating *The Grapes of Wrath, Philadelphia Story* and
Chaplin's *Great Dictator*) and launched Gladys, albeit in a small
and unrewarding part, on a Hollywood film career that was to
last her all the way through to *My Fair Lady* a quarter-century
later.

chapter twenty

1939=1941

THOUGH by Christmas 1939 there was still no other work
on the Californian horizon, Gladys was more than ever determined to stay there, as she explained in another letter to Joan:

I have never had an agent in my life before and so I can't
decide how bad Leland Hayward is, though his office keeps
telling me to hang on and they'll find me a picture sooner or
later; heaven only knows how long that will be. I feel pretty
helpless here as nobody seems to have heard of me, but they
all say things will improve in the New Year, and life is still so
cheap here that I can just about afford to hang on for another
month ... Philip wants me to go back to New York but I
think if any producer does remember my existence and want
me there they can always write and tell me ... Phil is
saving now, thank God, but I am really terrified about what
would happen if we were to be out of work together ever
again: he is so generous about money, and so foolish, that it
worries me but I am sure, in spite of my failure out here so
far, that I am right to hang on and see if my luck changes... I
am managing to send Johnnie some money now and again,
and of course the money for Granny and all that, but I wonder if you and Granny might come out here? It really would
be cheaper in the long run, though I suppose Granny would

have heart failure if we suggested moving her all the way to America: if only I could get one really good film then I could bring you all out – I keep wishing so hard, but nothing ever seems to happen ... the Hayward office are keeping me a dead secret, and Fay Bainter and Edna Best keep getting all the parts I should be playing: it really is most tiresome of them ... Doug Fairbanks senior died here very suddenly this week and the papers are full of funeral pictures of Sylvia and young Doug in mourning, Sylvia draped in heavy black but with her red painted toenails sticking through the end of her sandals which rather spoils the effect. They said it was to be a private service and in the church there were only two hundred of their most intimate friends and relatives! I shall be very thankful when this year's Christmas is all over – we have never been so divided up before and although we're going over to the Ian Hunters it just won't be the same. I am down to my last three hundred Sobranie cigarettes from England and all the American ones are filthy with cork things on the ends so I am hoping somebody will bring me some over ... let's pray to God for a good 1940.

God obliged, though not immediately: Gladys narrowly missed getting into both the Olivier *Pride and Prejudice* and *Tom Brown's Schooldays* that year, but she did get some good family news from England, where Joan was about to marry Robert Morley, the actor G had met and played poker with when he and her son John were together on Broadway in *Oscar Wilde* during the 1938 season:

Good heavens [she wrote to Joan] I do hope you will be very happy and please cable me the exact date so I can be with you in spirit. Robert had better bring you out here and then we can all be together: I am sure he could get a job as Cukor is still saying they should have had him for Mr Collins in *Pride and Prejudice* ... tell Robert he is my first ever son-in-law and I shall therefore expect a letter ... Philip says if you love him he must be all right, but Sally is very annoyed that she can't be there to be a bridesmaid ... they announced on the radio in New York that 'Gladys Cooper the famous actress has married Robert Morley' and that seems to have confused a lot of people so I am having to write lots of letters

190

now . . . please put some flowers for me on Gerald's grave this month, also Grandpa's and I'll send you the money if I ever get any again . . . Phil says John is doing very well in cabaret at the Algonquin and though people keep writing to me from England saying that he should go back and fight with the others, I really haven't the heart to persuade him to give up his New York life . . . I kept him out of danger all through the First War by driving you both down to Frinton, and I really don't want him to be killed in this one – it all seems to be so futile.

At the end of March she went to have a look at herself in *Rebecca*:

The premiere was a great success and we all seem to have got the most marvellous reviews but I really look quite terrible on the screen, a strange hunchbacked creature in an ill-fitting tweed suit out of whose mouth such a frightful grating noise comes that I thought something must have gone wrong with the soundtrack. If that's what I look like in films no wonder nobody else wants to hire me! The lights are in all the wrong places for my face and I look a most peculiar colour, but that may just be the print. Anyway, Jack says I'm worrying too much about it: he's out here rehearsing with Larry and Vivien for their *Romeo and Juliet* and tomorrow Phil at last arrives from New York, so we have borrowed a Union Jack from the Hunters to hang over the front door and welcome him to our little rented home!

Within a month of Phil's arrival in California, and still without any work in prospect for either of them, they had decided to buy a house there:

I know you'll think we're mad [she wrote to Joan] and I don't even dare think about how much money we've had to borrow from the bank, but it really is a very good speculation instead of paying out rent all the time, as we have been these past four years without getting anything back . . . the joy of having one's own place again really is tremendous, even if we can't afford to live there and have to rent it out: it's a charming house on Napoli Drive with a big, big garden looking out   191 over the Riviera Golf Club and the ocean in the distance, though it's only about five minutes away! The house is only just big enough for us but there's lots of room to build on for when you all come to stay . . . Constance Collier is going to lend us some furniture until we can afford to get ours shipped over . . . *Rebecca* has broken all the box-office records at Radio City in New York and I have got a new agent, so things may be looking up at last!

By the beginning of May, they were into 750 Napoli Drive, furnished largely by friends and Woolworths, Phil had taken to a daily round of golf with Fred Perry on the nearby course and G was writing irate letters home about her old friend Sir Seymour Hicks, who had published an article entitled *Gone With the Wind Up* attacking those British actors and directors who had chosen to remain in Hollywood:

Such a ridiculous thing for the old boy to do, and so unfair to most of us! What possible good could Phil and I do back in England now? We're both over fifty and we'd just be using up valuable resources and getting in the way . . . but Phil says that if we stay out of it we shall morally have lost any right to call ourselves British subjects after the war is over, though of course all that would change if America ever entered the war and many of us here think that's what we should be encouraging: then it would all be over so much faster. Noël and Duff Cooper and some others are already out here doing propaganda work and they want to move the children from the Actors' Orphanage out here too so May Whitty and I are forming a committee to raise the money . . . apart from that things seem rather aimless here and we all sit by the radio waiting for news from Europe and every bulletin just contradicts the last, so now I have taken up gardening to keep my mind off things . . . two days a week I go to the Red Cross British Relief Fund here and make pyjamas (you would laugh if you saw me sewing!): Mrs Ian Hunter and Mrs Boris Karloff and Mrs Melville Cooper are all in my group and we are doing our best, but I fear it isn't nearly enough . . . My name still means so little out here that I'm not even much good for raising any money, and when they asked for five hundred dollars from each of us for the Orphanage children and I realised I hadn't even got that in the bank I got very, very depressed: if only I could get one good film! The studios keep telling me to hang on, things will get better and they've lots of English films they're still planning to make but I'm still not getting a nibble from anywhere!

By midsummer 1940 Gladys had joined the rest of the expatriate British community around Hollywood in organizing a stage production there of the nine one-act plays that made up Coward's *Tonight at 8.30*; she was also, for the first and only time in her life, to help direct:

We are doing it for the British Relief fund, using all the film stars we can get and some R E A L actors too! I am so glad to hear that Buck is to marry again and I do hope he and Grace will be as happy as Phil and I still are, so it'll be third time lucky for us both! Philip has been offered 1500 dollars a week to do a radio series in Chicago next winter so I think he'll have to take that unless a play comes along, and if we can get by till then at least the winter will be paid for! . . . People who've seen me in *Rebecca* say they can't understand how I was once known as a famous British beauty unless there weren't many other beauties around at the time, and I must say I can't blame them . . . for the Coward plays I am playing the wife in *The Astonished Heart* with Basil Rathbone as the psychiatrist: he is awfully nice to direct and I am getting all the 'ham' out of him at last! Phil is in the *Family Album* play and I may also have to direct *Ways and Means* with Joan Fontaine and Brian Aherne though I don't fancy that much as they haven't an ounce of humour between them.

Nevertheless they raised over ten thousand pounds for the War Relief and Coward himself turned up at the theatre one night:

They are giving a party for him but I shall not go as I have refused to speak to him since he was so rude about John not being in the War. His plays have done me some good, however: the director Sam Wood saw me in *The Astonished Heart* and I have at long last got another film! He is doing *Kitty Foyle* with Ginger Rogers and I am to play the mother-in-

193

law: only a week's guarantee I am afraid, but at least the part is American and so I shall break down this awful barrier of being 'too English for my own good' which is what one casting director called me . . . it is good to hear all the news from England only of course your letters are being censored, especially the bit you wrote about the air raid over Reigate Hill!

By September, things in California were looking up at last:

I have started at R K O on the *Kitty Foyle* film and now there is talk of my playing Lady Nelson in the film that Larry and Vivien (who are married at last!) are going to do out here . . . I have been getting up at six every morning for *Kitty Foyle* and not getting home again till after eight at night which is very boring. Phil has given up the gardening because I say he does it so badly and so now he's staying on the golf course instead. Ginger Rogers is very nice, quite small though she looks so big on the screen, and there's also a very attractive man in the film called Dennis Morgan who plays my son. The studios at R K O are very uncomfortable, though, and I have an awful poky little dressing-room . . . Willy Bruce says I should complain that I'm a 'star' but I don't think it would do much good out here and I suppose I'm lucky to be working at all . . . we have got some new things called 'car stickers' with a Union Jack printed on them and written across it A L O N E A N D U N A F R A I D! and lots of shops we've taken them to are now sticking them up in their windows so nobody here can ever forget about England . . . the garden is really looking marvellous now and I do twelve hours digging every day I'm not called for *Kitty Foyle*: Phil finds he can only manage an hour or two and is furious with me for going on so long, says I must be turning into a man – all hard and rubbery! But I love it out there and we really are getting the house right at last.

Other houses were now less right: Buck's in Frinton had been bombed, and 'enemy action' was also held responsible for the loss of a large amount of Gladys's old Highgate furniture which she was trying to get shipped out to Hollywood, Gladys not being the kind of lady who believed that world wars should be allowed
to inhibit anything so crucial as the translatlantic shipping of

cupboards. Indeed much of the next thirty years of her life was to be spent arranging for the movement of innumerable packing cases from London to California: these cases would then frequently make the return trip a year or two later, often accompanied by chairs, pictures, dogs and assorted relatives, until towards the end of her Californian life G suddenly tired of the whole paraphernalia of programmes, photographs, press-cuttings, books and laundry bills and dumped the lot on a surprisingly grateful theatre department at the University of Southern California, where the more intriguing items are now stored for posterity as The Gladys Cooper Collection. One entire crate, now catalogued there as Mis Fin Pap which I take to mean miscellaneous financial papers, holds all the Playhouse bills: another, every script she ever worked in, and her family find it oddly reassuring that, after all those years criss-crossing the Atlantic underneath dog leads and old photographs of Owen Nares and programmes from the Gaiety, those papers have finally found themselves a secure and academically impeccable resting place where we can occasionally go to visit them.

Lady Hamilton (known in American cinemas somewhat more flamboyantly as *That Hamilton Woman*) was to be Alexander Korda's most important propaganda film and many believe the one that got him his knighthood as well as accusations in the American senate that the film was made 'as an incitement to War' which of course it was. Though Hungarian by birth Korda was by now more British than the British, and he persuaded his writers (R. C. Sherriff and Walter Reisch) to make the Nelson–Churchill and Napoleon–Hitler parallels as obvious as they could within the confines of a technically historical film. They made it in Hollywood within six October and November weeks of 1940, working at a hectic pace with the scriptwriters on the set trying to stay a few days ahead of the actors. The result was to be Korda's most critically and commercially successful film since *The Private Life of Henry VIII*, though during the shooting G had her doubts about the whole enterprise:

> I have quite a good part as Lady Nelson, but they are making me play her very disagreeable so as not to take the sympathy away from Vivien as Lady Hamilton! Nothing would induce me to see the rushes after the nightmares I had seeing myself in *Rebecca*, but Vivien and Larry both look very good and are

195

being awfully sweet to me . . . Quentin Reynolds is doing some very simple and touching radio commentaries from the bomb sites in London and making us understand what it must be like for you all there now, though we still feel terribly far away from it all . . . there are so many oranges on the trees in our garden I have to take them to the studios for lunch as otherwise the branches will break under their weight, but it is getting more and more impossible to stay here away from it all . . . Philip and I don't talk much about it but I know he feels the same as I do . . . we should be home with you except that I've got Sally and Gracie and Granny to support and I don't know how to do that except by staying here and trying

Hollywood 1941: as Lady Nelson with Vivien Leigh as 'Lady Hamilton' (background, Laurence Olivier as Lord Nelson)

to get some more film work . . . I know lots of our letters are being sunk on the way over but I'm hoping also to send some food parcels over to you soon, so let me know if they arrive!

That Hamilton Woman opened in April 1941 to generally glowing American and European reviews; it became a considerable box-office success as far away as South Africa and the USSR, and Churchill proclaimed it his favourite film: by August 1941 he'd had it screened five times. Korda was ordered to appear before the Senate to answer charges that the film, though made in Hollywood, belied American neutrality and he could have found himself in serious trouble had not the Senate hearing been fixed for mid-December of that year, by which time events at Pearl Harbor and America's entry into the war had made the charges somewhat academic.

In London a press campaign for the film read 'THRILL to the glamour of a famous beauty played by lovely Vivien Leigh; THRILL to the masterly performance of Laurence Olivier as England's naval hero Lord Nelson; THRILL to the deathless love story of two famous people; THRILL to the pageantry of Alexander Korda's presentation of a great period in English history; and THRILL to the superb acting of a superb drama in a living page of history'.

Many did, and Gladys got the best of her screen reviews to date. She was still professionally on her own, however; at a time when most of her friends and contemporaries within Hollywood's English colony were under the protective wing of a long-term contract with a single studio, Gladys was still freelancing, picking up the work when and where she could. The colony's unofficial Viceroy was then Sir C. Aubrey Smith and its social pecking order was as carefully arranged as life had been for the British imperial settlers in India a century earlier. On Sundays there was cricket, often played against native Americans, followed by a tea party to which only the British were invited: 'Gladys,' David Niven once heard Nigel Bruce remark in tones of some outrage, during one of these gatherings, 'there's an American on your lawn!'

197

chapter twenty-one

1941=1942

G LADYS herself fitted uneasily into the colony at first; though her theatre record back home was considerably more distinguished than almost any of theirs, that mattered as little to the resident British as to the American studio chiefs. All that concerned them was her standing within the film industry itself and this, though undoubtedly improving, was still not good. The colony had of course been much depleted by people like David Niven leaving for the war, and it was never again to regain its former pre-war stature: but middle-aged English character actresses were not among those being called up even now to fight for their country, and therefore within her own range of possible roles G was finding the competition as tough as ever – indeed more tough even than when she'd first arrived, since with the war now nearly two years old California was rapidly filling up with other actresses of hcr own age, sent out either by their husbands for safety or else there to bring up children in comparative tranquillity. All wanted work.

She did however get two more films in 1941: though constantly up against either Judith Anderson or Flora Robson for parts ('both of whom,' G considered, 'look like ailing parrots') she did manage to get herself into an Edgar Allan Poe chiller at Universal and one of the George Sanders *Falcon* quickies at RKO.

I saw Tallulah Bankhead in *The Little Foxes* which has been a great success though I can't imagine why unless it's because of the Ethel Barrymore imitations she does, though even they get a bit dull after the second act. The radio here [her letter to Joan continues] is now thoroughly unreliable: they told me you and Robert were doing a Christmas broadcast to us from London so I tuned in at 4.30 and we fiddled around with the dial for hours getting Italy and South America and a lot of filthy countries like that BUT NOT A WORD FROM LONDON so I wrote to the BBC in New York asking what you said and they said it was just Happy Christmas ... I miss you all very much: Gerald used to say I was a den mother and I like having all my cubs around me ... I have been made Chairman of my Red Cross sewing circle, I think because I have the loudest voice there, and last week we were all filmed at work for a British newsreel so if you go to the cinema soon you might see me ... the film I have done for Universal is called *The Black Cat*: it's what they call a B picture though I consider all my work here at the moment to be rather B. There is a funny little man in *The Black Cat* called Alan Ladd who wears very high heels to make him look taller only I don't understand why he doesn't fall over on them: he had a little part in *Citizen Kane* and they say he will do very well out here, so wonders never cease! Broderick Crawford is also in it and very nice!

'It is pleasant to see Miss Gladys Cooper in a part of some importance at last,' said *The Times* when *The Black Cat* opened in London in July 1941, 'though that is more than can be said for the film.'

Gladys had however already managed to forget that one and had decided to go back East for the summer:

Philip has got a job with Gertrude Lawrence playing the old du Maurier part in *Behold We Live* and I hope I might pick up some work on Broadway for the autumn: then by next summer the payments on this house will all have been made and it will be ours to sell or live in, depending on how the War goes. John has decided to go home and fight; though it frightens me I think this is probably for the best ... Jack is about to marry an actress called Jan Sterling and will then enlist in Canada unless America enters the war this year which looks more and more likely ... in that case of course they'll probably stay and join up in New York ... before we leave I am going to do a few days on another B picture, playing a murderess again, this one with George Sanders called *The Gay Falcon* back at R K O which I hate but still it's money! I dread getting the English papers now, they all seem to be full of people I once knew being killed ...

Gladys left California in July of that year, and motored east with Sally to Central City in Colorado where her son John was appearing in cabaret:

I hadn't seen him for eighteen months, so it was a great re-union and during his cabaret which is very good I was intro-duced as 'John Buckmaster's mother' which he said made a nice change from him always being known as 'Gladys Cooper's son' ... but this is a nasty dirty little city and John and Jack and his new wife Jan (who I don't much like) had a terrible car crash on the way out though they all seem to have survived ... I can't decide whether to go on to the East with Phil while he does the Gertie Lawrence play or to go back to Hollywood to see if I can get yet another bit in a B picture to see me through the autumn ... I hear David Merivale is also plan-ning to marry: what a lot of daughters-in-law Phil seems to be collecting this year: I do hope he likes them.

In the event, the lure of the sun and the sea and the garden still being all-powerful, Gladys returned to Hollywood where the film colony was still in a state of turmoil: Olivier had gone home now, and Fairbanks, and Niven of course, and the English actors left there were mainly those who'd been invalided out for one reason or another (Ronald Colman, Herbert Marshall, Basil Rathbone) or those like Willie Bruce and Cedric Hardwicke who were clearly too old to fight. The British embassy in Washington was still advising actors out there to stay put and carry on with their 'legitimate business of making pictures' but many were increasingly uncertain of the legitimacy of what they were up to. Meanwhile, at home in England, men like J. B. Priestley and Michael Balcon were still asking about the Hollywood 'deserters' and at the same time the British Consul in Los Angeles was

200

urging the expatriate British acting community to stay put and raise money for the allied charities rather than stampeding home. Things were in even more of a muddle than usual.

Gladys was still sending food and clothing parcels back to her sisters and daughter in England, as well as a little money when she could raise it; dollars were as scarce as ever, though, and with Phil still working in the East she decided to let 750 Napoli Drive and move with Sally into a small and cheaper house on 17th Street in Santa Monica. Soon after they did that, things began to improve again:

> We are getting two hundred and twenty-five dollars a month for Napoli Drive, nearly enough to live on as we only have to pay eighty-five for the one in Santa Monica though Phil says I have thrown him out of his house – so like a man. I am working now for nothing on a big film that is being done to aid British and American war charities: it is called *Forever and a Day* and it is made up of lots of different episodes written by people like Isherwood and James Hilton and Lonsdale and Keith Winter and John van Druten and R. C. Sherriff. The directors include René Clair and Cedric Hardwicke and Victor Saville and Herbert Wilcox and virtually everybody in Hollywood is in it: Charles Laughton, Herbert Marshall, Ray Milland, Anna Neagle, Claude Rains, Aubrey Smith, Jessie Matthews, May Whitty, Richard Haydn, Arthur Treacher, Nigel Bruce, Roland Young, Brian Aherne, Edward Everett Horton and hundreds of others. RKO have taken a year to make it and my episode is written by van Druten and directed by Edmund Goulding and they all say it's the first time I've looked all right and Victor Saville has promised me a job on the strength of it: Roland Young and I play bereaved parents.

The posters for *Forever and a Day* listed the cast alphabetically and announced '70 – count them – 70 of Hollywood's favourite Stars!' but cinema managers in Britain were warned not to bill any of them on the posters as most only appeared for a matter of seconds and would thus cause 'adverse audience reaction'. Gladys however had a longer role than most, and *Time* magazine though unhappy about the film's 'breathless' storyline (all about a London house and its adventures over two centuries) noted that 201

With Merle Oberon in Forever and a Day, *Hollywood's all-English star war effort*

'Gladys Cooper is startlingly good in a film which bears all the traces of having been composed by a well-intentioned but mediocre committee'.

From that she went straight into Anatole Litvak's *This Above All*, sadly the one and only film she was ever to make with Philip:

> Mine is a tiny part as the old Aunt, only about four lines and I can't imagine why they wanted to pay me for it, but Philip for once has got a really good role and they've also got Tyrone Power and Joan Fontaine and it's about Dunkirk and the war so it should be all right . . . John Barbirolli was here last week with Heifetz and Horowitz doing war concerts and we all went to listen and it was marvellous and very moving . . . I think you ought to call the new baby Adam: Sheridan sounds rather pompous unless he's going to be a writer, and even then I think I'd prefer Adam.

202

By now it was the beginning of 1942, one of her better years consisting as it did of two more films and a Broadway play. First though had come the news of America's entry into the war:

I was out in the garden all that weekend [wrote Gladys] and nobody told me America had declared war but I'm very glad they have and we're now all in this together . . . we have had some trial blackouts and it all seems to be going very well . . . a few people panicked and started to hoard food, but most have behaved very well and we've put up blackout curtains in the kitchen and sitting-room as they were the two rooms that didn't already have curtains . . . all the Japanese shopkeepers seem to have disappeared and vegetables cost a lot more but nothing else seems to have happened: . . . Basil Rathbone says I am wrong about Sheridan and it is really quite a good name: I thought perhaps Robert had been descended from the playwright but then Basil reminded me it's the name of the character he's playing in *The Man Who Came To Dinner* so that explains why you must have chosen it . . . Phil came up from San Francisco, where he's in a play, by Greyhound Bus to do some post-dubbing on *This Above All* and then he goes back to the Cornell company and they do one-night stands all the way across the country including Detroit and Seattle and then on to New York . . . the papers here are all full of poor Carole Lombard getting killed in that awful plane crash. . . .

The first of Gladys's 1942 pictures was *Eagle Squadron* at Universal and then, in April, came news of a rather better film: 'I am going to Warner's to be Bette Davis's seventy-year-old mother in a film called *Now, Voyager* and it is a really good part at last! Four weeks guarantee with the chance of going over six: I wear a wig and look just like my mother but Warner's is a very nice studio, unlike RKO. Irving Rapper the director used to work for Gilbert Miller and remembers coming to see me at the Playhouse so at least there's someone in America who knows about what I used to do there!'

chapter twenty-two

1942=1944

O F the thirty films that Gladys made actually in Hollywood, three were musicals, three were histories, a couple were comedies and almost all the others were contemporary 'dramas' of one kind or another, many distinctly B. In all, there are about half a dozen which have become 'classics' in the sense of constant television or arthouse revival, and in only about three of those did Gladys have a really distinctive role. *Now, Voyager*, was one of them. Made at Warner's in 1942 with a cast led by Bette Davis, Paul Henreid and Claude Rains, this was the 'Don't let's ask for the moon – we have the stars' film, one of the most expertly tear-jerking sentimental classics the American film industry in general and Irving Rapper in particular ever managed. Gladys and Miss Davis were to recognize, with a kind of wary mutual respect, their kindred spirits.

Both were, after all, 'strong women' at a time when this was a distinctly less than fashionable thing to be: both had built at least a part of their reputations on Maugham's *The Letter*, and Bette Davis was to remain a considerable fan of G's, writing on the card accompanying one of the largest of the floral tributes at her death the words 'She was a great Lady' as if recognizing not a rival exactly, since G's film career had started (as she herself always acknowledged) too late for real celluloid stardom, but instead a visiting member of some other but no less distinguished

204

royal family. G's reviews for *Now, Voyager* were among the best she ever got on film ('one of the most admirable performances of this or any other year in the cinema' said the *New Statesman*) and the film gained her the first of two Academy Award nominations that she was now to win in successive years.

Gladys never won an Oscar: 'the curious thing about that, though,' she once told me, 'is that nobody ever notices you haven't. So long as you get the nomination, and all the publicity surrounding that, the actual statue seems hardly to matter at all.'

In 1942, the competition was distinctly tough: the other nominees were Agnes Moorhead for *The Magnificent Ambersons*,

Testing at Warner Brothers, 1942

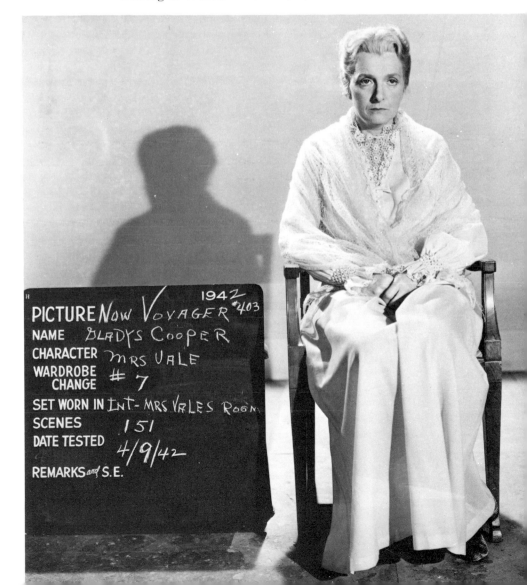

May Whitty for *Mrs Miniver*, Susan Peters for *Random Harvest* and the eventual winner, Teresa Wright, also for *Mrs Miniver* which scooped the pool that year (Greer Garson even beating Bette Davis). G herself was pretty sure during the shooting that they were on to a winner:

> I managed to get five weeks' work out of it which was pretty good: practically all my scenes are with Bette Davis who I couldn't have liked more. I only wish I liked her films more, but now I come to think of it I'm not sure I've seen many: I shall probably like them much better now that I know how very nice she is personally. . . last night we went to the British Relief Ball as there is a huge community here of retired Blackpool shopkeepers and one lady with the most amazing false teeth who said she had collected all my postcards since she was a child though I am sure she is a lot older than me really . . . Phil is now an Air Raid Warden but they haven't given him any equipment so he just goes out with a torch and shines it up at the sky to see if there are any planes about . . . I've been keeping up my canteen work for the Red Cross and one night I went down there and worked till midnight and then got back to the house and found a message to say they were filming three of my *Now, Voyager* scenes starting at six the next morning and of course I hadn't managed to learn any of them so I kept drying up all day which was really very embarrassing but Bette Davis was very good about it and they all pretended it hadn't happened; but that's what you get for doing war work out here! Phil is doing a lot of charity work for the Russian Refugees though I really don't approve of all that socialism and communism, and nor do I approve of Jack's wife Jan Sterling who is staying with us while he goes off to enlist in the Canadian Air Force . . . people do seem to be marrying the most extraordinary people these days, but Phil says I am just getting very intolerant in my old age and I suppose that's true! What on earth have they decided to knight Korda for? Losing more money in pictures than any other producer?

By mid-July, after a brief holiday in the desert which she thoroughly approved of, apart from the noise from a nearby Californian Air Force base, Gladys was back at Warner's:

A stinking little part in a really terrible Olivia de Havilland comedy called *Princess O'Rourke* with Robert Cummings and Jane Wyman; but I don't really mind playing bad parts at Warners because since *Now, Voyager* I am their white-haired girl and they give me a nicer dressing-room and seem pleased to have me back . . . it's a terrible little part as Olivia de Havilland's secretary, but two weeks' guarantee which will pay all my New York expenses and then some! It really is the most absurd little story and I have only about twelve words to say and they are so terrible I can never remember any of them . . . maddeningly I have just been offered two good jobs at Metro: you sit here for months and months looking for work and then the moment you get a play in New York they all offer you work! It is the most ridiculous place, but the weather is still marvellous and if Phil and I can make enough money then we should be able to get back into our house by the middle of next year!

Philip, now out of work, was taking a less resilient view of Californian life in letters to his children:

It has been awful to have to let the house just to pay the mortgage and taxes, though one day I am sure we will return in more fortunate circumstances and then there's room enough in the garden to build a house where all you kids can come and stay when the war is over . . . I play cricket a lot for C. Aubrey Smith's team against Los Angeles; I am very bad still but there is a charm about the cricket field these summer afternoons, like reading an old novel, which takes you temporarily out of the horror and the anxiety of the present and yet doesn't do you the kind of harm morphia and cocaine would do.

Meanwhile, in New York, Gladys was glad to get back to the live theatre after a long absence: the play was Emlyn Williams' *Morning Star*, already a success in London, and Gladys went into rehearsal with it during August 1942:

Quite a good little play and Guthrie McLintic is an exciting director but some of the cast – oh dear! There's a young man doing Emlyn's part called Gregory Peck, very good-looking   207 but I don't think he'll ever get it right, though I may be wrong . . . we open in Washington and then come in to the Morosco where we did *Call It A Day* . . . the weather is unbearable – I never thought I would hate heat but it isn't like California at all . . . I don't think I shall get the Oscar as they say May Whitty is up for it too this year, but nobody seems to care here at all anyway: funny when you think how much it matters out on that strange and silly planet called Hollywood . . .

Reviews for the play were not good, and they opened in a late September heatwave which also didn't help the business; by November, Gladys was back in Hollywood and back at RKO supporting Cary Grant in a comedy called *Mr Lucky*; this, Grant's first solo starring vehicle, was a ramshackle affair about an out-of-luck gambler who infiltrates a war relief outfit (run by Gladys) in the hope of escaping the draft, and it attracted some generally catastrophic reviews though there was the usual polite respect for G's involvement; she herself had no very great hopes for it: 'Cary Grant seems pleasant enough, and I have one or two faintly amusing scenes with him – all rather feeble really but I find it less of a strain than the gardening . . . Phil is doing *This Land Is Mine* with Charles Laughton and Maureen O'Hara: he had his birthday last week and Sally and I gave him a wonderful thing called a pop-up toaster! We have seven kittens now as well as the corgis and I think it might be nice to have a duck . . . just like Charlwood all over again!'

By the end of November there was not much going on in California, so little in fact that Gladys was able to devote eight airmail pages of a letter to the subject of my ears: I was just coming up to my first birthday at the time, and they appear to have been sticking out even more than in later life:

I have talked to lots of people here [wrote Gladys to Joan] and they all say you are NOT to worry: Clark Gable's ears stick out like a bat and haven't hurt his career at all; Jack's also stick out and he is regarded here as very good-looking indeed; babies grow around their heads, you see, and they end up looking all right later on; don't you remember how worried we all were about Danny Massey's big head until his body

208

grew too? Buck also had a funny-shaped head and he has never complained at all, at least not to me! . . .

Then, towards Christmas, good news: 'Phil and I are testing for *The Song of Bernadette* which Jennifer Jones is to do: a bestseller all about a nun I think, and I'm up for the Mother Superior while Phil is up for the Dean so we might be working together again which would be lovely.'

Philip lost out to Charles Bickford in the event, but G got the role of Sister Marie Therese and turned in the performance that was to win her the second of her three Academy Award nominations: on this occasion she was up against Paulette Goddard, Anne Revere and Lucile Watson and they were all beaten by Katina Paxinou in *For Whom The Bell Tolls*. *Bernadette* nevertheless remains among the best of Gladys's Hollywood work despite the lunacy of the publicity surrounding the film.

Fox had originally planned to use one of their contract artists, Anne Baxter, for the role of the half-starved French girl who in 1858 claimed to have had a vision of the Virgin Mary looking down at her from a grotto; Selznick however had Jennifer Jones as a protegée and persuaded the producer, William Perlberg, that it would be better to have an unknown actress without previous audience connotations for such a sacred role as that of a fourteen-year-old child with visions. The fact that Miss Jones had already acquired a husband and sons was remarkably unpublicized at the time, and the director Henry King, a man with presumably little fear of being struck by lightning, solemnly announced that at the final audition he had waved a long stick in the air, asking each of the finalists (of whom there were six) to imagine that it was a vision: 'only Jennifer,' he later announced, 'saw that vision'.

Armed with such qualifications and a powerful supporting cast (as well as G and Bickford the film featured Vincent Price, Lee J. Cobb, Anne Revere and Blanche Yurka) *The Song of Bernadette* was the full Hollywood-religious saga, complete with heavenly choirs and faraway looks in Miss Jones's eyes: 'there is a miracle here,' said the *New Statesman* critic, 'and that is that audiences will sit for two hours and forty-five minutes through such unutterable rubbish'. Generally however the film got very much better reviews than that, and it has stood the test of time rather better than later Hollywood assaults on religious belief. 209

With Jennifer Jones in The Song of Bernadette, *1943*

Moreover it did G untold amounts of good: soon after the shooting started, she got an offer from MGM:

> Imagine! Not just to do one film, which is all they usually offer, but instead what they call a 'term' contract: forty weeks in the year guaranteed, a cheque whether I work or not, only they have the right to reconsider every twelve months if they get bored of me. I think it must have been the Academy Award nomination that did it, that and getting this part in *Bernadette* at Fox! So our financial future is at last looking brighter: we'll be able to move back into the house on Napoli Drive and then despite income tax and the war

we'll all be able to get together again, either there or in England which is still what I call home. I dream now of the day when Gracie and Granny can come to live with me here and the rest of you come to stay while Robert [Morley, her son-in-law] becomes a Hollywood star! Things are really looking up now, and I'm also running a little theatre quite close to here; it only holds a hundred people but we are raising a lot of money for the Red Cross and we have also got eight hens now in the garden so there are lots of eggs when the RAF boys drop in . . .

Almost four years after she'd first moved to Hollywood, Gladys had at last begun to be a success there; her son John was by now in the American army, Jack was flying for the Canadians and Philip, his father, had resigned himself to the fact that he was never going to achieve G's albeit belated success in the studios and instead was contenting himself with odd stage jobs in the Servicemen's Theatre they were running. G's Metro contract was to last five years, and there's no doubt that she won it on the strength of her performance with Bette Davis in *Now, Voyager*: though she was then only in her early fifties and had made up to look twenty years older, Louis B. Mayer for one believed the make up and was more than a little taken aback at their first meeting: 'But Miss Cooper,' he said indignantly, peering at her across his executive desk, 'we thought you were so much older.'

What MGM wanted was yet another old British character actress and that in effect was what they got: almost all Gladys's Metro work in the next five years, from *The White Cliffs of Dover* all the way through a dozen films to *Madame Bovary* in 1949, was to consist of gentler variations on her *Now, Voyager* performance; yet the studio contract meant, for the first time in her American life, security and a chance to plan for the future, now it looked as though there was going to be one.

Meanwhile, on the *Bernadette* set, she was finding the strength to carry Jennifer Jones around in her arms and generally rather enjoying playing the jealous and spiteful Sister Vauzous: 'It's a very wordy part and I have to stand around all the time wearing heavy nun's clothes which give me a terrible backache, but I think it's what they call "showy" and I'll have the whole thing finished in three weeks, after which I go straight to Metro to start   211 my contract with *The White Cliffs of Dover* playing Irene Dunne's mother. I'm afraid I am always going to be playing somebody's mother there!'

By May the Merivales were back, animals and all, in Napoli Drive and a few weeks later Philip (who was already beginning to suffer the ill health that would end his life in less than three more years) was writing to his daughter in England:

> I wish to God I could have the whole lot of you out here where you could plunder the orange trees, swim in the Pacific and above all R E S T ... Our home, to which we returned a couple of months ago after an exile of one and a half years, is beginning to look very nice what with some cheap furniture we bought and some nice furniture we borrowed ... but I miss the family. There's no sense in having a home without kids in it – somebody to tease and occasionally to curse at. We have Larry Olivier's little boy Tarquin staying with us, his mother being without any help in the house and engaged at M G M from 7 am to 7 pm every day. He's a charming child and is doing his best to fulfil the functions of childhood – laughing and shouting and covering himself with tar and so on. Sally (now 13) has undertaken to look after him and is making a successful job of discipline ...

Philip was picking up occasional M G M work too ('a great saving on petrol if we both film at the same studio each morning') but G was finding M G M 'just like a factory: they have two hundred of us under contract and you have to fight to get anything done. Still, there are shops and a post office on the lot and people seem to spend their entire lives without going out of the gates – they even have a barber's shop!'

That summer, on a fortnight's leave from the Canadian Air Force, Jack took his new wife Jan Sterling to stay with his father and stepmother at Napoli Drive: it was not a success:

> Gladys still didn't care for Janey and there was something exhausting about being in a house with her for very long: she never liked to see a window or a door being closed, so the wind would howl through, and she liked to be able to hear the radio while she was gardening, so the volume was deafening. She also never sat down, which meant that you had to be on your

toes too: Gladys certainly wasn't the traditional kind of evil stepmother and Philip, the most romantic and poetic of men, could still have his days made or broken by a look from her. But she could be terribly small-minded and bitchy sometimes: that summer I'd just got my wings, and I think she was rather jealous that Phil's son had got on a bit better in the services than her own son so she just looked at my wings and said, 'Oh, I thought they'd be bigger.' I don't think she ever thought about being unkind, but she could be suddenly and mindlessly either cruel or tactless to the point where it took your breath away. I don't think she really ever wanted to go on making films, though financially of course it was a great relief to have the MGM contract: all she really wanted to do was work in that beloved garden of hers.

chapter twenty-three

1944–1948

1944 found Philip in New York doing *The Duke in Dark-ness* and Gladys in Hollywood doing retakes on *The White Cliffs of Dover* and then playing the Duchesse de Brancourt in *Mrs Parkington*. By now, as C. A. Lejeune remarked in the *Observer*, 'Miss Cooper is already a British period piece, working in those mythical Hollywood films in which an Englishman's house is always his castle, preferably gothic, and in which the titled classes keep log fires and a stiff upper lip while the working classes are evenly divided between reverent old retainers and music hall comics.' *Mrs Parkington* did give her the chance to break the mould for at least one picture ('Miss Cooper plays a drunken neurotic – in trousers!' exclaimed the *Sunday Times* in some astonishment) but she was seldom to be allowed such anti-typecasting by MGM who had a fixed idea about the role of elderly English ladies in movies – an idea apparently made up by a sort of composite of Lady Bracknell and May Whitty.

The MGM publicity machine was however grinding into action, and now, for the first time since she'd moved to Hollywood five years earlier, Gladys began to make regular appearances in the fan magazines: 'it is ironical,' wrote one, 'that with the fading of her good looks her fanmail is now increasing beyond anything she received as the most beautiful woman of the British stage. Hollywood believes that the most promising days of her career as a film actress are before her . . . the greatest part of her fanmail comes from members of the younger generation, and each letter is answered personally.'

CHARACTER ACTORS RULE THE ROOST AT MGM was the headline on a piece in the *Chicago Tribune* that year: 'Gladys Cooper, Charles Bickford, Una O'Connor and Philip Merivale are the backbone of our film industry,' it concluded, 'for too long we have taken the greatest actors and actresses from the theater without so much as saying thank you, put them into minor parts and they have regularly outshone "Dolly Dewdrop" or some other pretty face with no mind whatever . . . only the critics ever pick out the real troupers for praise, but the studios go on finding dim minds to try and build into stardom . . .'

Gladys was by now thoroughly settled back into 750 Napoli Drive and already making plans to build the little house by the pool in the garden which, as 770 Napoli, was to become her eventual Hollywood home until the late 1960s. A few streets away from there, on Amalfi Drive, lived the English actor and comedian and fish mimic Richard Haydn who (having made his name in everything from Noël Coward revues to war films) was to become the greatest and closest of her Californian friends despite one or two mysterious quarrels in their twenty-year alliance. For a radio tribute I was compiling just after her death in 1971, I asked Richard for his memories of Gladys in Pacific Palisades during and after the war:

> A garden near the Pacific, with the most marvellous view. Welsh corgis leaping and gambolling when you entered and somewhere a very determined but rather tuneless whistling, competing with Delius on the wireless. I can never quite reconcile Gladys Cooper under the spotlight with my neighbour under the sink, banging away at a clogged drain. I think of the courage and the beauty of her, but most of all I remember that whistling. I still pass the house almost every day, but never without wishing she were still there and I could drop in for tea and news of her family: I miss her very much, and I always shall.

But as the war in Europe drew to its close, she was getting distinctly homesick for England, a land she'd not seen since 1938; 215 her feeling of distance and lost contact was heightened in 1944 by the death of her mother, just at the time when it looked possible that the old lady might be able to be moved out to California to spend her last years with her daughter there. That was not to be, but early in 1945 Gladys got the chance she'd been waiting for since the very beginning of the war that was now almost over. Under the terms of her contract with MGM, if they had no immediate use for her she could be loaned out to other studios and her fee would then be split between herself and Metro. Miraculously, a film company called Two Cities wanted her to play Cedric Hardwicke's blind wife in *Beware of Pity*, a generally undistinguished Lilli Palmer–Albert Lieven romance set in Austria at the time of World War I. What mattered though was that the picture was to be made in England, and in March 1945 she therefore arrived in London having left Phil and Sally to look after the house on Napoli Drive.

'There is no trace of an American accent,' noted the *Evening Standard* diarist approvingly, 'and she looks young still for fifty-six – not at all like the old grey-haired lady we have seen in so many of her films! London, she thinks, is looking remarkably neat and tidy considering there's still a war on.'

The contract did mean however that she wasn't allowed to stay

With Joan and the author, back home again after the war: Berkshire,
1945

in England for a day longer than it took her to film her scenes with Hardwicke; she was though able during the shooting to see her son-in-law open as *The First Gentleman* and to go to a dinner party given in her honour by Buck at his club: Novello was another guest there, and the conversation could hardly fail to roam back across the forty years of their respective friend-ships and marriages.

In California, Philip was already missing her: 'I am so glad,' he wrote, 'that she is compelled to return by her MGM contract, for it would be hard for her to resist otherwise all the offers she is getting to appear in plays in London.'

Out West, Gladys was known as Trooper Cooper on account of her continuing war work with the Women's Ambulance and Defence Corps; she had left Sally (now all of fifteen) in charge of Phil and the house, and, recalls Sally, 'was rather indignant on her return to find that I'd become the hostess with the mostest, and didn't really want to give it all up. In those days we used to trek across America with all our belongings whenever either Gladys or Phil got a job in New York, and I always thought we should have been in wagon trains.'

John and Jack also spent part of the 1945 summer in California when they were on leave, and it was now that Jack first began to notice a distinct uneasiness in John's relationship with his mother:

> I shall never forget her coming back that time from England and looking at us all in the house and saying, 'You must all have had a lovely time – everyone does while Mum's away,' and then another morning John and I were standing in the drive watching her drive off somewhere and suddenly John breathed a great sigh of relief and said, 'Whenever I'm with her, I feel I'm always doing the wrong thing, whatever it is.' That was her own son, whom she adored: she was curiously unable, I think, to make even those she most loved feel that love very often.

But now the war was all but over, Gladys was no longer out selling bonds or driving ambulances at breakneck speed up and down the coast roads on 'exercises', and her little serviceman's theatre in Brentwood was disbanded. The furniture, or some of it, at last arrived from England, Val and her father arranged all the 217

With Greer Garson in The Valley of Decision *at the start of her long-term MGM contract, 1945*

books, and the house on Napoli Drive at last began to take on the aura of the big family home that the Merivales had been projecting and planning and wanting for so long.

Gladys spent the rest of 1945 at the studios doing such forgettable pictures as *The Valley of Decision* (Gregory Peck, her 'promising young man' from Broadway, and Greer Garson), *Love Letters* (Jennifer Jones and Joseph Cotten) and *The Green Years* (Charles Coburn and Tom Drake), cast almost always as the more or less lovable mother or grandmother of one of the leading characters. Philip at this time was getting rather more distinguished screen work in *Sister Carrie* and Orson Welles' *The Stranger*, but his Hollywood recognition had, sadly, come too late: he was already into the last twelve months of his life and in March 1946, a few months before his sixtieth birthday, he died of a heart ailment in the Good Samaritan Hospital, Los Angeles. Though she would seldom talk about it afterwards, there can be no doubt that his death was the greatest sadness of her long life.

They had been married less than nine years and much of that time had been spent in enforced separation on opposite sides of the United States: now, at the moment when the war had ended and it looked at last as though their lives were finally coming together into some sort of Californian pattern, along with their plans to build the family home, he was dead. Jack Merivale recalls:

For his last five days Gladys stayed at the hospital in downtown Los Angeles: her singleness of mind could only take in one thing and that was that her husband whom she loved was now dying. Theirs had been a good if irritable marriage: in so far as Gladys could give herself wholly to anyone, she'd given herself to my father and now, suddenly, she was to be left alone by his death. At his bedside she'd been looking a hundred and ninety: no colour, her whole face sunken underneath the sunburnt wrinkles. Then one evening Val and I, who were also at our father's bedside, asked the doctors if anything was likely to happen or if Phil would come out of his coma in the next hour or two and they said no, so we took Gladys out to a restaurant. We had to queue, I remember, for a table and when we finally sat down we managed to get Gladys's mind away from the hospital for a while; she began to talk about other things, about her childhood, about the Playhouse, and suddenly the years fell away from her and she looked dazzling, like a young girl again. By the time we got back to the hospital age and grief had caught up with her and she looked old and crumpled again, but those few minutes were quite unforgettable.

Philip had always said he fully expected to die with Gladys, almost certainly in a car, since he shared her own family's appalled view of her driving ability. 'She is impossible to live with,' he once said, 'and impossible to live without.' But now he'd gone first, leaving Gladys to live on for another twenty-five years without him: years which, though active and generally fairly happy, were never to be quite the same.

Predictably, she at first threw herself back into work: that year for Metro she did *The Cockeyed Miracle* with Frank Morgan and Keenan Wynn and then went straight on to play Lana Turner's mother in *Green Dolphin Street*, billed as 'a cavalcade of thrills and romance, MGM's most spectacular drama since *Gone With The Wind*'.

219

She also decided, again perhaps to keep her mind off the lonely aftermath of Philip's death, that Sally should be taken out of school and launched on an acting career of her own – one which started that year with a Californian and Broadway revival of *Lady Windermere's Fan* with a cast which also included Sal's half-brother John Buckmaster, her stepbrother Jack Merivale, Cornelia Otis Skinner, Estelle Winwood, Penelope Dudley Ward and, rather more surprisingly, Cecil Beaton making his stage debut as Cecil Graham.

They opened in California and then travelled to Broadway where they played the 1946–7 season; at the end of that run, Jack and Sally returned to Gladys in California leaving John to stay with friends near New York. It was then, via a phone call, that Gladys learnt her beloved son had suffered the first of the mental breakdowns which were to be a regular and increasingly violent part of their lives for the next ten years.

Gladys could never bring herself fully to accept the fact that her only son was now mentally unstable: shock treatment was at first able to contain his acutely schizophrenic condition, one G would invariably refer to as 'flu', and although others close to him were able to recognize the symptoms of his instability she kept her eyes determinedly closed to the possibility of mental illness in the family. It was simply not something one tolerated; both she and John's father, Buck, had after all come of a Victorian generation which regarded that kind of thing as a sign of weakness, something to be ignored or overcome rather than treated, and Gladys was never able to bring herself face to face with the truth about John's condition.

There is neither the place nor the expertise here for an analysis of that condition: briefly, the strains of a war in which he'd felt himself perhaps involved too distantly and too late, of a number of increasingly unhappy love affairs, and of maintaining a career which had began with rather too much glitter and not enough training, were proving too much for John, and under those pressures and the other pressure of being Gladys's son he was now, slowly but surely, to crack – temporarily at first, then for longer periods until in the late 1950s a series of increasingly effective drugs were able to bring him to his present and very controlled state.

The process was however a long, often violent and painful one and starting as it did so soon after her last husband's death it was

At her Pacific Palisade home in California with Sally and John, 1947

inevitably to cloud equally darkly Gladys's final years, years which were to be spent in almost everything but retirement.

Her 1947 films were something of an improvement for her and M G M, including as they did *Homecoming* with Clark Gable and Lana Turner and the Minnelli–Garland musical *The Pirate* for which she was cast as Aunt Inez. In the meantime she'd also been lent back to R K O for a David Niven–Cary Grant comedy called *The Bishop's Wife* which was to become the Royal Command film of 1948. Her reviews now were invariably good but brief, which was more or less what could be said for all her performances since she had settled into the routine of a Hollywood character actress: seldom was she asked to surprise the customers with a variant performance, and her films began now to merge into one extended grandmother so that she would often find it hard to put an actual name to the picture she was at any given moment shooting.

221

The Pirate (an old Lunt vehicle newly scored by Cole Porter) was however an exception, first because she'd never done a musical before and secondly because she was much taken with Judy Garland, to whom she taught the rudiments of the old Playhouse poker rules as a way of encouraging Miss Garland to get through one of the already recurrent crises in her professional and private life. She also took a distinct fancy to Gene Kelly.

That winter a visitor from her past, Ivor Novello, had come to stay at Napoli Drive: 'I've asked a friend to tea,' he told Gladys one morning. 'Who?' asked Gladys irritably, 'Garbo,' said Ivor. The two ladies got on remarkably well, Gladys noting with some approval that when Garbo came to tea it was she who did the washing up. Once the three of them went round to call on Niven. 'Who's that in the car, Gladys?' asked David, 'Only Garbo,' said G, and David looked as though she'd said only God.

But more and more frequently Gladys was now looking back over her shoulder towards the theatres of New York and London, all the more enticing since her MGM contract had made it virtually impossible for her to play in any of them. Money was no longer a problem, thanks to the continuing benevolence of Louis B. Mayer, but though all the wartime restrictions on travel were now lifted she was still finding it hard to escape the daily routine of the studios to which she was contracted. In England now there was a second grandchild to inspect (Annabel, my sister, had been born within a month or two of Phil's death in 1946) and she was longing to get home while at the same time rather hoping the Merivales and Morleys who'd spent the war in England would make their way out to the West coast. She'd been able to build now, as an unsentimental memorial to Philip, the pool house in the garden at Napoli Drive overlooking the golf course – a house to which she was herself to move in 1949 when my parents and sister and I invaded the big house, and where she was then to stay for the rest of her Californian life while the big house was first let to Ethel Barrymore and then eventually sold off.

It was just after they finished the prolonged and technically tricky filming of *The Pirate* in 1947 that Gladys got her first postwar chance to return to the theatre. In the mail from London came a script by Peter Ustinov: called *The Indifferent Shepherd*, a somewhat shaky early piece, it had been acquired by the impresario Henry Sherek (then presenting Robert in London in *Edward My Son*) and he offered it to Gladys who accepted it more as a travel voucher than as a script. She wanted to be in London, London was where this play was going to be, and that was more or less that. Henry Sherek, in an autobiography memorably subtitled *Malice in Wonderland*, takes up the story:

> Here was a great lady of the theatre. Whenever she made an exit, she always gave the impression that she had never in her life had to open a door for herself. We went straight into rehearsals, which were less than three weeks instead of the customary four, and there was no provincial tour . . . I looked forward eagerly to the first night and to the fine reception I knew she would get from the loyal London theatregoers (she had not played London for fully ten years) but when she stepped on to the stage the cheers and applause were so overwhelming that they threw her completely. I thought they were never going to end. Several times she tried to say her opening lines but they could not be heard because of the din. There were tears in her eyes, and as she was never remarkable for knowing her part, particularly with such short rehearsals, her emotions at this reception made it doubly difficult for her. The Ustinovs sat in a box with us and the prompter's voice seemed to us to vibrate shrilly through the theatre.

Ustinov himself recalled:

> She gave a performance of extraordinary power as a woman frustrated by the vacillations of a husband addicted to goodness. There has rarely been an actress who exuded more animal health, even in old age, or who was more fatally attractive, her deep and lovely voice cajoling or cruel, or both at once.

chapter twenty-four

1948=1951

The *Indifferent Shepherd* opened at the Criterion on February 5th, 1948 and ran a hundred performances: not a disaster, exactly, but then nor was it the professional homecoming Gladys might have wished. The first night was, as Sherek has indicated, an extraordinary testimony to the fact that London audiences despite ten years and a world war had not forgotten her. Many old friends and even contemporaries were dead now, including Agate, but for the *Sunday Times* Harold Hobson noted that 'on her first entrance Gladys Cooper received a tremendous and prolonged ovation, an ovation that would have satisfied Irving or even Mr Danny Kaye. Not the least moving thing in the evening was the superb stillness with which Miss Cooper accepted this ovation without acknowledging it. No Greek statue could have been more coldly magnificent, yet as the applause died away there was the faint flicker of a smile at the corners of the mouth.' *The Observer* however noted that by Act Three the proceedings had slowed to 'a calamitous crawl while lines are being groped for' and they had closed by the middle of May. Though glad to be back in the bosom of her English family at last, this was not an entirely happy time for Gladys: her loyal and loving old dresser, Motty, had died during the rehearsals and soon after they opened G was robbed of three thousand pounds' worth of jewellery, virtually all she had, from her London flat. The haul included a bracelet given her by the Duke of Westminster, a fur coat and several pairs of nylon stockings. 'What are you going to do about it?' asked Robert in some alarm, 'Have dinner,' said Gladys, who was never one to dwell on her disasters.

Soon it would be time for her to return to Hollywood and the last year of her Metro contract; Sally was to stay in London and carve out a career for herself in the English theatre while John and Jack commuted across the Atlantic doing plays and, in Jack's case, also a number of films. This was now defiantly a family of second-generation actors, while Robert, having married into it and being also a playwright, was under instructions to write Gladys a script:

> By no means everyone can write a play for his mother-in-law, and even if he could, it wouldn't do him any good. You cannot get rid of your mother-in-law by simply writing a play and telling her to go away and act it. The average mother-in-law can't act – and what's more, won't. If you want to get rid of her, better by far the old-fashioned arsenic-in-the-tea or burning house routine. Even supposing you genuinely wish to please her, she would rather have her usual mink coat or box of comfits this Christmas. Plays, even when delicately bound by the Typewriting Agency, are always a bit of a disappointment. They wrap well, but once you've said that, that's about all there is to say. No, take my advice. This Christmas give her something to eat, not something to act.
>
> My case, of course, is different. I have a mother-in-law who acts to eat – that is, when she remembers to do either. I have just finished a play for her – or rather Ronald Gow and I have just finished it and I must say it looks fine from here [called *The Full Treatment*, it was eventually and briefly to be staged at the Q Theatre with Ambrosine Phillpotts in the role written for Gladys and Sally also among the cast, though never G herself]. It has come back from the typist in a smart, stiff cover, with only the title on the front page and a row of those curiously beautiful starry dots which I can never quite manage on my machine. Tomorrow it will fly to California where you might think mother-in-law Gladys Cooper is impatiently awaiting it. But you would be wrong. She will read it, of course – or, at any rate, some of it – as soon as it arrives, and then probably put it aside for a month or two,

225

and go back to her garden. But one morning, sooner or later, she will come indoors from those impossible flower-beds and, getting out her enormous horn-rimmed spectacles, she will sit down on the porch overlooking the golf course and start reading a play. Something, perhaps a dragon-fly or the scent of a flower, or even the bark of a dog, has reminded Gladys that it's time to be off. This is the time when I trust my play will be at the top of the pile (surely nepotism must count for something), for Gladys is apt to choose a play as she chooses a plane – casually and for the same reason: a desire to go places. It may be to New York to see her son, or London to see her daughter, or Hawaii just to see Hawaii. And on these occasions she travels on the first available flight with the first available play. As a rule, the plane proves the more reliable vehicle . . . but she remains to remind us of the days when the Theatre didn't take itself too seriously and was in consequence a great deal more amusing. Those days, actors took

With Judy Garland in Minelli's eccentric Gene Kelly musical,
The Pirate, *1948*

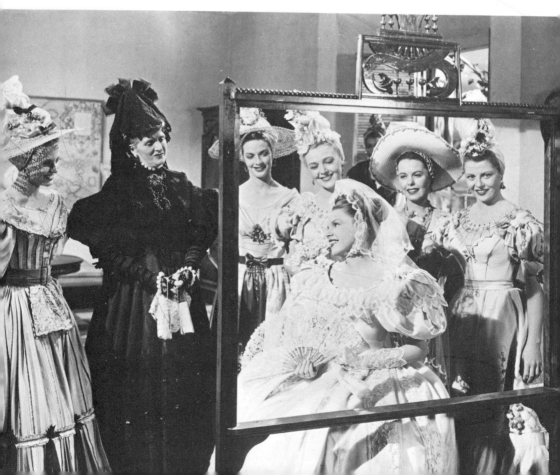

the first job that came along because they wanted to act . . .
they were pitchforked into plays and sometimes of course
pitchforked out again; but on the whole Gladys's generation
were happier, healthier and wiser than we are about the
Theatre today.

Back in California in 1949, Gladys gathered us all around her
for the first time and we spent a happy summer en route to
Australia where my father was to play *Edward My Son*: my own
recollections of that eight-year-old summer three decades ago are
now no more than a cheerful haze of sunshine and swimming and
visits to the hallowed MGM lot where G was then making
The Secret Garden with Margaret O'Brien and Herbert Marshall
and Dean Stockwell ('Miss Cooper at her most tightlipped as the
housekeeper' said the reviews) but Robert's recollections are
more specific:

She could be very sharp at times. She was not good at feeling
sorry for people, perhaps because she never felt sorry for
herself. If you were in trouble, you got out of it, with her help
of course but it was up to you in the end. If you got ill, you
got better. She was, in her way, something of a health fiend.
She didn't eat much. She worshipped the sun. When we were
staying with her in California she would come back from the
studios at dusk and start cooking our dinner and then, when
everything was in hand, she would disappear and a moment
later sweep across the patio, wrapped in towelling, for her
evening swim. Ten minutes later she would be back and five
minutes after that she would reappear in the sort of shift dress
of which she was so fond, gold bangles on her arms, her hair
and her make-up immaculate, to mix a final round of daiquiris
before she took the lamb from the spit. How is it done, I used
to ask myself. How can she be so elegant? If she was vain
about anything it was about her cooking. Two things you
were never allowed to criticise – her marmalade and her
driving. Both, I always felt privately, left a good deal to
chance. But about everything else she was eminently reasonable. How good an actress she thought herself to be, how
seriously she took her profession, I was never sure. She acted
like she did everything else, naturally. But of one thing I
am very certain. She was immensely proud of the affection   227

and gratitude of her public: she answered every letter, she acknowledged every compliment and no day was too cold or too wet for her to pause as she came out of the stage door, or in later years the supermarket in Henley, to have a chat to a faithful patron who wished to compliment her on some past performance in the theatre or on the screen or on television or on just being Gladys Cooper.

From California we all, including Gladys, flew by seaplane to Honolulu and spent a month on its deserted beaches, deserted because of a shipping strike; then we went on to Sydney and she returned to the house on Napoli Drive to do *Madame Bovary*, one of Metro's rare brushes with the French classics. A starry cast was led by Jennifer Jones, Van Heflin, Louis Jourdan 'and' said the billing 'James Mason as Gustave Flaubert (the author)'. 'Less nauseating than many Hollywood attempts at the classics,' said the *Manchester Guardian*, and on that note Gladys ended her five years with Metro. She was to make five more films in Hollywood and three in Britain during the fifties and sixties.

Freed from Metro's clutches, she spent the winter of 1949 at Napoli Drive: her children John and Sally and her stepchildren Jack and Val joined her there and the two houses could still be used as the extended family home that Phil had first envisaged in the early 1940s, though not for much longer. Our generation of grandchildren were never really able to spend more time there, the children and stepchildren were increasingly to be caught up in their own careers and families, and Gladys herself would now be dividing her time almost equally between the little house there and the wooden riverside home (Barn Elms) she was soon to buy in Henley-on-Thames for her English visits.

She first found this when she came over at the beginning of 1950 to do *The Hat Trick*, a shaky cricketing comedy by Tom Browne which only ran for six weeks. 'What on earth,' asked Robert in G's dressing-room after the first night, 'made you choose this one?' 'Oh I don't know,' replied Gladys, 'I just thought it might be nice to be in London when you all got back from Australia.'

Gladys had now turned sixty but was in no frame of mind or financial situation to consider retirement: instead, after *The Hat Trick* closed, she flew back to Hollywood to warm over her

228 Mother Superior performance from *Bernadette* and give it again,

With Joan, Sheridan and Robert Morley in the sea off Waikiki Beach, Honolulu, 1948

in slightly less severe form, for a screen version of *Bonaventure* known in America rather curiously as *Thunder on the Hill*: 'I find Miss Cooper,' wrote the film critic of the *Spectator*, 'strangely cast. I confess I do not know a single nun, and yet an inner voice here prompts me to believe that neither she nor Miss Claudette Colbert is what you might call a nun type. Their natural sophistication can be smothered in serge up to a point, but their voices 229 sound strangely unholy. Ann Blyth doesn't seem all that holy either.'

But whatever Gladys was doing in *Bonaventure* was at least rather better than what she was doing next: a Cornel Wilde pot-boiler at RKO called variously *At Sword's Point* or *Sons of the Musketeers* and uniquely terrible in either guise.

What she needed, on stage or screen, in America or England, was a good script and the one that turned up, none too soon, was from and by her old friend and sparring partner from their pre-war years, Noël Coward. She had in the meantime decided not to do Robert's specially-written *Full Treatment*, considering that the part really wasn't quite good enough, and took herself for a brief holiday to Jamaica. Her passion for islands, preferably with sandy beaches and hot climates, had already led her to negotiate for an acre or two of Hawaii and now she was also to buy land in Jamaica which would lie there throughout the Fifties, a plot unbuilt but reserved against the day when she might feel like settling there and putting up some kind of house. She never did, and the plots of land were eventually sold off again, but on this first Jamaican visit in 1951 she was to find the island positively loaded with old friends: Ivor was there, a few months away from his death, and her old Playhouse designer Edward Molyneux, and John and Sally, and Bea Lillie, and Richard Haydn from Pacific Palisades, and Adrianne Allen and, wrote Gladys, 'a very nice brother of Peter Fleming's who seems to be writing a thriller'; the 'thriller' was *Casino Royale*, first of the James Bond books. This Jamaican winter was the last gathering of the pre-war showbusiness clans.

Back in New York by the middle of 1951 (the Californian house had been let to Peter Bull) she was wondering whether or not she could get the Edith Evans part in *Waters of the Moon* for Broadway, but seemed undecided about her career: so undecided in fact that she promptly returned to Jamaica to see if it was as nice in the summer as in the winter. It wasn't: 'We have just,' she wrote to Joan on August 20th, 'had the greatest hurricane in Jamaica's history: it has done sixteen million pounds worth of damage to houses and was most unpleasant, though Sally and I are all right! No electricity or water for five days and we shall all have to work to raise money for the different charities ... just like the war!'

230   When Gladys did finally get off the island and back to London,

it was to rehearse *Relative Values*, the new comedy by Noël Coward; she and the Master had renewed their friendship that previous Christmas in Jamaica, a friendship which now went back nearly forty years to their first uneasy meeting in Davos. In the interim they'd never actually worked together, though they had signed autographs side by side at innumerable first nights and charity garden parties. Cole Lesley, Noël's most constant friend and aide, remembers himself going to one of the Actor's Orphanage parties in the very early 1930s where G, one of his earliest idols, appeared to be handing out carnations. Coley, gazing in some awe at Gladys, took one and was about to depart when in stentorian tones she announced that the charge would be half a crown for charity. That left him just sixpence to get through the rest of the week, but he still has the carnation – pressed lovingly into a scrapbook and guarded across forty years.

Now she and Noël were to be working together for the first time, on the comedy he'd written the previous winter in Jamaica about Felicity, Countess of Marshwood who finds to her considerable horror that her son and heir is to marry a Hollywood film star who, as if that weren't ghastly enough, also turns out to be her maid's long-lost sister. The play was to give both Noël (who was also directing) and Gladys their first real success after a recent run of London disasters, and was to give Gladys not only her one great post-war triumph in the West End but also her first real success there since *The Shining Hour* almost twenty years earlier. But the joint victory did not come without a considerable struggle, as Cole Lesley relates:

A firm and enduring friendship had built itself up between Gladys and Noël, and this was now to be put to its severest test; Gladys could not learn her words and her part was enormously long. Especially in his comedy dialogue, not one of his carefully chosen words must be misplaced, or another word substituted, and to listen to Gladys stumbling became torture for Noël; counting rehearsals and the pre-London tour he suffered two-and-a-half months of this torture. Gladys, with her many years of stardom and experience, seldom actually dried up, but filled in the many gaps with *er, er, er*, which was even more painful to his ear. We went up to the opening night in Newcastle, in agony because of her insecurity, though she herself flew brilliantly through the play with every out-

231

ward sign of star-sized assurance . . . Theatres were packed all through the tour, but even as late as the week in Brighton, the list of Gladys's mistakes amounted during one performance to no less than twenty-eight including when, instead of saying she was going into the study, she announced that she was going into the understudy. Good trooper that she was, she rose word-perfect to the occasion of the first night in London, and she and the play got an ovation at the end.

This one and only joint Coward–Cooper venture opened on November 28th, 1951: 'a play that glitters and sparkles', wrote Alan Dent, and Harold Hobson added, 'what really matters in this play is the dowager Countess. To her Mr Coward has given the very best of his wit: and to this Miss Cooper has added the incisiveness of her attack and the brightest of her radiance. Marie Tempest herself was never more masterfully glittering than Miss Cooper in this play: it is a performance to draw the town and the country.'

And it did, for all of four hundred and seventy-seven performances.

chapter twenty-five

1952=1954

THOUGH she was to do a dozen later plays, never again in London (and only in New York with *The Chalk Garden*) did Gladys have the kind of tumultuous success she had with *Relative Values*: Noël's play re-established her as a leading player in the West End for those who had begun to think Californian sunstroke was affecting her choice of plays, and introduced her as an already *grande dame* to a whole new generation of theatre-goers. Her irritation with Noël in rehearsal ('Ridiculous' she'd said; 'he expects me to be word perfect at the very first run-through'; 'It's not the first run through I worry about,' retorted Noël. 'it's the first night') melted in the warmth of their shared success. It was during the tour, recalled Gladys later, that she became known once and forever to Noël as the Hag:

> We had a very enterprising publicity lady who was always sending round the local newspapers to photograph us. I photograph rather badly in stage makeup because I use a rather dark makeup which isn't good for cameras: the most hideous photographs of me were always appearing in local papers after we'd opened. One particularly revolting picture came out, and I got the usual sort of anonymous letter saying 'You old hag, why don't you go back to America?' so I told Noël who fell about with laughter. The night we opened I had

The last of her many homes: Barn Elms on the towpath at Henley-on-Thames

flowers from him and a note reading, 'Why don't you go back to America, you old hag, and take my play with you?'

In fact Gladys never did *Relative Values* on Broadway, reckoning that a year and a half in London was perhaps enough of a good thing; but while she was playing at the Savoy in the following year, Noël was to come into her life once more with, as she said later, 'an act of typical and tremendous generosity'. In February 1952 her son John, having just finished a highly successful and critically acclaimed Broadway run as the Dauphin in *St Joan*, had the worst and most violent of his mental breakdowns; after a chase through the streets of Manhattan he was arrested by police who charged him with felonious assault and the illegal possession of two knives which he was alleged to have brandished at the police.

The story broke in the English papers and for Gladys, having to play every night a light comedy five thousand miles away from her only son and in many ways the most loved of all her children, the strain was up to breaking point. The rest of the company, led by Judy Campbell and Angela Baddeley, gave what support they could, but sympathy was neither enough nor something that G could readily accept: she and Buck, together in London in their sixties as they had been in their twenties, took the view that what was wrong with their only son must be something physical and short-term rather than mental and lasting, and there was to be no dissuading them.

In New York, John was committed to the Bellevue Hospital for the criminally insane, from where his release was eventually engineered by Jack Merivale and Noël together with Adrianne Allen's second husband Bill Whitney: the Cooper ranks had closed and managed to get John out of immediate trouble on condition he left the United States forever, which he then did. Gladys's letter to Noël read simply, 'I shall never forget nor cease to be deeply, deeply grateful to you for all you have done. I am torn with anxiety and heartbroken by the knowledge of the unhappiness of my beloved John, but the Countess in your play is merry as a grig eight times a week . . . laugh, clown, laugh.'

By now she was living at Barn Elms in Henley, the Thameside house that was to become her last home; from there she would drive daily and at breakneck speed to the Savoy Theatre ('the only hope,' Philip had said, 'would be for us all to die in the car with her'). MGM had taken to providing a chauffeur and forbidding her to drive at all, a ban the family in England tried to impose on her without success until, at the very end of her life, she did give in and allow herself to be driven to the theatre. That was, for most of us, the first sign that the end was approaching.

But at this time Gladys still took considerable if misplaced pride in her driving: convertibles were what she liked best, preferably large American convertibles, which she could drive with the top down (even in an English autumn) and the radio blaring a kind of warning to oncoming traffic that they'd be advised to steer clear. Gladys steered anywhere but clear: several times she had criss-crossed the United States in this fashion, accompanied by increasingly nervous relatives and dogs until either Jack or Val would insist on doing the driving themselves. On these journeys Gladys seldom stopped for food or sleep, regarding such stops as signs of weakness: if you were going somewhere then you went there, and it was as simple as that. On one celebrated occasion after she'd been driving for about two days and nights even she felt the need of refreshment and stopped at a motel where she discovered that the entire dining-room had been taken over for the annual dinner of General Motors. Other non-car workers were being turned away: not G, who sent for the head waiter. 'You won't know me,' she explained, 'but I'm an old English actress and I happen to be a great friend of the General's, who would like me to eat here.' She got a table.

That was one of the other remarkable things about Gladys: she could never see alternatives or possible defeats; she ruled out 'either/or' decisions just as she ruled out of her life the things that didn't suit her – illness, exhaustion, fear, old age, loneliness, failure, were things that didn't suit her and that therefore she refused to acknowledge. It was in a way a charmed life, but the charm was all of her own making: luck, she once told me, is something you make happen, not something that just does of its own accord.

The rest of 1952 she spent in England, playing *Relative Values* and building herself a new life around Henley: Gracie, her born-deaf sister, was now living with her again, as was Sally between theatre and other engagements. Her other daughter Joan was living five miles away in Wargrave where there was now a new and third Morley grandchild, Wilton, available for inspections and the occasional outing. Gradually, in the years that followed, the whole family was to congregate around Gladys: when Sally married, when I married, and when her stepdaughter Rosamund came home from Canada in the early sixties, we all instinctively settled in houses within a ten-mile radius of Barn Elms and that house, her house, was soon just as full of dogs and children and cats and ducks and visiting friends as ever Charlwood or The Grove or Napoli Drive had been.

There was the beginning of a feeling now that G was coming home to stay; though she was not in fact to give up Napoli Drive completely for another ten years, more and more of her time would be spent in Henley as Hollywood closed up around her. The woman who had once been the very height of Molyneux fashion now seemed to take no interest at all in her appearance and yet to remain incredibly elegant, even when wearing shifts and a curious hat she'd bought for ninety-nine cents in a Toronto Woolworth's, when she'd suddenly remembered she was going to meet the Queen Mother at the races there. True the face was lined now, wrinkled by the Californian and Jamaican sun, but the

236

cheekbones were high and the backbone was erect and she was looking, as always, straight ahead and remarkable.

Even had she been an introspective lady, and she was anything but that, there was a lot to be said now for not looking too deeply inside herself: privately she'd lost, in different ways, the two men (Philip and John) who mattered to her most, and publicly she was finding it increasingly hard to sustain her interest in a career which had always lacked the classical distinction of a Thorndike or an Evans. Not that the career itself was in much trouble: merely her own feeling of commitment to it. Other things, as Guthrie had said of G before the war, always seemed to matter to her so much more than acting ever did.

She had, as her stepdaughter Rosamund once pointed out, an extraordinary ability to hold families together: Coopers, Merivales, Morleys and eventually Hardys (for Sally, like her sister, was also to marry an actor called Robert) were held together during her lifetime by the shared experience of her energies and enthusiasms, and relationships that might eventually have soured were kept fresh and loving by her splendid ability to disappear across oceans before anyone could ever tire of her. Deep down, I think she was still Peter Pan.

Her interest in gardening was now rewarded by the naming of a Gladys Cooper tulip, a tough little bloom that used to come

The naming of the Gladys Cooper tulip, Chessington, 1951

up time after time much like her, but a couple of English winters had been enough for her and so, when *Relative Values* closed, she took herself back to Jamaica for the Christmas of 1952. There was now a certain amount of doubt in her own mind as to where she belonged: England was where the family now all seemed to be living, but in America (despite *Relative Values*) she was still in some ways a better name and a bigger star thanks to the continued after-effects of various MGM campaigns. Then there was Jamaica, where she still planned to build a house one day, and Canada where she would visit her stepdaughter Rosamund and her two young daughters.

There no longer seemed to be any films on offer now that Metro had dropped their option on her contract, but she was getting occasional one-shot television plays on both sides of the Atlantic (her TV debut had been for the BBC in 1950 as the Queen Mother in Rattigan's *Adventure Story*) and by the beginning of 1953 there was talk of another play in the West End.

This was *A Question of Fact*, Wynyard Browne's first since *The Holly and the Ivy*: the story of a public schoolmaster discovering that his father has been hanged for murder offered strong dramatic roles to Paul Scofield (as the schoolmaster) and Pamela Brown and G as, respectively, his wife and mother. Gladys didn't in fact come on until the middle of the second act, and somewhat unnerved Pamela Brown at the dress rehearsal by going up to her in the first interval and saying, 'That was lovely, dear; I'd always wondered what the first act was about, perhaps I should have read it.' Paul Scofield remembers:

> An extraordinary relaxation: Gladys had style and zest but her relaxation and her beauty were what made her stage quality so special. She was like a superb athlete, always apparently at a peak of health and energy and always seeming to enjoy every moment of her hours on the stage, though always one felt that what mattered most to her was her family life away from the theatre. I loved this about her, as it didn't seem to detract from her skill. Sometimes we'd talk about her old days at the Playhouse, and it all sounded so carefree and insouciant and beautifully light-hearted – 'I didn't like the designer's cushions,' she'd say, 'so I brought my own from home.' And then going straight back to a game of poker in the greenroom after coming off stage. It wasn't

238

that she had no nerves at all, it was that she also had an athlete's relaxation and control. She was very sensitive to act with, responsive to any small unexpected change, and somehow delighted with the interchange of thought, her eyes huge and happy. She was so relaxed that, apart from the evidence of her immaculately groomed appearance, she seemed entirely unselfconscious: she made her first entrance on the first night still sucking a Polo mint she'd forgotten to take out of her mouth, so that on her first line it shot straight out across the stage and she didn't bat an eyelid. I really did love her.

Frith Banbury, the play's director, found himself in her dressing-room one hot summer afternoon about six months into the run:

She suddenly turned to me and said, 'You know, I really hate acting,' and I said, 'If you hate it, how come that you do it so well?' and she said, 'Well, I have to do what I can do to the best of my ability. The only thing I know how to do is act, so I have to do that as well as I possibly can.' We ran about eight months and I would say that of all the big stars I ever worked with, she was the one who most consistently gave full value for money at every performance. I used to go in now and again to watch: her performance hardly varied at all: I think this was because she regarded it as a duty, as a job that had to be done. Whether one actually liked doing it or not was beside the point. Personally, I'm inclined to think that she was a very much better actress than she ever gave herself credit for.

A Question of Fact took Gladys through most of 1954, and when the run at the Piccadilly came to an end she went into one of her rare English films: a Rattigan screenplay based on his comedy *Who Is Sylvia?* but called for the cinema *The Man Who Loved Redheads*. In neither incarnation was this a success, though G did have one touchingly-written scene as the wife of an ageing rake played by John Justin.

What she lacked now in her professional life was any real sense of purpose: always before there had been children to bring up, or the Playhouse to keep going, or the Californian house to pay for. Now the work was just there to be done, and this perhaps more   239 than anything else accounted for an increasing inclination to repeat with a certain mechanical precision her more successful performances. She could still be, as T. C. Worsley had once written, as finely tuned as any other musical instrument; but there were not many good new notes to play.

Lonsdale died in that year, another reminder for Gladys that the old days were fast drawing in, and she wrote a touching *Times* obituary for him: 'By the small circle of his intimate friends to which I had the privilege of belonging, Freddy will indeed be sadly missed ... of all the men I have known in the theatre who achieved dazzling success, he remained the least dazzled. He was also a born diplomat: during rehearsals of *Cheyney*, when a discussion went on (as it did most of the time) about whether Gerald du Maurier or I had the better part, he tactfully told some people that I had and others that Gerald had. The one who really had the best part in that play was Ronald Squire; as, of course, the author knew all the time.'

There was a temptation, even then, to recall in conversation the best rather than the worst of Gladys; Robert would therefore try occasionally to list the things that others would find most objectionable about her:

'Love me, love my family' is one of Gladys's favourite mottoes. She carts us round with her, and is frankly astonished at the consternation she causes at the dinner tables of her friends and acquaintances. One might suppose that by now they would be prepared for the invasion, but they seem never to be. 'I knew you wouldn't mind,' she says, 'so I've brought Jack, John, Sally, Val, Joan, Robert and Sheridan. Annabel couldn't come, I'm afraid; in any case, she is rather young for dinner parties.' Our hosts do what they can. 'I know I shouldn't say it,' says Gladys once we've left, 'but I didn't think there was quite enough dinner. It's my one meal in the day and I am still hungry. I wonder if it's too late to go and look up Mabel? She can't have seen Sally since she was a baby.' It is useless then for Sally to suggest that perhaps Mabel hasn't wanted to. Gladys, her children, her step-children, her grandchildren and her in-laws are not only welcome but eagerly awaited at any time anywhere – at least in Gladys's opinion. Combined with this persistent optimism as to her eventual welcome is her persistent habit of coming

240

upon policemen unexpectedly – unexpectedly, that is, as far as she is concerned. The policeman has usually observed her approach from a considerable distance and has just had the time to take necessary steps to save life and limb. It is at such moments that Gladys is superb. Before the policeman has had time to enquire whether she knows that this is a one-way street going the other way, or expostulate with her as to the speed of her approach, she welcomes him as an old and trusted ally. 'Just the man I wanted to see: how thoughtful of you to be standing there. I am on my way to Brighton, rather late for a matinee; if you were me, how would you go?' In a moment the policeman is sitting beside her, conducting her through the traffic and on to the Brighton road.

Back in the 1920s there had been an old music-hall song which started, eccentrically enough.

> *'He's only a fly*
> *You can swear like a trooper*
> *But he can do the Charleston*
> *On the face of Gladys Cooper.*
> *Could Lloyd George do it?*
> *Could Ramsay do it?*
> *Could Churchill do it?*
> *Why, no, no, no!'*

Nobody was doing the Charleston much in 1954; Ramsay was dead, and so was Lloyd George. Gladys and Churchill were however still very much around.

chapter twenty-six

1954-1957

GLADYS spent her sixty-sixth birthday that year, 1954, doing a BBC radio production of her old *Second Mrs Tanqueray*: from there she went straight into rehearsal for a new play by Michael Burn called *The Night of the Ball*. A starry cast (Wendy Hiller, Tony Britton, Robert Harris, Jill Bennett) were directed by Joseph Losey who seemed to a number of the company distinctly out of sympathy with a play which the *Guardian* described as 'a sumptuous Pinero plot heavily overlaid with Chekhovian sympathy'. *The Times* wished the whole thing could have been turned into an Ivor Novello musical, and other papers objected to 'such meaningless splendour' while Milton Shulman thought it 'a period piece of the wrong period and a problem play about no definable problem'. All in all, it was not much of a way for Gladys to begin her fiftieth year on the stage.

The play was remarkable for one thing, though, and that was the start of Gladys's friendship with Wendy Hiller, a friendship that was to be one of the closest and most enduring of her later years.

One of the most intriguing things about Gladys [says Dame Wendy now], was the way that unlike most people she grew warmer as she got older. I remember her first as a rather distant, glittering, shimmering figure but she seemed then to

242

Back to the West End: with Jill Bennett in Night of the Ball, *New Theatre, 1955*

acquire a kind of patience, an ability to live with ordinary mortals and not be as impatient of them as she once had been. She still wasn't able to give her private self away, if there ever was a private self, but she 'gentled' a lot. Doing the *Night of the Ball* tour became an occasion because of Gladys: one night coming out of the stage door she was for some reason carrying a whole lot of bath buns and cottage loaves, and somebody asked for her autograph, so as I was standing behind her I said, 'Madam, let me hold the bread,' and after that I always called her Madam and she called me Frobisher because she thought that a suitable name for her maid.

243

They opened at the New Theatre in January and were off by March, but by then Gladys knew that she had something better lying ahead – the role of Mrs St Maugham in Enid Bagnold's *The Chalk Garden*, a new and autumnal comedy (or possibly a Chekhovian thriller, depending on which side of the Atlantic you saw it) which was to give G her greatest post-war success on Broadway and, briefly, in the West End as well.

George Cukor, the pre-eminent 'woman's director' and a long-time fan of G's, was hired to direct *The Chalk Garden*; Siobhan McKenna was to play the sinister governess Miss Madrigal, and rehearsals started in New York in an August heatwave. All, as Miss Bagnold was to relate, did not go well:

> Before the first rehearsal Gladys had called me Enid. After it, Miss Bagnold. Later, Lady Jones. As I ascended in social position and went down in contempt I realised she had classed me as a social character who by luck (and possibly ghosted) had got some fool to put on my play. And as my oddly-contrived words were appalling to memorize, I believe she said on the telephone to New York (during the Boston or Philadelphia try-out) 'We're out here in a lot of nonsense!' I forgive her.
>
> Now Gladys is an old hand. She had owned her own theatre; she had been in management. We were about the same age but I was inexperienced. We were both positive characters and I annoyed her from the start.

Things went from bad to worse: though Cukor was happy with Gladys, after a brief row with the management he departed in mid-rehearsal. While they were casting around for another director Bagnold herself took a hand:

> I was put on to the stage. 'Lady Jones' – God help me. I eyed Gladys. For the moment she didn't speak. What I knew I could do was what I had longed to do – point out meanings mislaid here and there. Deep things not said lightly. I was surprised at the response I got. Siobhan understood half an indication. How quick they are, actors, once they have got over the muddle of the first week. But suddenly (Gladys's voice) 'Goodbye!' (from the wings). 'See you on the First Night!'

G had always taken the view that playwrights rated somewhere in the theatre hierarchy above the night fireman but not much: Maugham had never had the impertinence to interfere with the way she did his plays, so thirty years later she was hardly likely to take notes from Bagnold. Another director was found (Albert Marre, whom Bagnold didn't much care for: 'his name is on the programme for ever. Like an Augustus John signed by Landseer') and the pre-Broadway tour continued amid sustained quarrelling. Beaton's set was considered to be too white, there were nights when it seemed as usual that Gladys was never going to learn it, and when they opened at the Ethel Barrymore in New York on October 26th, 1955 and found themselves the greatest smash hit of that Broadway season, nobody seemed more surprised than the author herself:

> The curtain went up – and *who* had written that dancing play? That play I hadn't seen yet. Gladys 'knew her words'. But oh, so much more than that! It was a gay, enjoying Gladys, the difficult, halting words running like liquid amber, her timing magical, with a golden authority for laughter, the right laughter. The chuckle that says to itself: 'I know, I know!' It was a balloon of a play. It rose in the warm air to the ceiling.
>
> At one of the intervals I heard Noël Coward get up in the stalls and say to a woman with him: 'For those who love words, darling! For those who love words . . .' It was Gladys's evening. Did I get to her dressing-room? I can't remember. I think I didn't: I was afraid she'd throw me out.

The *New Yorker* wrote of G's 'wonderful exhibition of scatter-brained sophistication' and for the first and last time in her long career she was the toast of that particular city: *The Chalk Garden* ran through to April 1956 by which time it had already opened in London (with Edith Evans and Peggy Ashcroft in the roles created by G and Siobhan McKenna) where Tynan called it, 'the finest artificial comedy to have flowed from an English pen since the death of Congreve'.

Gladys stayed in New York for the summer, doing a couple of television dramas for NBC; then, in August, while she was staying with Rex Harrison on Long Island, came an agonized phone call from Binkie Beaumont of the H.M. Tennent management in   245

London. Dame Edith Evans had been taken suddenly ill, was out of *The Chalk Garden* and would be for several more weeks: could Gladys take it over for a while? A trooper to the last, she was on the next plane out of New York, clutching the dresses Beaton had designed for her. The next morning the English director of the play, John Gielgud, met her at the theatre:

> She had been flying all night, but she came in to look at the set and meet the English cast: we'd already had the understudy on for a night or two, and I asked Gladys when she'd like to start, thinking she'd say in about a week. She looked at me in blank amazement: 'Tonight, of course; that's why I've come.' She went straight to the hairdresser, was back by 2.30, we had one dress rehearsal and that was that. She winged her way through the Monday night like an elegant bull in a china shop and in her dressing-room after the curtain had come down she said, 'I see exactly what the problem is: we played it in New York as the House of Cuckoos and you've done it as the House of Regrets. I'll start rehearsing it your way in the morning.' And she did.

Gladys played on for six more weeks at the Haymarket and revived the play there at the end of her life; despite its initial teething troubles and the early quarrels with Bagnold, the two ladies were to become firm friends later and the play remained Gladys's favourite of all her post-war work – she bitterly minded losing the role in the (as it turned out, appalling) film to Edith Evans, particularly as she was for several months under the impression that it had been promised to her.

She continued to play the part of Mrs St Maugham on the road in America for nearly a year after her brief Haymarket take-over, and worked with a number of stage grand-daughters of whom her favourite was undoubtedly Judith Stott. But it was the actress who created the role in America, Betsy von Furstenberg, who wrote (for the *New York Times* when Gladys died) one of the most touching of all the accounts of what it had been like to work with her:

> I only knew Gladys when she was already old – old in years, for she was not old in any conventional sense. She was totally enviable – her vitality, her beauty, her astuteness. If one

could grow more like Gladys as one grew older, then growing old would be desirable. When I met her, she was starring with Siobhan McKenna in *The Chalk Garden* and I, who had just had my first child, was playing her incorrigible fourteen-year-old grand-daughter. She was Grandloo and I was Laurel, and that was the only play that has entirely lived up to what I expected from the theater. We walked in an enchanted land and, to me at least, it was not work, not that play. Gladys would come on stage and whisper to me the results of the *64 Dollar Question* which was on the TV in her dressing-room, and it didn't break the spell. And when something funny happened, she'd squeeze my hand hard to keep us from breaking up. I remember her touch as distinctly as I remember my mother's. Gladys's was a cool, dry hand full of firm affection. I adored her and I idolised her – but, then, everyone I know who knew her feels the same way. We shared an affinity for Welsh corgis and pale colors of unusual hues – and yoghurt, preferably in the jar. Gladys thought nothing of driving across the country by herself. She didn't pamper her looks or avoid the sun. But the lines that she had didn't mar her beauty a bit – it was strong, and the sun and wind suited it. I guess the most characteristic thing about how Gladys looked was the way she carried her head – up and jutted slightly forward. She had enormous deep blue eyes full of intelligence and ready for mischief, for Gladys at her most dignified was never above a giggle. She was neither petty nor clumsy nor nagging. She had largesse. Hers was the definite decision – utter rejection or complete acceptance, but always accepting life as it came, realistically, with enthusiasm and a grain of salt . . . in my copy of *The Chalk Garden* Gladys wrote to me, 'She is like a flower,' a quote from the play. I return the compliment now – *she* was like a flower, a strong beautiful rose, in those dusty pink hues that became her so.

All told, Gladys was to play *The Chalk Garden* for more than two of her last fifteen years; she'd tour it around, pausing briefly for other projects. She was beginning to do several one-shot television dramas now in New York or London or Toronto, often plays like *Waters of the Moon* which she'd always wanted to do in the theatre, and she'd pause for occasional holidays with friends and/or relatives across North America. Staying with her

247

stepdaughter Rosamund in Canada around this time, she decided that even a fortnight was too long to be utterly idle and enrolled in a downtown business school for a typing course, so that her other relatives might at last be able to read her letters to them. She left, however, when the instructor objected to the length of her fingernails.

As she approached her seventieth birthday, Gladys was slipping now into the role of a Grande Dame: the actual title wasn't to be hers for another decade, and like Thorndike she retained a kind of brisk efficiency in and out of the theatre which precluded too much awe in others. Her refusal to think of the theatre in terms other than 'going to work' meant that her career now lacked the classical dignity of her contemporary Dames, and though I believe there was a large amount of very good work that she could have been doing in the dowager line in these years, the younger generation of directors and playwrights had grown up in her Californian absence and were inclined to think of her too seldom and for too little. As a result, she ended up in a considerable amount of theatrical rubbish including, early in 1957, a uniquely disastrous musical called *The Crystal Heart*.

Almost everything that could go wrong here did so: *The Crystal Heart* was an ambitious and (for its time) expensive show costing over thirty thousand pounds. For it, Gladys, in a plot of such stunning banality that I have miraculously managed to forget it, was required to both sing and dance; the fact that she'd done neither since her days at the Gaiety half a century earlier seemed not to alarm anyone, least of all Gladys. On the tour, during a strenuous dance routine, she cracked a bone in her chest which meant that she opened at the Saville on painkillers. The first night was not a success; it was indeed one of the rare postwar occasions on which a West End show has been booed not only at curtain fall but a long time before it. 'Like watching Christians thrown to the lions,' wrote Shulman in the *Standard*. 'What a lovely afternoon,' said Dilys Laye, on stage. 'Not a very lovely evening,' came the reply from the gallery. The cast battled on; Gladys did a song about a Bluebird (a singularly unfortunate choice) and finally won the evening on points, though it was a near thing. 'Gladys Cooper,' wrote Harold Hobson in the following *Sunday Times* (by which time the show had closed after only five performances) 'responded to the audience's catcalls with magnificent venom. At the close, such victory as there was lay with her for the tremendous curtsy, defiant, lovely and imperial, with which, like a spirited Miranda kneeling to Caliban, she provocatively challenged the theatre.'

Sharing Noël Coward's belief that the great thing to do after a flop is to sail away, G returned to California: in these last two decades of her life she was to spend nearly as much time crossing the Atlantic as on either side of it, but the Californian sun was still a powerful magnet. A good many of her older friends were now dying off or departing from there, but she was still capable of new friendships. Her devotion to a good male profile was as strong as it ever had been, and among the new generation of actors whom she befriended at this time were Paul Newman and Dirk Bogarde, who recalls:

> She had all the charm of an electric carving knife: she was precise, hard, efficient, very cool, very beautiful and I was terrified of her. She once hit me on the head for talking too much, and yet we did manage to become very great friends. Perhaps that was because we never had to work together. I loathed Hollywood, but she loved it: she loved being warm, and swimming, and she had a house where she collected the English, like a sort of colony: but by now the people she'd known were all disappearing and they were lowering the Union Jack and I don't think she liked the new Hollywood, the radio and television city, nearly as well as the old studio city she'd known. She had a passion for making marmalade and chutney, and I always knew her as the Marmalade Aunt: one of her more curious habits was cooking a lot and eating very little, so you'd find yourself having a meal of hers while she was swallowing a carton of yoghurt in the kitchen.
>
> But what she liked best about California was that she could live entirely out of doors: cooking at the barbecue, swimming, gardening, driving with the roof down. She'd hardly ever talk about her work, or indeed mine, though she did say that she'd once seen me in a film and thought my head was too small.
>
> I never saw her in England looking quite as radiantly happy as she could be in California when the sun was shining: she hung on to that house as long as she dared, until she was almost eighty, and later in England when it was raining and there was a fire to light and the grandchildren to look after at Henley she'd sometimes catch my eye, and I knew she was thinking about California.

Terence Rattigan's all-star cast for the film of Separate Tables: *Gladys, Wendy Hiller, David Niven, Deborah Kerr, Rita Hayworth, Burt Lancaster and (above them) Felix Aylmer and Kathleen Nesbitt*

There was a baby alligator at Napoli Drive to look after now, and a mynah bird, and the chance of another film, this one rather more distinguished than her last half-dozen: Rattigan's stage success *Separate Tables*, in which she was to play Mrs Railton-Bell, the part of the domineering mother created on the stage by Phyllis Neilson-Terry. Rattigan's two one-act plays were to be telescoped into one ninety-minute film, and though the demands of the domestic American box-office meant that Burt Lancaster and Rita Hayworth had to be cast, disastrously, in two of the leading roles, the rest of the casting made the film the last great united stand of the Hollywood English: Deborah Kerr, David Niven, Gladys and Cathleen Nesbitt were joined by Wendy Hiller, Felix Aylmer, and May Hallatt from the original stage production. The result, said John McCarten in the *New Yorker* was, 'a dilapidated version of one of those segmented, portmanteau dramas like *Grand Hotel*'. Other critics thought it fell uneasily between stage and screen, England (its original setting was a south-coast hotel) and America, and Derek Prouse for the *Sunday Times* concluded that 'Bournemouth, California looks to me like a pretty bleak place'.

Yet the film did well at the box-office, it won both Wendy Hiller and David Niven Academy Awards and managed to retain a certain distinction: during the shooting of his big scene Niven looked up to see Gladys, Wendy, Cathleen and Aylmer all watching him. 'Tried by a jury of my peers,' he wrote, 'and found guilty.'

During the filming, Cathleen Nesbitt went to stay at Napoli Drive with Gladys; physically not unalike, and both destined to live well into their eighties, their paths were only professionally to cross for this one film and one television play, though both were at different times to play Mrs Higgins in *My Fair Lady* and Mrs St Maugham in *The Chalk Garden*, Cathleen Nesbitt finishing the last tour when G's illness made it impossible for her to go on.

> She was the only woman [says Cathleen Nesbitt] I have ever managed to stay with and not quarrel: she knew how to leave one alone as a guest and that was a great art. Every morning when I woke up she'd already be in the pool, and she managed to pay for the heating of it by the overtime on *Separate Tables*. 'Goody goody,' she'd say as we did another retake, 'more money for the pool.' She was a most unconceited woman

251

not overburdened with a sense of humour but warm and very, very helpful if you were in any kind of immediate trouble.

She didn't tolerate fools gladly [says Wendy Hiller, with G on this film and soon to be in another play with her] so the great thing when she was around was to avoid being foolish. There was never any quiet around her, and she amazingly never seemed to need a nap: I used to call her the Silver Dynamo. We outnumbered the Americans on the set 9 to 2, which was just as well as Gladys never knew a line and it was all Burt Lancaster's own money that we were using up with the re-takes. As soon as he and Rita Hayworth went into their scenes Gladys used to take off her glasses and fall into a deep sleep in a corner of the set, which I did think was rather naughty and certainly used to unnerve Rita, a poor darling dancing girl who was already rather lost in the film.

Deborah Kerr, whose only film with Gladys this was, once asked her on the set what she thought of the then-fashionable Method school of acting. 'I don't understand it, dear; one just goes on and one is, that's all there is to acting.'

chapter twenty-seven

1957-1961

F OLLOWING *Separate Tables* she did a day or two as the
Mother Superior in a catastrophic Carroll Baker film version of
The Miracle, mercifully never given a wide release, and then
spent a happy summer at the La Jolla Playhouse in San Diego, a
theatre she was often to work at during her last few Californian
summers, sometimes in dramatized readings (*Under Milk Wood*
was one such) sometimes in fully-fledged productions: this year it
was Graham Greene's *The Potting Shed*, playing the part Sybil
Thorndike had recently created for Broadway.

Then it was time to return to Henley, where there was now a
new figure in her life, and the last of the really important ones –
the actor soon to marry her daughter Sally, Robert Hardy:

> I expected to meet something extraordinary in the way of a
> personality, having only ever seen her on the stage in plays
> like *A Question of Fact* where she made me cry immoderately,
> and I suspect the rest of the audience too; and so I was a little
> bit frightened when first we met, though the fright disap-
> peared almost straight away. She came across the room with
> her arms out, as ever, and I was made to feel absolutely and
> perfectly at home. We talked, I remember, for some reason
> about animals and how she loved them: I asked her once how 253

she could then bring herself to wear mink and she said, 'Because they're such disgusting little creatures, but I'd never wear leopard.'

I also remember that first weekend a feeling, curiously enough, of her loneliness: we were all there, Sally and Gracie and I, and she was busy and brilliant and joyous and yet I was very conscious that here was a woman who had trained herself to manage on her own. She never depended on other people to the extent that most of us do; she adored other people and enjoyed them, but she could live alone.

I was still married at the time to my first wife, and Gladys didn't altogether approve of my friendship with her daughter so we used to have occasional terrible rows: she was never going to make it easy for people. I remember at the end of one of those rows her suddenly and heartbreakingly saying, 'All my life I've had to try and live independently, and make my own decisions, and that's why I am now perhaps a rather difficult person to live with.' But we got along together marvellously after Sally and I married and had our two daughters, Emma and Justine: they with her had something very magical going, something I don't really understand, but they were closeted together in the last years of her life a very great deal and she would pass on herself to them in all sorts of ways, the ways that old Victorian nannies and grand-mothers would pass themselves on to another generation with rhymes and stories and games.

When Emma was christened we invited her grandfather, Neville Pearson, whom Gladys hadn't seen or spoken to for thirty years since their divorce, to come to the service and after it he went over to talk to Gladys and the two of them seemed to be getting along marvellously. After he'd gone Gladys turned to me and said, 'Such a nice old man: who was he?' and to this day I've never known whether or not she was serious.

The first thing Gladys did back in London after *Separate Tables* was a rather fey comedy by Judy Campbell (writing as 'J. M. Fulton') called *The Bright One* about a schoolmistress on a Greek tour who finds that her body has become inhabited by the goddess Phaea. 'The whole affair,' wrote Milton Shulman when they opened at the disastrously large Winter Garden on Decem-

With Sally and her daughters Emma and Justine Hardy, Henley, 1967

ber 10th, 1958, 'is coated with such a thick crust of sugary whimsy that it could well prove a dangerous evening for diabetics.'

The director of *The Bright One* was Rex Harrison, working on it in between eight performances a week at Drury Lane in *My Fair Lady*, and playing the star role of the schoolmistress was his then wife Kay Kendall. Like Vivien Leigh, she was a lady for whom Gladys had a rather special affection; all three of them had after all spent much of their careers trying to persuade audiences and critics that they could act as well as they looked. But what Gladys knew now, because Rex Harrison had told her and almost no one else, was that Kay Kendall was dying of leukaemia: she had indeed less than another year to live, and it was partly to keep her occupied and from discovering the truth that he had put her into this play.

Miss Kendall gave, on the first night, a performance of iridescent magic and charm but it wasn't enough to save a hopelessly   255 flawed last act and, despite Mr Harrison's protests, and indeed a certain amount of his own money, the Jack Minster management whipped the play off within ten days. It was to be Miss Kendall's last appearance on the stage.

Then it was back to California, to see how the house was and which of the old friends were still there: Isherwood, she found, and Don Bachardy who made her the subject of one of his first portrait drawings; but increasingly now she was inclined to spend only a few weeks a year in California before travelling on to more exotic locations, accompanied as often as not by Robert Morley:

> I have flown with her in small aeroplanes across the Pacific. I have been driven by her across the High Sierras in a car which either she didn't understand or which didn't want to understand her. I have even watched from what I hoped was a safe distance while she photographed a particularly grizzly bear in close-up. Miss Cooper is a great one with a camera. Normally she shoots her subjects from a distance: she is essentially a background girl. As we sit afterwards looking at the results it is seldom possible to identify the tiny figure seated at the café table or waving from the water's edge: 'I think,' she will remark, 'that must be Cyril Ritchard . . . or James Mason . . . oh no, of course not, it's Irene Dunne.' But on this particular occasion she marched right up to the bear with her camera and almost looked down its throat. I don't remember how the bear came out. As usual, I came out rather badly, staying in the car and rolling up all the windows so that I would be unable to hear her cries for help and thus at least have saved my own skin. 'I wasn't frightened,' I lied to her as she got back in the car having taken her close-up of the bear, 'I was just obeying the notice. It says DO NOT LEAVE YOUR CAR DO NOT APPROACH THE BEARS.' 'If you are going to take any notice of notices,' said Gladys, 'it will quite spoil my holiday.'

A few weeks later we were walking together along a beach in Acapulco when we came upon a high wall which enclosed a large villa standing by itself on a small cliff overlooking the Pacific. 'We must find out who lives here,' said Gladys, 'it's just the kind of house I should like to build for myself one day.' We climbed up the little path. Immediately a dog started to bark. 'You're not thinking of going in?' I asked nervously. 'Just a dog,' said Gladys, 'doing his job of guarding the house,' and in that voice she reserves exclusively for animals, be they crododiles, hamsters or monkeys, she attempted to quiet the invisible watchdog. Then, having signally failed to reassure either the dog or myself, she pushed open the gate. She was about to enter when the sound of rifle shots caused her to pause. I don't know to this day who fired at her: I had taken to my heels and was by then running into the sea.

1960 brought Gladys back to London to do a play called *Look On Tempests* which was to give Vanessa Redgrave her first good starring role in the West End. Joan Henry's plot, courageously for its time, considered the effects on a wife (Vanessa) and a mother (Gladys) of a man's trial for homosexual assault, and though it was not to prove a great commercial success, this was undoubtedly one of the better plays of G's postwar years. In Vanessa at that time she recognized a faintly kindred spirit: a woman of courage and tenacity setting out on the career she too had chosen, though she would I suspect have had rather less sympathy for the later Miss Redgrave: Gladys's politics were of a hazy kind, though she was a staunch monarchist who believed in larger-than-life leaders. Churchill was thus a hero more for his size than his politics, and she had little time for minor or local differences of political opinion. Kennedy she approved of because he looked and sounded good, and had the sense to get a decent haircut. Gladys was conservative rather than Conservative, but her instincts were quirkily personal: Nancy Mitford took the view that both G and Robert (Morley) were undoubtedly Communist, though in truth any politician who'd stood on a platform of wildlife preservation and no speed limits for motorways could certainly have won her vote.

Reviews for both Gladys and Vanessa Redgrave were very good indeed, but there was a distinct hostility at that time to the play's theme and they were off within a month which meant that not one of Gladys's last three London shows (*Look On Tempests, The Bright One, The Crystal Heart*) had survived four weeks on stage. Other ladies of seventy-one might have taken what seemed now to be a fairly loud hint and given up the ghost: but then Gladys was not other ladies.

Retirement, she told a *Sunday Times* reporter, was not 257

With a young Vanessa Redgrave in Look on Tempests, *Comedy Theatre, 1960*

possible: 'I have neither the money nor the inclination for it': instead she went back to California where she picked up a little television work and a summer season at the La Jolla Playhouse and spent a happy few months by the pool debating whether or not to join a scheme for the mass adoption of homeless ducks. By now she'd acquired so many parking or speeding tickets out there that the Beverly Hills police were threatening to take her car away, but apart from that her life there was much as it always had been: barbecues by the pool for visiting English actors and relatives and friends, shopping at the Farmer's Market, doing a few days at the studios whenever the offers came along.

She began to feel now, perhaps rightly, that in California she was at least appreciated: not only was her acting better paid out there but it was also, in the nature of television, not subject to overnight reviews or closure the following Saturday. She took to television drama like one of her own ducks to water: short takes meant not having to learn a great many lines all at once, and there was now a kind of reverence for Gladys around Hollywood which she was never really to find at the end of her life in London.

There was also not a great deal at this time to keep her even privately in England: Sally had not yet had the two daughters who were to be the last great joys of G's life and yet both she and Joan were wrapped up in their own marriages and John was now settled into the clinic where he would spend the latter half of his life refusing to see either of his parents, both of whom he blamed for his breakdowns. Yet even had John not cracked, children in their thirties and forties and fifties were not the kind of children with whom Gladys could make a life; of her Merivale step-children, David had been killed in Africa, Val had recently died of cancer and the other two were leading their own separate existences: Rosamund married with her own children in Canada, Jack now living with Vivien Leigh. The rest of us, the grand-children, were still in school or college which just left her two sisters: Gracie of course, who still lived most of her life with Gladys in an increasingly irritable yet deeply loving relationship, and Doris with whom Gladys had quarrelled some years earlier, a quarrel that was sadly never to be fully made up.

With the exception of Gracie, whose stone deafness since birth G had now taken to regarding as a sort of eccentric front ('she could hear perfectly well if only she'd try harder' I once heard her tell an astonished doctor) there was thus now nobody who really   259 depended on Gladys for their existence: everybody else seemed to be leading lives of their own in which, though constantly welcome and much loved, G could never really play the leading role she'd been so accustomed to playing for so many years. A lady who believed deeply in independence, she had nevertheless acquired through her life a varying but generally large number of dependants and, now that they had almost all fallen away from her for one reason or another, she felt strangely rootless, going wherever the wind blew her and hoping only that it was going to be sunny when she arrived.

One of the most touching and magical things about Gladys in this last decade of her life was the renewal of her friendship with her first husband: Buck too had been thrice married, he too had lost one partner through early and unexpected death and now, though still married to his third wife Grace, he was in fact living alone, back at his club. There he would give Gladys lunch whenever she was in town, arrange parties to celebrate her first nights, and generally behave towards her not as an ex-husband (they had been divorced all of forty years) but as an intensely proud elder brother. Though now on the verge of his eightieth birthday and virtually crippled by arthritis he still ran Buck's Club with a rule of iron, prodding less favoured members in the ribs with one of his sticks; but to see him there in the 1960s, lunching with Gladys and starting one of those endlessly circular conversations about friends they could neither of them now quite recollect, is one of the most joyous of all my grandparental memories.

Early in 1961, she came home for another play: called *The Bird of Time*, it was an account of two women (Gladys and the late Diana Wynyard) living out their lives alone on neighbouring houseboats in India after their British compatriates and governors have all departed. Memories of Maugham and all the work Gladys had done with him were never far from the surface here, but despite some generally disdainful reviews the play was strong enough to last out the summer at the Savoy. 'As clear as frost,' wrote Philip Hope-Wallace in *The Guardian* of Gladys in this: 'the Lady Bracknell of the Orient,' thereby reminding a record producer that, curiously, Gladys had never actually played Lady Bracknell anywhere. She promptly did so on a set of LPs for him and was quite surprisingly bad in what must have seemed 'natural' casting, until you reflect that appearances aren't every-

Savoy Theatre, 1961: as Mrs Gantry in The Bird of Time

thing. Gladys might have looked right for Lady Bracknell: on disc she sounds desperately modern and down-to-earth. Artificiality was never something she could cope with, even in the theatre.

Night after night, fans would gather at the Savoy stage door again to watch Gladys leave: she'd autograph their programmes with that amazing flourish which had become half a century earlier the best-known postcard signature in the land, and sometimes, if she wasn't in a hurry to zoom home in her Thunderbird and cook herself dinner or catch the late film on television, she'd pause to listen while they told her how she reminded them of all their yesterdays.

'Quite old women hobble up to me nowadays on crutches,' G once told me indignantly, 'and tell me they remember me from their childhood: one night a woman just stood there, her eyes full of tears, saying, "Oh, Miss Cooper," over and over again. I suppose I reminded her of something, though God knows what.'

The first half of the twentieth century, I told Gladys; but I don't think she ever believed me.

chapter twenty-eight

1962=1967

WHEN *The Bird of Time* closed Gladys got the offer of what was to be her last Broadway appearance, playing the aged Mrs Moore in the dramatization of E. M. Forster's *A Passage to India*. Her performance in this won her the nomination for a Tony Award and the morning after they opened at the end of January 1962 Walter Kerr wrote of her 'proud and unrelenting performance' opposite Eric Portman. John Chapman said that 'she captured perfectly the almost ghostly but shattering impact of India upon a world-weary but still sensitive soul' and in this, her hundred and fiftieth stage role, Gladys found a distinguished and distinctive way to bring her Broadway career to its close.

Not that there was ever any thought in her own mind of giving up:

> I think perhaps I should go to make films in Italy [she was writing to Joan from New York that winter, her seventy-third,] as I have just seen the most incredibly handsome man they seem to have there called Mastroianni. He really is dishy, so good-looking that I sat through his whole film twice just to have another look at him! When this play closes in April I think I shall drive out to California, taking it very slowly I promise, and then in June I've got a TV of *Question of Fact* to do in Toronto though that will only take a week so I shall fly there and back . . .

263

She had decided to try and save a little of the tax by staying out of the country for the rest of the 1962–3 year, and spent most of it doing what she called 'bits and pieces': a guest shot (alongside George C. Scott, Frank Sinatra, Tony Curtis, Burt Lancaster, Robert Mitchum and Herbert Marshall) in a camp and ludicrously complex John Huston thriller called *The List of Adrian Messenger* for which G's performance as a drunken dowager was about the best excuse, and then a number of television drama specials including Mrs Higgins to James Donald's Henry in a Hallmark *Pygmalion*.

Her cross-country drive from New York to Santa Monica was to be the last of many, and by her standards uneventful:

> I did over 500 miles every day, alone, and never drove after dark. I left Texas one morning at 94 degrees and when I got into Arizona that evening it was down to less than 30! It was cold, too, in the Grand Canyon and I just missed going down the mule track on a mule as I arrived there at 9.30 in the morning and they'd set off at nine, so I walked down it instead for miles. I also stopped off to have a look at the Painted Desert and the Petrified Forest. The roads are wonderful, all turnpikes, and driving across the States is just like going through about seven different countries in a week and how nice all the people are to one, so much nicer than those ghastly New Yorkers!

While she was on the West Coast she did a Dick Powell show and a Hitchcock TV thriller; she also embarked on a brisk correspondence with her younger grandson Wilton, now ten, who'd written to tell her that at school he had been told his grandmother had been the Marilyn Monroe of her day: 'Quite untrue and a great insult to me,' replied Gladys. 'No two people could be less alike as actresses or as women; I suppose it is true that I was the pinup girl of my time and she of hers B U T I W A S PINNED UP FOR QUITE DIFFERENT REASONS!'

Christmas 1962 she spent, for the last time, in Jamaica: by January she was back in New York doing the Hallmark *Pygmalion* and considering two rather good offers she'd just had: one was to play the Queen Mother in a new Noël Coward musical (*The Girl Who Came to Supper*) and the other was to continue playing Mrs Higgins only this time not for television – for the screen version of 264   *My Fair Lady* instead.

Ascot Gavotte: with Jeremy Brett, Audrey Hepburn and Rex Harrison in Cukor's film of My Fair Lady, *dressed by Cecil Beaton (1964)*

She couldn't however do the Coward musical and the film of *My Fair Lady* at the same time, and so she chose the latter since there was a guarantee of two thousand dollars a week for at least two months: Cukor was to direct, and other old friends on the film included Cecil Beaton as the designer, Rex Harrison as Professor Higgins and Wilfrid Hyde-White in the old Robert Coote role as Pickering. All that plus Stanley Holloway (as Doolittle), an old music-hall trouper who'd started with her in pre-World War I London, made it an irresistible project and made up for the disappointment in that year of being offered the *Chalk Garden* film and then having the offer abruptly withdrawn when it was decided Dame Edith should play it. By March, as Cecil Beaton's diary for 1963 indicates, plans were well advanced for the filming of *My Fair Lady*:

> Gladys Cooper (our Mrs Higgins) had come to George (Cukor's) room at Warner's with a pot of marmalade which she had made from the oranges grown in her garden, and a sheaf of early photographs of herself, taken at the time she was England's greatest beauty and the First Lady of the stage. These are to be used in connexion with a pre-Raphaelite portrait to be placed in Higgins's study.
>
> Gladys has a marvellous way of facing the onslaught of the years. No excuses. Her eyes may have lost some of their lustre but none of their intensity. She does not give her past beauty a thought. She's too interested in everything else. She looks at you with seeing eyes. She breathes in fresh air. She radiates health, and her complexion is so burnt by the sun that it has become like a walnut. She told us what she eats ('If you really want to know: hot water and lemon, first thing. Then a huge cup of milky coffee and prunes for breakfast. Only yogurt for lunch. And then I cook myself a proper meal for night'). She's Spartan and self-disciplined . . . pressed to tell us about her theories on her acting, she pooh-poohed. 'Oh, I don't think about it. After all these years I just try to get out there and be heard and hurry through it as quickly as possible and then go home.' Although her loveliness made her the great picture postcard favourite and a household name throughout England, Gladys never had the easy, pampered life of a famous beauty. Adulation, and tributes in the form of jewellery or flowers have seldom come her way. At the height

of her glory, her mother came to her dressing-room and said, 'You're too thin, dear! You're all nose!'

Though the role of Mrs Higgins is not an unduly large one (it was the only part she and Zena Dare and Cathleen Nesbitt were all to play, just as Mrs St Maugham in *The Chalk Garden* was the only one undertaken by Gladys, Sybil Thorndike and Edith Evans on different continents) the filming of *My Fair Lady* was slow and occupied Gladys all through the summer of 1963. I was with her then for a week or two in California, on my way to work at the University of Hawaii, and this was the first time that I'd begun to think of her as an old woman. Not that she seemed unduly fragile, which she never did, but because suddenly around Pacific Palisades and the Warner's lot she was being treated like some immensely distinguished visiting dowager instead of one of the workers: 'it is quite extraordinary,' said Gladys to me one morning as we hurtled down the freeway in the wrong lane and I cowered in the passenger seat next to her, 'that in Hollywood the less one actually does in a film, the more they respect one.'

By now her friendship with the director George Cukor was at its height:

I never really knew her [says Cukor] in the days of her great London fame, but I was always struck by her utter lack of vanity and by the way she avoided all the pitfalls of the ageing character actress. She was essentially very untheatrical: none of the nonsense that so often afflicts grandes dames, and instead an intense kind of energy that I've only ever seen equalled by Kate Hepburn. She'd arrive a little late on the set, usually because she'd taken the wrong exit off the motorway, but she'd be clutching peace offerings of home-made marmalade. Houses and gardens always fascinated her, more than people I think, and she was, in a way, the first of the feminists: it infuriated her that women were so seldom allowed to become real stars in Hollywood. 'If only I could play old men,' she used to say, 'the parts are so much better for them.' She wasn't at all gushing: I remember during the *Chalk Garden* rehearsals she really couldn't bear Bagnold and Selznick because they were so feminine and amateur in their approach to the theatre. She was like a man: tough.

267

But she also had enormous style and knew it: never actually malicious, but very impatient with anything which struck her as unnecessary or inefficient. She'd been through it all, but never talked about the past unless you asked direct questions and then she'd answer very precisely, technically.

Her film career had really come too late for her own beauty which was fading by the time she reached California: yet she remained a Queen in her own right, and when she was on screen in *My Fair Lady* there was no doubt that she was the most important person there, which was precisely the effect I wanted.

She carried herself with distinction, and without regrets: she was brusque and businesslike and although she always had her own point of view, she didn't spill over: she left you with your own opinions and in no doubt of hers. There was class there, real class.

When the filming of *My Fair Lady* was drawing to a close she began to think the end really had come to her Californian life: there seemed to be no other work around, Sally now had the first of her daughters and G was longing to get home and be with the family there. She was in fact on the verge of putting Napoli Drive on the market, a sale she'd been working herself up to for several months, when on November 7th a telegram arrived there from David Niven's Four-Star television production company: CAN OFFER THREE YEAR DEAL FOR SERIES TO BE CALLED THE ROGUES GUARANTEE YOU APPEAR IN NOT LESS THAN HALF THE EPISODES EACH SEASON ONE THOUSAND DOLLARS FOR FIRST DAY'S WORK THEN THREE THOUSAND FIVE HUNDRED IF IT GOES BEYOND SIX DAYS COSTARS NIVEN CHARLES BOYER ROBERT COOTE GIG YOUNG PLEASE SAY YES.

G said yes; it was the best television deal she'd ever been offered, indeed the only series, and it was to run on American and British television throughout 1964–6: a stylish sequence of comedy thrillers in which Gladys played the matriarch of a family of gentlemen crooks, the series took her right back to the golden days of *Mrs Cheyney*. The dialogue was admittedly somewhat sub-Lonsdale, but the storylines were good and because the series was made by a company partly owned by Boyer and Niven it was done with care and style and charm and elegance at a time when such qualities were not regularly to be found much elsewhere in American television.

The Rogues launched Gladys on a whole new lease of her career, and it was one she much enjoyed: asked once at the end of her life if, looking back across eighty years, she had any real regrets she said, 'Only one: I wish they'd never stopped *The Rogues*.' Working with such old friends as Niven and Cootey meant that she was well looked after on the set, and her part in each episode was never so long as to create real learning problems. I asked Niven once what G had been like on *The Rogues*:

> Extraordinary: very quick, very stylish, never quite got the lines right, but that didn't seem to matter too much because she gave us all a kind of style to work towards: she set the tone for the series by just being around it, and that was very important. I don't think we'd ever have had such a success without her.

Gladys basked in this Indian summer of her career: her reviews for *My Fair Lady* were good ('a flawless delight,' said Dilys Powell, 'all brisk, managing, upper-class good manners') and *The Rogues* was bringing in loving letters from all over the world including one from Edward Halliday who fifteen years earlier had painted the portrait of her which hung above her fireplace throughout the series. 'One entire episode,' Halliday told me later, 'centred round this portrait and the man supposed to have painted it, who had become an international drug pedlar and a thoroughly bad lot. *The Rogues* saw to it that he came to a sticky end, while the real artist remains alive and well and is living a blameless life in St John's Wood.'

My Fair Lady won Gladys the third and last of her Academy Award nominations ('always the bridesmaid' she wrote to me, 'never the bloody bride') and the offer of one more musical, the one that was to be her last Hollywood movie. But before that there were more *Rogues* to do, Sally and Emma to stay, and the house to think about: when she wasn't actually living there it could be rented out to the likes of Juliet Mills and Vanessa Redgrave while they were filming in Hollywood, but the upkeep was no longer as cheap as it once had been and now, at seventy-seven, Gladys had reluctantly decided that it was time to quit the Californian life forever and settle down in England with her new and beloved Hardy grandchildren.

269

First, though, there was one more film to make there: called *The Happiest Millionaire*, this was a Tommy Steele–Greer Garson–Fred MacMurray musical based on a successful Broadway comedy of a few seasons before. For it, Gladys had to sing a duet with Geraldine Page ('the only bright spot in a dismal Philadelphia story' said *Time Magazine*) but the best thing for her about the picture was that it was being made by Disney, which meant that she was given a free book of tickets to Disneyland by Walt himself and could therefore spend many happy Sundays there, occasionally taking younger relatives and friends but sometimes just taking herself for the sheer joy of what was then the greatest playground on earth.

But it was now the autumn of 1966, and there was a distinct chill in the air. Gladys had finally decided to leave: the house went to Marti Stevens, most of the contents were shipped home or given in huge cardboard boxes to the University of Southern California. The writer Gavin Lambert went along to see her in G's last days at Napoli Drive:

> Colman, Aubrey Smith, Clifton Webb, the cricket eleven, they'd all gone by now and Gladys Cooper seemed the last of the colonial settlers in Hollywood: she knew it was all over, and I think she was keen now to get back to her family in England where she knew she could still get work in the theatre. She had no patience with decay or loneliness, or failure, and she was not one to stay around after the party was over. She'd belonged really to MGM at the height of its Anglophilia and now that was all over and Hollywood had become a youth industry the old colony simply couldn't survive and I think she was very wise to get out when she did – otherwise she'd just have ended up like Helen Hayes, doing parodies of herself on television forever. Gladys was a very cool lady, and she knew when to stop something, in her acting and in her life. You remember that moment in *Rebecca* where she looks at Joan Fontaine and realises she's in the wrong dress? Other actresses would have gone overboard at that moment and ruined it: Gladys understood about restraint and she also managed to keep her head well above the rubbish she was often given to do on the screen. She kept her head and her distance, and that was what made her as an actress.

Gladys had five years left now, and she was to spend almost all of them living at Barn Elms and working in the London theatre: the first thing she did, as if to mark her homecoming, was a revival of Maugham's *The Sacred Flame*. Wendy Hiller, who was in the cast with her, remembers:

> I longed to ask Gladys at that time how she'd managed to grow old with no apparent awareness or bitterness at the passing of the years: all she'd ever say about her age was, 'I don't want to lose the expectation, the forward-looking bit about life – that's what keeps you going.' If anyone ever slammed the door on her past it was Gladys. How many lives had she led by then? Half a dozen? Yet none of them seemed

With the tiger from Daktari, *Hollywood, 1965*

to matter now; I remember Edith Evans once telling me that Gladys's beauty had stopped the buses in her youth: but she knew now, by instinct, that if she was going to survive into her eighties that would mean getting on and not looking back. Sometimes she'd talk to me about the old days, about Ivor and how they'd eat fish and chips together and her face would light up like a young girl's: mostly, though, she lived for the moment.

They started the *Sacred Flame* revival at the Yvonne Arnaud Theatre in Guildford for a short 1966 season, and then took it in to the Duke of York's in February 1967 where despite generally respectful reviews and, in my own view, a performance of stunning and haunting authority from Gladys in the role of the mother, they survived less than seven weeks before being replaced by the first of the Ayckbourn comedies.

But that summer was one of celebration: on the tenth of June it was announced in the Queen's Birthday Honours that G was henceforth to be known as Dame Gladys Cooper. She was the fourteenth actress to become a Dame and, in the view of a good many of us inside and outside the family, the honour had come not a moment too soon. Gladys was then seventy-eight, admittedly also the age at which Ellen Terry got her D B E in 1925; but since that time Edith Evans had been given hers at fifty-eight and Sybil Thorndike and Peggy Ashcroft theirs at forty-nine. Margaret Rutherford had also been given the honour earlier and younger than G, as had both Flora Robson and Judith Anderson. Gladys however had been made to wait, partly perhaps because of her decision to spend nearly thirty years away from the country and partly perhaps because other people seemed to adopt her own refusal to take her career very seriously.

Now, at last, she was Dame Gladys, and more than five hundred letters and messages poured into Barn Elms including a telegram from the staff of the Henley post office who, having sent nearly a hundred cables on to her from all over the world, decided to add their own. It was, if she needed it, powerful reassurance that she'd not been forgotten and was welcome home.

That autumn she did an eight-week provincial tour in a Hugh and Margaret Williams comedy, *Let's All Go Down The Strand*, which reached the Phoenix in October: 'lamentable' wrote

272

Michael Billington in *The Times* and that was the general critical consensus about a slender little drawing-room comedy concerned with Home Counties divorce. But if the play did nothing else (which it didn't) it did bring in for Gladys the best single review of her sixty years in the theatre. It came from Harold Hobson in the *Sunday Times*:

> In my opinion, Gladys Cooper is one of the two greatest actresses on the British stage; in fact, one of the four greatest I have ever seen anywhere. No actress in my experience has so cool, so lithe, so swiftly still, so splendid a pride both of body and mind . . . unfortunately she is merely on the periphery of this snobbish, querulous and dull little drama.

Almost unable to believe what I was reading, since good reviews of that nature had never exactly been a feature of my grandmother's stage career, I rang her to see if she'd read it too: 'Oh yes, darling, I have – but then Hobson's so often wrong, isn't he?' I never dared ask whether she meant about her performance or about the play.

chapter twenty-nine

1968=1971

WHEN that run ended in the spring of 1968, Gladys was already coming up to her eightieth birthday; we were seeing more of each other now than at any other time in my life, as regular Sunday teas were held at Barn Elms (indoors if wet) and there'd be gatherings to celebrate family occasions or the annual Henley Regatta which was rowed just the other side of her garden fence. We now had Hugo our first child, her first (and in fact only) great-grandson, and that as usual made life easier with Gladys: she and my wife had taken a deep and instinctive dislike to each other when we first married, the kind of dislike G took on occasion to anyone fearless or foolhardy enough to marry into her family, but the dislike was miraculously overcome the moment children could be produced . . . evidence, presumably, that the marriage was going to last and that she'd therefore have to settle down and like it, which she invariably then did.

During the week, winter or summer, you'd see her around the streets of Henley hurling shopping and dogs and grandchildren into the back of an enormous and open-topped Thunderbird, at the wheel of which she'd then put the fear of God into local residents as she hurtled back over the bridge and down the narrow lane to Barn Elms. In the summer, if she wasn't playing, she'd drive the five miles across to my parents' house in Wargrave at dusk and plunge into water considerably colder than anything she could have known in California:

With her grand-daughter Emma Hardy and her great-grandson Hugo Morley, 1967

I still look up from my desk sometimes [says my father] and wonder why she isn't coming over the lawn to plunge into the pool long after the rest of us had decided it was too cold ... there was, even in the last three or four years, a marvellous and touching energy about everything she did: I don't think she had time to jog back or to regret that she wasn't, towards the end, the great star that she'd once been. She accepted that, partly because she hadn't got a very good memory and partly because she only ever wanted to live for the morrow. She swam, you know, and she gardened, the way other people play Hamlet: with a tremendous intensity and courage. But when she talked about the theatre, and about the people she'd worked with, it was always in terms of the fun she'd had with them, not of the performances any of them had actually given. Those, I think, she'd entirely forgotten by now ... at home she was the sort of woman who 275 could lift sofas, and when she was around you weren't encouraged to do anything . . . if you got up to help she'd say, 'No, no, dear, stay where you are, you'll only get in the way otherwise.' She had an ability to look a thousand dollars in a cheap drug-store dress, and because she always looked smart she couldn't understand why the rest of the world didn't also. Illness she thought was a mortal sin, and not one she approved of; she herself never took even an aspirin, suspecting they were dangerous drugs. She happened to have a wonderful constitution, coupled with a certain lack of imagination about the effects of ill-health on others.

By the autumn of 1968 she was ready to do another play, and the one that came along was Ira Wallach's *Out of the Question*, a curious little comedy about an impoverished scientist trying to convince an American university that his family life did not make him an unsuitable man for one of their jobs. Michael Denison played the scientist, with Dulcie Gray as his wife and Gladys as a bossy next-door neighbour with a couple of good scenes. A number of critics spent their columns debating whether Ira Wallach could be an anagram for Hugh and Margaret Williams, an easier alternative than considering the plot, but despite some generally dismissive notices this was a magic little piece which managed to hang on at the St Martin's well into 1969.

A month or two after the opening night came December 18th, 1968, Gladys's eightieth birthday. The family decided that this called for some sort of celebration, and with the considerable help of the Denisons and the management it was arranged that for this one night the theatre should be entirely filled with G's friends, and that at some point early in the proceedings Robert, my father, should appear on stage with a tray of champagne glasses. The play itself was then abandoned and we all took Gladys across the road to the Ivy for dinner. Michael Denison:

Gladys was amazed and appalled and delighted in roughly that order: she had no idea what was going on, or that the people in front weren't the usual paying customers. When Robert appeared on stage, she first tried to carry on with the show, thinking the audience would be more than a little mystified otherwise, then as we were going back to the dressing-rooms she murmured, 'Most unprofessional: besides, I'm on a percentage so what happens to tonight's takings, may I ask?' But deep down she was really rather delighted, though she wasn't the kind of lady to let it show too much.

Others were less delighted: this was almost certainly the first (and maybe also the last) time that a show had been interrupted for such a celebration, and the following day's *Evening Standard* carried an irate if somewhat straightlaced letter from James Roose-Evans, founder of the Hampstead Theatre Club:

> Sir: Is the theatregoing public to be deflected at the last moment from seeing a production for which they have booked, merely to indulge the wilful humour of Robert Morley who wishes to play a private family in-joke on his mother-in-law? This is no way to pay homage to the distinguished career of Dame Gladys Cooper. Can our theatre afford the precedent?

In fact our theatre seems to have survived the precedent, and far from people 'being deflected at the last moment' we had already offered paying customers their money back or an alternative date some weeks later, as the whole manoeuvre was planned with the military precision of *This Is Your Life*.

The publicity also did the play itself no lasting harm, and by the end of January they had, amazingly, broken all the St Martin's box-office records. Gladys and the Denisons stayed with *Out Of The Question* through the first half of 1969, G wandering further and further from the text until Denison took to clapping his hands and murmuring 'Olé' when, like a particularly exorbitant Spanish dancer, 'she'd finally come back to earth from her solo and get us back into the text of the play. She had the gift not of eternal youth but of eternal courage, and that made her a marvellous stage companion.'

After that play closed G made what was to be her last journey out to California, staying now with Marti Stevens in the house she had sold her at Napoli Drive and where Miss Stevens still lives:

She was nothing like a Dame, that's for sure: one Friday in the summer of 1969 she rang me and said she was on her way to California for the weekend and could she stay? That night I had Rattigan and Michael Wilding and Margaret Leighton to dinner and the door on to the verandah flew open and there she was saying, 'Well, Mum's home!' So we stayed up talking until about two in the morning when, bedraggled and bleary eyed, Rattigan and the Wildings left but Gladys, not apparently noticing that she'd just crossed eight thousand miles, carried on talking for another hour or so, bright as a button on champagne. We finally got to bed about four, and I remembered that she was an early riser so I set my alarm for seven thinking I'd be up in time to get her breakfast and as I groped my way to the kitchen there she was, naked, lying by the pool having already been for a swim and noticed that I wasn't taking proper care of her marmalade tree. I don't think anybody ever explained to her about being eighty. That day, still with only about two hours' sleep, she'd agreed to do the *Dick Cavett Show* on television in Los Angeles, but she said she'd some friends she'd quite like to see, so could I please arrange a dinner party for about 11.30 that night when she got back from the studio? She was like the Pied Piper to me: sharp and astringent as champagne and just as unforgettable.

Back in England that year she did one last film, playing an aged aunt in an eminently forgettable disaster called *A Nice Girl Like Me*. Now, at the very end of her life and career, G was once again a really good box-office name: she could command £1000 for a single TV episode of *Emergency Ward 10* and was finding that her age, her Damehood, and the fact that a whole new generation had got to know her as tele-face via *The Rogues* all contributed to the wave of popular enthusiasm on the crest of which she was to end her life. Like Sybil Thorndike, like Edith Evans, she had survived, and audiences have always liked a survivor.

One of her most loyal and consistent admirers, Hugh Williams, now had another job for her: he and his playwright wife Margaret had cobbled together an admittedly rather shaky drawing-room comedy called *His, Hers and Theirs* in which there was the part of a balloon-clutching county grandmother which appeared to have been written not only for Gladys but about her too. They opened in December 1969 to reviews which were good for Gladys but poor for the play, and a few days after the opening night

Her last screen appearance, with Barbara Ferris

co-author and co-star Hugh Williams, a friend of G's from their
Playhouse days and the only man apart from Maugham to write
with her in mind, suddenly died. In the best theatrical tradition
it was decided that the show must go on, and the director Murray
Macdonald and G persuaded her old friend Roland Culver to take
over the Williams role with only a day or two's rehearsal.
Roland and his wife Nan were among the greatest and closest
of G's post-war friends, and had lived with her through some of
John's most violent attacks. They'd stayed several months at
Napoli Drive in the time when Culver too had a contract in
Hollywood, and he first worked with G as early as 1925:

> I understudied the butler in *Iris* and one afternoon he was ill
> and I had to go on for him and as I opened the double doors   279

to announce somebody, Gladys looked up and said 'Good God'. They were the first words she ever said to me on a stage: I suppose she'd never seen me backstage and wondered what I was doing there. As an actress she always lacked dedication, and people may wonder now why she did so few of the classics – no Shaw, for instance, and precious little Shakespeare. The answer is that in her time as an actress-manager, reviving the classics was simply not something one did, unless of course you happened to be working at the Vic which she never was. Her career was based, like her life, on the survival of the fittest, and she was usually the fittest. I was already into my seventieth year when she rang up to say would I take over from Tam Williams, and with his son Simon in the cast it wasn't an exactly easy job to go in so soon after the death and say Tam's lines, especially knowing how close he and Gladys had always been. I tried at first to point out that I was far too old: the character was meant to be a middle-aged romantic and even Tam had been pushing his luck a bit. 'Nonsense dear,' said Gladys, 'put on a nice toupée and you'll be quite all right. Can you open on Saturday?' She was very intolerant of old age: in her view you went on till you dropped, just as Tam had done.

Gladys's programme note for *His, Hers and Theirs* was in fact written for her by my father, since she refused to commit anything ever to print, but it summarized better than she ever could her own feelings about her life and work:

Who cares how old I am? Who cares how long ago it was since I first played Peter Pan? Who remembers me as the Novice in *The Dove Uncaged*? I don't even remember myself as Pamela in *The Pursuit of Pamela* so why on earth should you? Why do theatre programmes always concentrate on the past? This is the performance that matters. This is the challenge . . . the theatre today is as much a part of my life as it ever was, but I am not I suppose a dedicated actress, there's always too much else going on. Children and grandchildren and great-grandchildren and houses and gardens and dogs and cats and marmalade and curries . . .

She was currently occupied in trying to sink a pool into her garden at Barn Elms, the last of her many building and land-

His, Hers and Theirs, *Apollo Theatre, December 1969*

scaping projects and the only one she never quite managed, though she did get as far as a fountain and a sort of goldfish pond into which the younger grandchildren and great-grandchildren spent 1970 and 1971 falling with sickening regularity. She now had only one more play to do, and it would be a revival of her one post-war classic *The Chalk Garden*.

She never had much patience with the increasing signs of old age in her contemporaries, though for Sybil Thorndike, who had come to her eightieth birthday party at the St Martin's when she herself was already eighty-six, and for Ellaline Terriss who had survived an entire century, G had nothing but love and respect. For Edith Evans, her feelings were, as Cecil Beaton recalls, rather more mixed:

> Gladys was unsympathetic when she heard that Edith had been forced to withdraw from a play at Chichester. 'Her trouble is that she thinks too much about the theatre. She should go out and forget it, but she's so ingrained and self-centred she has no interests except her performance. I have my grandchildren and all sorts of other interests to keep me going, and I don't think about my part once I'm outside the theatre. I don't think about myself at all if I can help it. A young man rang me up for an interview once on "The Psychology of Acting". I said I didn't know anything about it. I was far too busy housekeeping and living my life; and as far as the theatre is concerned, if I'm working I just feel jolly lucky that I've got a good job.'

Buck was dead now, and her beloved Vivien Leigh, and every post seemed to bring in the news that one or other of G's octogenarian contemporaries was disappearing into the void: she refused, typically, to think much about that. Death, when it came, would just have to be coped with the way that her life had always been, and that's all there was to it. That penultimate summer of 1970 she took her two younger grand-daughters Emma and Justine down to Cornwall for a week or two, where she found one of the oldest and closest and most loving of her friends, Gerald's daughter Daphne du Maurier:

> She took a house quite near me and she'd come over for lunch
> with these two little girls whom quite clearly she adored,

and seeing her with them one suddenly realised that they were then what mattered to her far above anything she'd ever done on the stage. One day she came without them, and we talked about Gerald and the old days for a while, and then suddenly she was up and saying she must get back to the beach where Sal and the girls were. I offered to drive her, as it was a mile or two away, but she said no, she'd rather walk and that was the last I saw of her, cloth hat crammed down over her ears, setting off for a swim with the grandchildren.

A year after my grandmother died, Daphne du Maurier published a novel called *Rule Britannia*: the central characters were a girl called Emma and her grandmother, a famous though retired actress who organizes an entire Resistance movement when England is invaded by America. She dedicated it 'for Glads – a promise, with love'.

Back in Henley, Gladys prepared to revive *The Chalk Garden* at the Yvonne Arnaud Theatre, Guildford. At about this time I published the only profile I ever wrote of G in her lifetime. It was in the *Sunday Times*, who headlined it 'Gladys Cooper: Toast of the Century': 'I don't care for the title,' said Gladys afterwards, 'next I suppose we'll be having all that rubbish about Stage Door Johnnies drinking champagne from one's slipper.' But for the piece I had persuaded her to think about which period of her life had in fact been the happiest:

Oh, the Playhouse, without a doubt: I enjoyed running that theatre more than anything else in my career, I suppose because it was the only time I have ever really felt in charge of anything. It all depended on me, in a way that other theatres and film studios never really have. In those days we had no real competition, you see, from television or the cinema: theatre was a part of people's lives, not only the rich but people who paid a shilling to sit up in the gallery. The only thing I regret about that period is that one never had the time to travel: through the Playhouse I met people like King Alfonso of Spain and I'd love to have seen what his country looked like before the war.

The future? I don't really think much about that, now, though I've always wanted to do a television series about a lady vet who has a lot of strange animals to look after. **283**

Robert and Sally Hardy with their daughters Emma and Justine

Nobody ever seems to have written it for me. Whatever happens, I'll go on working as long as I can; somehow I don't see myself in a wheelchair being looked after by some nice old retired dresser in a flat in Brighton, do you?

I didn't.

The Chalk Garden revival opened at Guildford in November 1970. In the company, playing her daughter, was G's own step-daughter Rosamund Merivale:

I'd been off the stage for nearly twenty years and it was Gladys's idea that I should return in this, so naturally I was very touched. We opened at Guildford and then did a long tour through that winter, and increasingly it was obvious that her chest was troubling her: I'd be staying in adjacent hotel rooms and through the wall at night there'd be that terrible cough, but then the next day she'd murmur something about 'Doctor Theatre' and play on regardless. She was as intolerant of her own failing health as she'd always been of other people's.

In fact what Gladys was suffering from was cancer of the lung, though typically she herself reckoned it was nothing more than a spot of recurrent and troublesome pneumonia. *The Chalk Garden* company were laid off early in 1971 because no London theatre could be found for them, and Gladys went into her last television job, a few episodes of the soap-opera series *The Doctors*.

Then, towards the end of April, the Theatre Royal Haymarket (the play's old home) fell vacant and the revival was put in there for the summer. Reviews were grudgingly good: 'Miss Cooper,' said the *Observer*'s Ronald Bryden, 'is an actress whose art consists of growing more and more like herself.' 'She brilliantly abuses the privileges of old age,' wrote another critic, while John Barber for the *Telegraph* added that hers was, 'a glittering portrait of high egotistical grandeur'. The play was treated now rather more respectfully than on its first outing in London, and Irving Wardle in *The Times* wrote of G's 'parchment features crinkling into radiant welcomes and surly pouts, moving when you least expect it from absent-minded distraction to complete mastery of the situation with undiminished vigour and agile timing'.

285

What Gladys now thought of her own acting, in so far as she thought about it at all which wasn't often, is anybody's guess; soon after she died, though, I did find among her scattered papers an article about the actress Maxine Elliott who in 1908 had given some advice to stagestruck young girls. G had underlined in her unmistakable hand the following passage:

> You must have serious ambition and reasonable qualifications – the constitution of a horse, the skin of a rhinoceros and that which is perhaps the best definition of genius, an infinite capacity for taking pains . . . remember that Nature on the stage bears no resemblance to Nature, and the actor who succeeds in being just natural has travelled far in art only to find out how little he knows. Nobody can teach you to seem a real being on the stage. The spirit comes from within, and it is only the individual note or expression that gives one's work the smallest value.

The Chalk Garden played on at the Haymarket to good tourist business throughout the summer of 1971, and the management then decided that it and the company could stand another tour. A few south-coast dates were booked, then Billingham, and then the intention was to go on to a fortnight in Toronto. Gladys only got as far as Billingham: at the end of a week in the theatre there her health had suddenly collapsed to the point where she was taken into Guy's Hospital for treatment. Cathleen Nesbitt was brought in to complete the *Chalk Garden* tour, and Gladys's rage and frustration and unhappiness at being 'off' after a sixty-year career in which she had missed less than half a dozen performances was best expressed in a letter written on October 5th, 1971 to the play's author, Enid Bagnold:

> When I was at the Playhouse I played with cracked ribs due to a motor crash, I played with a broken arm due to a skiing accident, I played with a bound-up hand due to a monkey bite, I played once standing up for a whole week because my back hurt so much I couldn't sit down, and on one first night I played while I was actually having a miscarriage . . . in those days they called me the iron lady. Now I have alas proved that even iron can crack.

Her stage farewell: Mrs St Maugham in the revival of The Chalk
Garden, *Theatre Royal Haymarket, 1971*

If Gladys did ever realize she was now dying, it wasn't until the last few days: in these last few weeks, though she was to spend more time in bed than ever before in her life, there were also days when she was up and about at Barn Elms carrying on almost as though nothing had ever happened. In late September the writer Christopher Matthew, an old friend of mine and by now an old friend of hers too, telephoned to see how she was bearing up:

> She sounded rather faint at first, but that I discovered was because she was putting on a funny voice to deter strangers: when I asked how she was she said pretty exhausted, and I said I supposed that was because of her daily walk along the towpath, and she said no, more probably because she'd just moved the grand piano into the other room. Alone. She didn't believe in asking for help, even then.

A few months earlier Gladys and Chris had been at the first night of an Alan Ayckbourn play my father was doing at the Lyric; afterwards there was a party and G was asked if she'd like to sit next to the Swiss ambassador. 'I don't think I will,' she confided to Chris in a voice all too clearly audible to His Excellency, 'it's such a bore sitting next to people who don't speak the language.'

As October turned into November it became clear that Gladys was not going to get any better: she herself was still making plans to go away somewhere, however, and Roland Culver suggested that Brighton might be nice: 'Brighton? Brighton? Are you mad? I expect to be in Jamaica for Christmas.' But she wasn't.

> On the last night of her life [wrote my father later,] my splendid and courageous mother-in-law rose from her bed and, making her way, not without considerable effort, to her dressing-table, proceeded to brush her hair and make up her celebrated face. Then, gazing into the mirror for what was to prove the very last time, she remarked to her nurse, 'If this is what virus pneumonia does to one, I really don't think I shall bother to have it again.' She got back into bed, and presently died in her sleep.

It was November 16th, 1971, and Gladys was almost exactly a month away from her eighty-third birthday.

288

Tributes came in from all over the world: in print, in letters, in telegrams and some written on the backs of the innumerable post-cards for which she'd posed sixty years earlier. *Time* magazine noted that only a week before her death she'd written to them in an outburst of rage about the musicals *Hair* and *Jesus Christ Superstar* ('The theatre having sunk to the depths of filth and obscenity both in sight and sound, is the church now to do like-wise? Is there no Christianity left, no morals, no standards, no faith?') and it was more than a little typical that her last word on the theatre should have been about its present and future rather than its past.

Olivier said the theatre had lost one of its greatest hurdlers; Sybil Thorndike spoke of 'a bright and dazzling friend and a darling girl', and *The Times* wrote of 'an Edwardian beauty who became an actress of distinction and intelligence'.

Letters came in hundreds from Hollywood, from New York, from all over the world, some written by those who'd starred in her films or played with her in the theatre, others from total strangers who just wanted us to know that they'd miss her, too. Most wrote in amazement, not that she'd died so quickly but that she'd died at all: 'indestructible' is a word that turns up in more than fifty of the letters including one from the late Hugo Dyson, Emeritus Fellow in my time at Merton College Oxford:

I remember her first at my prep school when I started to collect her picture postcards: I had them with me on the Western Front, and what a mitigation they were to shell fire! I never met her, but across half a century she taught me how much more there is to womanhood than beauty and charm; she was one of the light-bringers of our time.

The day after she died they dimmed the lights outside the theatres along Shaftesbury Avenue, a tribute accorded to less than half a dozen players this century, and there was a small family funeral at the little church in Remenham near where she'd lived for the last twenty years of her life.

Gladys left three children, five grandchildren, two great-grandchildren, some pretty unforgettable memories and just over £34,000. At the very end of her life I'd once asked her if there was anything, anything at all, she was really afraid of: 'Only a long illness,' she'd replied, 'or spending the rest of one's life in a

289

wheelchair.' It was good to know she'd been spared that, as well as the indignities of an old age she had never really been prepared to accept as her own. Once, taking some of the grandchildren to the cinema in Henley, she had presented her money to the lady at the box-office. 'O A P?' asked the lady. 'No,' replied Gladys, 'I think we'd all prefer to sit in the stalls.'

On what would have been her eighty-third birthday, December 18th, 1971, there was a memorial service at the actors' church, St Paul's in Covent Garden. My father gave the address, Stanley Holloway read from *Pilgrim's Progress*, Celia Johnson read a Shakespearian sonnet and Ian Wallace was the soloist: the list of those in church read like a Who's Who of the British theatre and they included Dame Sybil Thorndike, then already well into her ninetieth year; as she was leaving, she turned to us all and said, 'What a lovely party: and how very much Gladys would have enjoyed it.'

Gladys Cooper, 1888–1971, says the sign on the wooden bench by the Thames at Henley which is her only memorial: at nearly eighty-three years it was a long life, but even so not I think long enough for G herself. Or for me.

(Opposite) At Barn Elms, 1970   291

Appendix

GLADYS COOPER: THE CAREER

1: **Plays** (theatres are in London unless otherwise indicated)

(Gladys Cooper born December 18th, 1888).

1905 (debut): Bluebell in *Bluebell in Fairyland* (Theatre Royal, Colchester).
1906: Lady Swan in *The Belle of Mayfair* (Vaudeville).
Mavis in *Babes in the Wood* (Theatre Royal, Edinburgh).
1907: Eva in *The Girls of Gottenberg* (Gaiety).
Molly in *Babes in the Wood* (Theatre Royal, Glasgow).
1908: Touring Newspaper Beauty in *Havana* (Gaiety).
1909: Lady Connie in *Our Miss Gibbs* (Gaiety).
Toured with Seymour Hicks in *Papa's Wife.*
Sadie von Tromp in *The Dollar Princess* (Daly's).
Lady Elizabeth in *Our Miss Gibbs* (Gaiety).
1911: Cecily Cardew in *The Importance of Being Earnest* (St James's).
Sylvia Fawsitt in *The Ogre* (St James's).
Violet Robinson in *Man and Superman* (Criterion).
1912: Ann in *The Pigeon* (Royalty).
Columbina in *The Dove Uncaged* (Royalty).
Muriel Pym in *Milestones* (Royalty).
Barbara Weir in *The Odd Man Out* (Royalty). **293**

Catherine Hervey in *The Kiss* (Criterion).
Beauty in *Everywoman* (Drury Lane).

1913: Dora in *Diplomacy* (Wyndham's).
Josie Richards in *Broadway Jones* (Theatre Royal, Bradford).
Pamela in *The Pursuit of Pamela* (Royalty).

1914: Mrs Rodney Carlish in *Peggy and Her Husband* (Royalty).
Anne, Nina, Annette, Antje, Annie, Anna and Anita in *My Lady's Dress* (Royalty).
Susy in *The Silver King* (His Majesty's).
She in *The Bridal Suite* (Coliseum).
Troop tour in France with Seymour Hicks's Concert Party.

1915: Lady Lilian Garson in *Half An Hour* (Coliseum).

1916: Emily Delmar in *Please Help Emily* (Playhouse).
Lady Agatha Lazenby in *The Admirable Crichton* (Coliseum and London Opera House).
Helen Steele in *The Misleading Lady* (Playhouse).

1917: Entered into management with Frank Curzon at the Playhouse.
Mabel Vere in *Wanted a Husband* (Playhouse).
Clara de Foenix in *Trelawny of the Wells* (New).
Marya Varenka in *The Yellow Ticket* (Playhouse).
Marjory Seaton in *The Man from Blankley's* (His Majesty's).

1918: Eloise Farrington in *The Naughty Wife* (Playhouse).

1919: Victoria in *Home and Beauty* (Playhouse).

1920: Anne in *My Lady's Dress* (Playhouse and Royalty).
Rosalie in *Wedding Bells* (Playhouse).

1921: Joy in *The Betrothal* (Gaiety).
Olivia in *Olivia* (Aldwych).
Miralda Clement in *If* (Ambassador's).
Anne Hunniwell and Mrs Reagan in *The Sign on the Door* (Playhouse).

1922: Paula in *The Second Mrs Tanqueray* (Playhouse).

1923: Magda in *Magda* (Playhouse).
Kiki in *Enter Kiki* (Playhouse).
Peter in *Peter Pan* (Adelphi).

1924: Dora in *Diplomacy* (Adelphi).
Celia in *The Ware Case* (Adelphi).
Peter in *Peter Pan* (Adelphi).

294   1925: Iris Bellamy in *Iris* (Adelphi).

Anne in *My Lady's Dress* (Adelphi).

Mrs Cheyney in *The Last of Mrs Cheyney* (St James's).

Ginette in *L'Ecole Des Cocottes* (Princes').

1927: Becomes sole lessee of The Playhouse.

Leslie Crosbie in *The Letter* (Playhouse).

Jeanne de Baudricourt in *The Wandering Jew* (Drury Lane).

1928: National tour of *The Letter*.

Ginette in *Excelsior* (Playhouse).

1929: Stella Tabret in *The Sacred Flame* (Playhouse).

1930: Clemency Warlock in *Cynara* (Playhouse).

1931: Wanda Heriot in *The Pelican* (Playhouse).

Kitty Fane in *The Painted Veil* (Playhouse).

1932: Princess Narcissa in *King, Queen, Knave* (Playhouse).

Lucy Haydon in *Dr Pygmalion* (Playhouse).

Carola in *Firebird* (Playhouse).

Phyllis Benton in *Bulldog Drummond* (Adelphi).

1933: Jane Marquis in *Flies in the Sun* (Playhouse).

Jane Claydon in *The Rats of Norway* (Playhouse).

Gave up management of the Playhouse.

Aspasia in *Acropolis* (Lyric).

1934: Mariella Linden in *The Shining Hour* (Royal Alexandra, Toronto; Booth, New York; St James's, London).

1935: Desdemona in *Othello* (Ethel Barrymore, NY).

Lady Macbeth in *Macbeth* (Ethel Barrymore, NY).

1936: Dorothy Hilton in *Call It A Day* (Morosco, NY and tour).

Janet Tardy in *Chevaleresque* (later *White Christmas*) (Locust Valley, USA).

1937: Liesa Bergmann in *Close Quarters* (US and Canada tour).

Laura Lorimer in *Goodbye to Yesterday* (Phoenix).

1938: Fran Dodsworth in *Dodsworth* (Palace).

Olivia in *Twelfth Night* (Open Air, Regent's Park).

Lysistrata in *Lysistrata* (Open Air, Regent's Park).

Rosalind in *As You Like It* (Open Air, Regent's Park).

Oberon in *A Midsummer Night's Dream* (Open Air, Regent's Park).

Tiny Fox Collier in *Spring Meeting* (UK tour, then His Majesty's Montreal and Morosco, New York).

1942: Mrs Parrilow in *The Morning Star* (Morosco, NY).

1948: Melanie Aspen in *The Indifferent Shepherd* (Criterion).

1950: Edith Fenton in *The Hat Trick* (Duke of York's).

1951: Felicity, Countess of Marshwood in *Relative Values* (Savoy).
1953: Grace Smith in *A Question of Fact* (Piccadilly).
Palladium Midnight Matinée. *The Shopgirl Princess* (with Jack Buchanan).
1955: Lady Yarmouth in *The Night of the Ball* (New).
Mrs St Maugham in *The Chalk Garden* (Ethel Barrymore, NY).
1956: Mrs St Maugham in *The Chalk Garden* (Theatre Royal Haymarket and US tour).
Palladium Midnight Matinée: Sketch (with Robert Morley).
1957: Mistress Phoebe Ricketts in *The Crystal Heart* (Saville).
Mrs Callifer in *The Potting Shed* (La Jolla Playhouse, USA).
1958: Dame Mildred in *The Bright One* (Winter Garden).
1960: Mrs Vincent in *Look on Tempests* (Comedy).
1961: Mrs Gantry in *The Bird of Time* (Savoy).
1962: Mrs Moore in *A Passage to India* (Ambassador, NY).
1966: Mrs Tabret in *The Sacred Flame* (Yvonne Arnaud, Guildford).
1967: Mrs Tabret in *The Sacred Flame* (Duke of York's).
Prudence Slater in *Let's All Go Down the Strand* (Phoenix and tour).
1968: Emma Littlewood in *Out of the Question* (St Martin's and tour).
1969: Lydia in *His, Hers and Theirs* (Apollo and tour).
1970: Mrs St Maugham in *The Chalk Garden* (Yvonne Arnaud, Guildford, and tour).
1971: Mrs St Maugham in *The Chalk Garden* (Theatre Royal, Haymarket, and tour).

(Gladys Cooper died November 16th, 1971).

2: Films (Dates here refer to first British or American release).

1913: *The Eleventh Commandment* (Kisch-Barker). Dir: James Welch. With Vincent Clive, Ronald Notcutt.
1914: *Dandy Donovan, The Gentleman Cracksman* (Cunard). Dir: Walter Walter. With Owen Nares, Thomas Meighan.
1916: *The Real Thing at Last* (British Actors Company). Dir: L. C. Macbean. With Edmund Gwenn, Owen Nares,

Godfrey Tearle, Nelson Keys, Ernest Thesiger.

1916: *The Sorrows of Satan* (Samuelson). Dir: Alexander Butler. With Owen Nares, Cecil Humphreys, Lionel d'Aragon, Minna Grey.

1917: *Masks add Faces* (Ideal). Dir: Fred Paul. With Sir Johnston Forbes-Robertson, Gerald du Maurier, Irene Vanbrugh, Ben Webster, George Bernard Shaw, Charles Hawtrey, J. M. Barrie, Joan Buckmaster.
My Lady's Dress (Samuelson). Dir: Alexander Butler. With Malcolm Cherry, Alice de Winton, Andre Beaulieu, Leal Douglas.

1920: *Unmarried* (Granger's Exclusives). Dir: Rex Wilson. With Gerald du Maurier, Edmund Gwenn, Lady Diana Cooper.

1922: *The Bohemian Girl* (Alliance). Dir: Harley Knoles. With Ivor Novello, C. Aubrey Smith, Ellen Terry, Constance Collier, Gibb McLaughlin.

1923: *Bonnie Prince Charlie* (Gaumont-British). Dir: C. C. Calvert. With Ivor Novello, Hugh Miller, Lewis Gilbert, Arthur Wontner, A. B. Imeson.

1935: *The Iron Duke* (Gaumont-British). Dir: Victor Saville. With George Arliss, Ellaline Terriss, A. E. Matthews, Emlyn Williams, Allan Aynesworth.

1940: *Rebecca* (United Artists). Dir: Alfred Hitchcock. With Laurence Olivier, Joan Fontaine, George Sanders, Judith Anderson, Nigel Bruce, C. Aubrey Smith.
Kitty Foyle (RKO). Dir: Sam Wood. With Ginger Rogers, Dennis Morgan, James Craig, Eduardo Ciannelli.

1941: *Lady Hamilton* (US: *That Hamilton Woman*) (United Artists). Dir: Alexander Korda. With Vivien Leigh, Laurence Olivier, Alan Mowbray, Sara Allgood.
The Black Cat (Universal). Dir: Albert S. Rogell. With Basil Rathbone, Broderick Crawford, Bela Lugosi, Gale Sondergaard, Alan Ladd.
The Gay Falcon (RKO). Dir: Irving Reis. With George Sanders, Wendy Barrie, Anne Hunter, Turhan Bey.

1942: *This Above All* (20th Century Fox). Dir: Anatole Litvak. With Joan Fontaine, Tyrone Power, Thomas Mitchell, Nigel Bruce, Philip Merivale, Alexander Knox, Melville Cooper, Jill Esmond.
Eagle Squadron (Universal). Dir: Arthur Lubin. With

Robert Stack, Diana Barrymore, John Loder, Eddie Albert, Nigel Bruce, Isobel Elsom.

Now, Voyager (Warner's). Dir: Irving Rapper. With Bette Davis, Paul Henreid, Claude Rains, Bonita Granville, Ilka Chase.

1943: *Forever and a Day* (RKO). Dir: Clair, Goulding, Hardwicke, Lloyd, Saville, Stevenson and Wilcox. With Brian Aherne, Charles Laughton, Herbert Marshall, Ray Milland, Anna Neagle, Merle Oberon, C. Aubrey Smith, Claude Rains, Ian Hunter, Richard Haydn, Jessie Matthews, Victor McLaglen, Robert Coote, etc.

Mr Lucky (RKO). Dir: H. C. Potter. With Cary Grant, Laraine Day, Charles Bickford, Vladimir Sokoloff.

Princess O'Rourke (Warner's). Dir: Norman Krasna. With Olivia de Havilland, Robert Cummings, Charles Coburn, Jack Carson, Jane Wyman.

The Song of Bernadette (20th Century Fox). Dir: Henry King. With Jennifer Jones, Charles Bickford, Vincent Price, Lee J. Cobb, Alan Napier.

1944: *The White Cliffs of Dover* (MGM). Dir: Clarence Brown. With Irene Dunne, Frank Morgan, Roddy McDowall, Van Johnson, May Whitty, Peter Lawford, C. Aubrey Smith, Jill Esmond.

Mrs Parkington (MGM). Dir: Tay Garnett. With Greer Garson, Walter Pidgeon, Agnes Moorhead, Tom Drake, Dan Duryea, Hugh Marlowe.

1945: *The Valley of Decision* (MGM). Dir: Tay Garnett. With Greer Garson, Gregory Peck, Donald Crisp, Lionel Barrymore, Jessica Tandy.

Love Letters (Paramount). Dir: William Dieterle. With Jennifer Jones, Joseph Cotten, Anita Louise, Cecil Kellaway, Reginald Denny.

1946: *The Green Years* (MGM). Dir: Victor Saville. With Charles Coburn, Tom Drake, Hume Cronyn, Dean Stockwell, Jessica Tandy, Richard Haydn.

The Cockeyed Miracle (MGM). Dir: S. Sylvan Simon. With Frank Morgan, Keenan Wynn, Audrey Totter, Cecil Kellaway.

1947: *Green Dolphin Street* (MGM). Dir: Victor Saville. With Lana Turner, Van Heflin, Donna Reed, Frank Morgan, May Whitty, Moyna McGill.

Beware of Pity (Two Cities). Dir: Maurice Elvey. With Lilli Palmer, Albert Lieven, Cedric Hardwicke, Emrys Jones, Ernest Thesiger.

The Bishop's Wife (RKO). Dir: Henry Koster. With Cary Grant, Loretta Young, David Niven, Monty Woolley, Elsa Lanchester, Regis Toomey.

1948: *The Homecoming* (MGM). Dir: Mervyn LeRoy. With Clark Gable, Lana Turner, Anne Baxter, John Hodiak, Cameron Mitchell.

The Pirate (MGM). Dir: Vincente Minnelli. With Gene Kelly, Judy Garland, Walter Slezak, Reginald Owen, George Zucco.

1949: *The Secret Garden* (MGM). Dir: Fred M. Wilcox. With Margaret O'Brien, Herbert Marshall, Dean Stockwell, Elsa Lanchester, Reginald Owen.

Madame Bovary (MGM). Dir: Vincente Minnelli. With Jennifer Jones, Louis Jourdan, James Mason, Van Heflin, Gene Lockhart, George Zucco.

1951: *Thunder on the Hill* (UK: *Bonaventure*) (United-International). Dir: Douglas Sirk. With Claudette Colbert, Ann Blyth, Robert Douglas, Anne Crawford, Philip Friend.

1952: *At Sword's Point* (UK: *Sons of the Musketeers*) (RKO). Dir: Lewis Allen. With Cornel Wilde, Maureen O'Hara, Robert Douglas, Alan Hale.

1955: *The Man Who Loved Redheads* (United Artists). Dir: Harold French. With John Justin, Moira Shearer, Roland Culver, Denholm Elliott, Harry Andrews.

1958: *Separate Tables* (United Artists). Dir: Delbert Mann. With Burt Lancaster, Rita Hayworth, David Niven, Deborah Kerr, Wendy Hiller, Cathleen Nesbitt, Felix Aylmer, Rod Taylor.

The Miracle (Warner's). Dir: Irving Rapper. With Carroll Baker, Roger Moore, Walter Slezak, Katina Paxinou, Vittorio Gassman.

1963: *The List of Adrian Messenger* (Universal). Dir: John Huston. With George C. Scott, Dana Wynter, Clive Brook, Herbert Marshall, Frank Sinatra, Tony Curtis, Kirk Douglas, Burt Lancaster, Robert Mitchum, Jack Merivale.

1964: *My Fair Lady* (Warner's). Dir: George Cukor. With Rex Harrison, Audrey Hepburn, Stanley Holloway, Wilfrid Hyde-White, Jeremy Brett.

1967: *The Happiest Millionaire* (Disney). Dir: Norman Tokar. With Tommy Steele, Greer Garson, Fred MacMurray, Geraldine Page, Hermione Baddeley.

1969: *A Nice Girl Like Me* (Avco Embassy). Dir: Desmond Davis. With Barbara Ferris, Harry Andrews, James Villiers, Joyce Carey, Fabia Drake.

3: Television, radio and recordings.

TELEVISION:

1950 (debut): *Adventure Story* (BBC).

1956: *Sister* (NBC).

1957: *The Tichborne Claimant* (NBC), *Circle of the Day* (NBC), *The Mystery of Thirteen* (NBC).

1958: *A Day by the Sea* (ITV), *Verdict of Three* (CBS).

1961: *Lucky Strike* (BBC).

1963: *Pygmalion* (Hallmark Hall of Fame).
If the Crown Fits (ATV).

Also: *They Hanged My Saintly Billy, Waters of the Moon, A Question of Fact* (CBC Canada) and frequent appearances in the Dick Powell, Alfred Hitchcock, *Daktari, Girl from Uncle* and *Twilight Zone* drama series. GB: *Emergency Ward 10, The Doctors*, etc. Also occasional panel game and chat show appearances.

1964–66: Regular appearances in *The Rogues* with David Niven, Charles Boyer, Robert Coote, etc.

RADIO:

1954: *The Second Mrs Tanqueray* (BBC 'Star Choice' series). Other appearances in many drama and interview series.

RECORDINGS:

1961: Lady Bracknell in *The Importance of Being Earnest*.

1967: Aunt Mary in *The Happiest Millionaire* (duet with Geraldine Page).

Bibliography

The following is a list of those books which proved most useful to me while I was researching and writing this biography; some afforded anecdotes or direct quotations, many more were used as background material and for cross-checking references and dates and opinions. To all the authors, executors and publishers I am most grateful.

AGATE, JAMES: *Ego*, Hamish Hamilton 1935.
—— *Around Cinemas*, Home and Van Thal 1948.
BAGNOLD, ENID: *Autobiography*, Heinemann 1969.
BALL, ROBERT HAMILTON: *Shakespeare on Silent Film*, Allen and Unwin 1968.
BARKER, FELIX: *The Oliviers*, Hamish Hamilton 1953.
BARNES, KENNETH: *Welcome, Good Friends*, Peter Davies 1958.
BAXTER, BEVERLEY: *First Nights and Footlights*, Hutchinson 1955.
BEATON, CECIL: *Beaton's My Fair Lady*, Weidenfeld and Nicolson 1968.
The Parting Years, Weidenfeld and Nicolson 1978.
BEHLMER, RUDY: *Memo from David O. Selznick*, Macmillan 1973.
BLAKELOCK, DENYS: *Round the Next Corner*, Gollancz 1967.
BRAUN, ERIC: *Deborah Kerr*, W. H. Allen 1977.
BROWN, JOHN MASON: *Two on the Aisle*, W. W. Norton 1938.
BUCKMASTER, HERBERT: *Buck's Book*, Grayson and Grayson 1933.

CASSON, JOHN: *Lewis and Sybil*, Collins 1972.

COLLIER, CONSTANCE: *Harlequinade*, John Lane, the Bodley Head 1929.

COLMAN, JULIET BENITA: *A Very Private Person*, W. H. Allen 1975.

COOPER, GLADYS: *Gladys Cooper*, Hutchinson 1931.

COTTRELL, JOHN: *Laurence Olivier*, Weidenfeld and Nicolson 1975.

COWARD, NOËL: *Present Indicative*, Heinemann 1937.

CURTIS, ANTHONY: *The Pattern of Maugham*, Hamish Hamilton 1974.

—— (ed.) *The Rise and Fall of the Matinée Idol*, Weidenfeld and Nicolson 1974.

DARK, SIDNEY: *The Life of Sir Arthur Pearson*, Hodder and Stoughton 1922.

DARLINGTON, W. A.: *6 Thousand and One Nights*, Harrap 1960.

DAVIS, BETTE: *The Lonely Life*, Macdonald 1963.

DESCHNER, DONALD: *The Films of Cary Grant*, Citadel 1974.

DONALDSON, FRANCES: *Freddy Lonsdale*, Heinemann 1967.

—— *The Actor Managers*, Weidenfeld and Nicolson 1970.

DU MAURIER, ANGELA: *It's Only the Sister*, Peter Davies 1951.

DU MAURIER, DAPHNE: *Gerald*, Gollancz 1934.

—— *Rule Britannia*, Gollancz 1972.

EDWARDS, ANNE: *Vivien Leigh*, W. H. Allen 1977.

FORBES, BRYAN: *Ned's Girl*, Elm Tree 1977.

GARRETT, GERARD: *The Films of David Niven*, LSP Books 1975.

GIELGUD, JOHN: *Early Stages*, Macmillan 1939.

GUTHRIE, TYRONE: *A Life in the Theatre*, Hamish Hamilton 1959.

HADDON, ARCHIBALD: *Green Room Gossip*, Stanley Paul 1922.

HALLIWELL, LESLIE: *The Filmgoer's Companion* (4th Ed.), Hart-Davis MacGibbon 1974.

HARRISON, REX: *Rex*, Macmillan 1974.

HAWTREY, CHARLES: *The Truth at Last*, Thornton Butterworth 1924.

HICKS, SEYMOUR: *Night Lights* Cassell 1936.

HYMAN, ALAN: *The Gaiety Years*, Cassell 1975.

JOHNS, ERIC: *Dames of the Theatre*, W. H. Allen 1974.

KULIK, KAROL: *Alexander Korda*, W. H. Allen 1975.

LAMBERT, GAVIN: *On Cukor*, W. H. Allen 1973.

LESLEY, COLE: *The Life of Noël Coward,* Jonathan Cape 1976.

LORAINE, WINIFRED: *Robert Loraine,* Collins 1938.

LOW, RACHAEL: *The History of the British Film 1914–18,* Allen & Unwin 1971.

—— *The History of the British Film 1918–29,* Allen & Unwin 1971.

MACKAIL, DENIS: *The Story of J M B,* Peter Davies 1941.

MacQUEEN POPE, W: *Ivor,* Hutchinson 1951.

MANDER, RAYMOND and MITCHENSON, JOE: *Theatrical Companion to Shaw,* Rockliff 1954.

—— *Theatrical Companion to Maugham,* Rockliff 1955.

—— *Lost Theatres of London,* Hart-Davis 1968.

MARSHALL, MICHAEL: *Top Hat and Tails,* Elm Tree 1978.

MASON, A. E. W.: *Sir George Alexander and The St James's Theatre,* Macmillan 1955.

MATTHEWS, A. E.: *Matty,* Hutchinson 1952.

MCDOWALL, RODDY: *Double Exposure,* Delacorte Press 1966.

MINNELLI, VINCENTE: *I Remember it Well,* Angus and Robertson 1974.

MORLEY, ROBERT: *A Musing Morley,* Robson 1974.

—— *Morley Marvels,* Robson 1976.

NESBITT, CATHLEEN: *A Little Love and Good Company,* Faber 1975.

NOBLE, PETER: *Ivor Novello,* Falcon Press 1951.

OSBORNE, ROBERT: *Academy Awards Illustrated,* LSP Books 1969.

PARISH, J. R. and BOWERS, R. L.: *The MGM Stock Company,* Arlington House 1973.

STINE, WHITNEY: *Mother Goddam,* W. H. Allen 1975.

STOKES, SEWELL: *Without Veils,* Peter Davies 1953.

TERRIS, ELLALINE: *Just a Little Bit of String,* Hutchinson 1955.

TREWIN, J. C.: *Edith Evans,* Rockliff 1954.

—— (with Mander and Mitchenson) *The Gay Twenties,* Macdonald 1958.

—— *The Roaring Thirties,* Macdonald 1960.

TRUFFAUT, FRANCIS: *Alfred Hitchcock,* Secker and Warburg 1967.

USTINOV, PETER: *Dear Me,* Heinemann 1977.

WILSON, A. E.: *Playgoer's Pilgrimage,* Stanley Paul 1938.

WORSLEY, T. C.: *The Fugitive Art,* John Lehmann 1952.

Index